MEDIA, FEMINISM, CULTURAL STUDIES

Stepping Forward: Essays, Lectures and Interviews
by Wolfgang Iser

Wild Zones: Pornography, Art and Feminism
by Kelly Ives

Global Media Warning: Explorations of Radio, Television and the Press
by Oliver Whitehorne

'Cosmo Woman': The World of Women's Magazines
by Oliver Whitehorne

Andrea Dworkin
by Jeremy Mark Robinson

Cixous, Irigaray, Kristeva: The Jouissance of French Feminism
by Kelly Ives

Sex in Art: Pornography and Pleasure in Painting and Sculpture
by Cassidy Hughes

*The Erotic Object: Sexuality in Sculpture
From Prehistory to the Present Day*
by Susan Quinnell

Women in Pop Music
by Helen Challis

Detonation Britain: Nuclear War in the UK
by Jeremy Mark Robinson

Julia Kristeva: Art, Love, Melancholy, Philosophy, Semiotics
by Kelly Ives

Luce Irigaray: Lips, Kissing, and the Politics of Sexual Difference
by Kelly Ives

Helene Cixous I Love You: The Jouissance of Writing
by Kelly Ives

The Poetry of Cinema
by John Madden

The Sacred Cinema of Andrei Tarkovsky
by Jeremy Mark Robinson

Disney Business, Disney Films, Disney Lands
Daniel Cerruti

Feminism and Shakespeare
by B.D. Barnacle

Thomas Hardy and John Cowper Powys

Wessex Revisited

Thomas Hardy and John Cowper Powys

Wessex Revisited

Jeremy Mark Robinson

CRESCENT MOON

CRESCENT MOON PUBLISHING
P.O. Box 393
Maidstone
Kent, ME14 5XU
United Kingdom

First published 1991. Second edition 2008.
© Jeremy Mark Robinson 1991 2008.

Printed and bound in Great Britain.
Set in Book Antiqua 9 on 14pt and Gill Sans display.
Designed by Radiance Graphics.

The right of Jeremy Mark Robinson to be identified as the author of *Thomas Hardy' and John Cowper Powys* has been asserted generally in accordance with sections 77 and 78 of the Copyright, Designs and Patents Act 1988.

All rights reserved. No part of this book may be reprinted or reproduced, stored in a retrieval system, or transmitted, in any form or by any means, electronic, mechanical, photocopying, recording or otherwise, without permission from the publisher.

British Library Cataloguing in Publication data available

ISBN-13 9781861711236

CONTENTS

	Introduction 15
1	John Cowper Powys In Context 24
2	John Cowper Powys's Wessex Quartet 31
3	The Wessex of John Cowper Powys and Thomas Hardy 62
4	The Ecstasy of Landscape 82
5	The Mythology of Sensualism 98
6	Nature In Thomas Hardy's Fiction 125
7	The Visions of Thomas Hardy and John Cowper Powys 139
8	Paganism and Folklore 159
9	Love 172
10	The Oedipal Rebellion 187
11	The Transcendence of Work 196
12	Philosophy 206
13	The Metaphysics of Style 216
14	Thomas Hardy Goes To the Cinema 224
15	Conclusion: Thomas Hardy, John Cowper Powys and D.H. Lawrence 236
	Bibliography 245

Thomas Hardy (courtesy of Dorset County Museum)

John Cowper Powys (National Portrait Gallery, London)

Marnhull in Dorset, maybe an inspiration for Marlott in *Tess* (Dorset County Museum)

Woodland, New Forest
(This and other photos by Jeremy Robinson)

Landscape near Kimmeridge, Dorset

Stonehenge, Wiltshire

West Dorset seascape

Introduction

What are my books but one long plea against 'man's inhumanity to man' – to woman – and to the lower animals? Whatever may be the inherent good or evil of life, it is certain that men make it much worse than it need be.

Thomas Hardy, 1904[1]

---

1 In F. Pinion, *A Hardy Companion*, p. 178.

Thomas Hardy is now 'Thomas Hardy', a cultural icon, a discourse, a text, an industry. He is a catalyst for meditations on ruralism. He is the creator of 'Hardy's Wessex'. He is the catalyst for a mass of cultural and commercial products: in film, television, radio, magazines, journals, newspapers, festivals, tours, lectures, courses, summer schools, holidays, degrees, shops, cafes, exams, maps, guides, walks and meetings.

As Rochester in Kent has its Dickens Festival, and Stratford its Shakespeare industry, so Dorset has been transmuted by Hardy's imaginative power into the 'Hardy Country', a poetic place called 'Wessex'. Dorset has been transformed with a themepark mentality into a literary wonderland. An ordinary houses becomes (in awed tones) the house against which Tess leaned for warmth.

Like Shakespeare, Dickens and Lawrence, Hardy has become something much more than a 'great writer'. He is now a national treasure, part of the national heritage. There are many reasons for this. He combines a piercing nostalgia for the English country side with a set of romantic stories so simple that anyone can identify with them. Ruralism is back-to-nature, green, eco-friendly, quaintly rustic, lyrical. All of those qualities that make Wordsworth so popular, combined with romance and drama of occasionally Shakespearean depth and scope, are found in Hardy.

It is surely this deft mix of romance and nostalgia that makes Hardy and his Wessex so popular with all kinds of readers. The nature/ landscape/ rural/ romantic aspects of Hardy are exalted – in the tourist industry, in the TV and film adaptions, in advertizing – while the deeper, bitter and more polemical Hardy is politely ignored. The 'Thomas Hardy' the nation loves and the media promotes is the rural romance writer who creates books of 'character and environment'.

Love certainly is Thomas Hardy's primary concern, but it is love affected by all kinds of other factors – personality, circumstance, accident, 'Fate', environment, labour, landscape, history, genealogy, ambition, enculturation, deception, education, religion, folklore and so on.

Thomas Hardy's influences were many: Shakespeare, the *Bible*, Shelley, Keats, Scott, Turner, Milton, Sophocles, Darwin and Mill. He is now one of the five most popular British authors. The reasons for his enduring popularity are usually given as follows: his romance and tales of passion, intrigue and relationships; his nostalgia for earlier times; his ruralism and country style; his evocations of vanished ways of life; his Wessex; his fully-rounded characters; his easily-approachable texts; his poetic style; his influential poetry; the rigorous philosophical and religious discourses; his sense of drama; his sense of tragedy (that is sometimes Shakespearean); the ideological, social and psychological discourses (which can be analyzed from psychoanalytic, New Critical, semantic, Marxist, feminist or post-structural viewpoints); the literary life in the letters and autobiography; his humanism; the timeless evocations of nature; his sense of drama which is sometimes as great as that of Classic Greek and Elizabethan tragedy.

All these factors make Hardy popular. They are endlessly perpetuated in films, TV, radio series, and in the tourist industry. The public loves Hardy for his nostalgic ruralism and romance. The academics and critics and philosophers and sociologists and anthropologists like him because they analyze him in so many different ways (and maybe use him a vehicle for their own philosophies). Feminists can have a field-day with Tess and Sue; psychologists can study his characters' typologies and motives; post-structuralists can look at his texts and cultural information; Marxists can discuss his materialist discourse; sociologists and historians can look at his 'peasants', his rural web and changing world; cineastes can delight in his cinematic style; critics can look at his poetry and fiction and his influence on later literature; theologians and philosophers can wade into Mill, Darwin, Nietzsche, Schopenhauer, Gnosticism, atheism, existentialism, paganism, politics and Christianity, and so on.

This study looks at 'Thomas Hardy' from an old-fashioned, poetic perspective. It does not use formal semiology, structuralism, deconstruction, Marxism, psychoanalysis, linguistics or feminism.

The intention here is to revisit the fiction and ideas and landscapes of Hardy and John Cowper, to revisit Wessex, the country of the heart, the landscape of the soul, the spirit of place as it has been charted by these two British novelists. Powys was an exile – his Wessex novels were written in America, although his spiritual homeland was always Britain, or more particularly, Wessex and Wales. Hardy created his Wessex from the inside. His Wessex is a construct of the imagination, of a waking dreamer.

Other writers have written of Wessex. Lawrence Durrell spent some time in Milkwell, near Shaftesbury in Dorset, working on *Justine*. He wrote: 'dammit here I am for a few months in the heart of the Hardy country where the people talk in the identical tiresome moralising way they do in Hardy'.[2] Rider Haggard wrote of the 'southern, sea-bordered shire of Dorset'.[3] Durrell, Stevenson, Verlaine, Lawrence, Shelley and Beardsley were all connected with Bournemouth. Keats was supposedly at Lulworth Cove (Hardy commemorates the occasion in a poem). Jane Austen popularized Bath and Lyme Regis. In *Persuasion* she wrote of 'the very beautiful line of cliffs stretching out of the east' of Lyme Regis (chapter 11). T.S. Eliot was associated with East Coker, Walter Raleigh and Thomas Wyatt were at Sherborne. George Herbert was at Bemerton. Fielding was at East Stour. Roger Bacon was born in Ilchester, and T.E. Lawrence lived at Clouds Hill. The Wordsworths and Coleridge walked in the Quantocks, Somerset, and stayed at Racedown Lodge, near Pilsdon Pen, Dorset. The other Powyses – Llewelyn and T.F. – wrote of Dorset. William Barnes was a powerful presence in Dorchester. Hardy and Powys did not have Wessex to themselves, though no one has exalted the place as much as Hardy.

Among contemporary writers, Naipaul has eulogized Wiltshire Plain, Golding has used Salisbury Cathedral as the model for his *The Spire*, Durrell lampooned Bournemouth (in *Livia*), Peter Ackroyd satirized West Dorset around Marshwood Vale, and John Fowles has produced a synthetic Hardyan novel set in Lyme Regis.

This study began as a reworking of an earlier book on Powys, *Sensualism and Mythology: The Wessex Novels of John Cowper Powys* (Crescent Moon 1990). As the book grew, I realized there was much more to be said about Thomas Hardy (an earlier study had appeared in 1989 – *Love and Tragedy: A Study of Thomas Hardy*, Crescent Moon 1989). The exploration here is of the two Wessexscapes of Hardy and Powys, and how they interconnect.

D.H. Lawrence is used to provide a third reference-point. Hardy is the base of the structure of this book. He provides the traditional Victorian

---

[2] *The Durrell-Miller Letters*, p. 280.
[3] *A Farmer's Year*, 1899, p. 1257.

foundation upon which subsequent regional fiction is built. Lawrence forms a bridge between Hardy and Powys, while Powys moves into his own peculiar kind of modernism.

Hardy is a rich field of discourses. The more you delve into his works, the more you find to discuss. The wealth of Hardy criticism proves this. Hardy has become an *Ur*-Hardy (like the *Ur*-Tess). He is a cultural phenomenon, one of the few British writers who keeps on expanding (like Shakespeare, Chaucer, Dickens, Brontë and Lawrence). Hardy has many eyes – the poet's eye, the painter's eye, the philosopher's eye, the critic's eye and so on. Hence the discussion here of some aspects related to Hardy's Wessexland: his painterly and visionary sensibility, his attitude to work and class, to feminism and sexual politics, his sense of Nature and nature-mysticism, his relation to other nature-poets, his poetic style, his philosophy, his use of myth, religion and folklore, his psychological discourse, and his sense of love and tragedy. Finally, there is a discussion of the film and television versions of his fiction, and the many creative problems these involve.

The discussion of Hardy and the rural tradition can be extended in any direction – from Wessex to topography and the 'spirit of place', which is present in every writer, or from Hardy's meditations of love into the vast area of feminism and sexual politics, or into anthropology, sociology, politics, or into painting and art history. Hardy is such a prodigious source of material, a multiplicity of approaches and discourses. He is a launchpad for all kinds of explorations into the deep space of culture.

We acknowledge how provisional all this critical work is – how vague, how subject to change and fashion. Hardy wrote in a Preface to a selection of poems by one of his gurus, William Barnes: 'But criticism is so easy, and art so hard; criticism so flimsy, and the life-seer's voice so lasting' (Per, p. 81). Certainly, some artists have become *seers*, in the Rimbaudian sense. Now Plato and the *Bible* and other ancient classics are regarded as great works of fiction, as ancient novels. More recently, the works of British critics such as Ruskin, Pater, Arnold and Eliot are fast becoming mythologized.

'All art is only approximate' wrote Hardy (Life, p. 169). Deeper and more accurately, Weston La Barre has written:

All values, moral and intellectual, are constructs of human experience and need. So also are æsthetic values. It is understandable that art should have the overwhelming power that it does over sentient human beings. In art men of all times are kin. For art, always and everywhere, speaks with secret power to the human condition. (*The Ghost Dance*, p. 114)

The revolution in Hardy and Powys is inside, in the interior landscape of the soul. The revolution comes from within. Their Wessexscapes, for all their studied accuracy, are poeticized psychological constructs. They do not pretend, as Lawrence sometimes does, to be able to change the world. Theirs is an art of individual psychic change. The transformations are slow or revelatory, but they occur in the individual, not in the crowd. Hardy and Powys do not have great statements to make, or any easy answers. They are not social prophets, like Blake or Shaw. They make instead passionate but highly individualized claims for 'loving-kindness', for Shakespearean tenderness.

André Gide spoke of two kinds of novel. The first is objective, it visualizes and interprets. The second is experiential and emotional – dreaming in prose. Thomas Hardy combines the two, while Powys is very much a writer of the stream-of-consciousness novel. Of this kind of waking dreamer Gide wrote:

> everything derives from him. He is the only one to vouch for the truth he reveals, and the only judge. All the heaven and hell of his characters is in him. It is not himself that he depicts, but he could have become what he depicts if he had not become everything himself.[4]

John Cowper Powys is clearly a dreamworker, someone involved, like Anais Nin or Rilke or Auster, in the re-invention of themselves through creative work. In the game of self-invention, Hardy tries to keep his distance, to keep himself detached. He is, however, fully enmeshed now with his Wessex, with contemporary Dorset, and with an international urban nostalgia for the simpler ways of rural living – living in the Paradisal Golden Age of the rustic Past, the dream-country, more spiritual than material, more poetic than topographic, more mythic than

---
4 *The Journals of André Gide*, II, p. 392.

historic, more soul than body, more spirit than place.

A word about the critical approach. I have kept quotes to a minimum, quoting only from Hardy and Powys where possible. The reader is referred to the bibliography for full details of texts used.

Some critics of Hardy have proved useful, particularly Alcorn, Goode, Bullen, Pinion, Salter, Jagdish Dave, Widdowson, Brooks, Guerard and Lawrence.

John Cowper Powys studies are much rarer – Humfrey, Knight, Cavaliero, Krissdottir, Fawkner, Coates, Collins and Wilson are the core critics. What Powys criticism needs is a wealth of new approaches, not more close readings of the novels – we have enough of those already. Now we need postmodernist approaches, feminist readings, Marxist, political and materialist analyses, comparisons with other magical realists (Borges, Marquez *et al*), comparisons with the magical feminists who use Arthurian, pagan and fairy tale imagery – Sarah Maitland, Angela Carter, Jeanette Winterson, Isabelle Allende, and Anais Nin.

Powys criticism needs to be opened out. It is too narrow, too traditional. It lags behind contemporary techniques. Powys needs some of the treatment that Hardy and Shakespeare receive. New studies are gradually appearing, but they are too cliquey. They should explore and explode, not regurgitate. Curiously lacking in Powys criticism is a serious exploration of his cultural position in relation to other writers and thinkers.

Thomas Hardy on the other hand gets excellent treatment critically. Hardy criticism is a vast field now. The complexity of some of the articles now appearing is bewildering. The old Hardy critical book used to be laid out in the following manner: Chapter 1: Introduction, 2: The Man and His Life, 3: His Thought and Wessex, 4: The Major Novels, 5: The Minor Fiction, 6: The Poetry, 7: The Dynasts, 8: Conclusion. These typical Hardy books always had a picture of Hardy printed somewhere (usually in the frontispiece) as if no one knew by now what he looked like.

The books on Hardy's Wessex are disappointing. They list the real and fictional places, and note the correspondences between them. They do not get to grips with the poetry and ideology of his Wessexland. Instead, they exalt the topography and get annoyed when Hardy deviates from the norm. 'Hardy got it wrong when he said place X was five miles from place Y' they moan. This is not the point at all. Hardy's Wessex is *poetic*, it is *imaginative*. He stated this a number of times.

Thomas Hardy takes up the landscape of Wessex and moulds it, sculpts it into the poetic shape suited to his dramatic discourse. It is a 'border country', a country of the soul. Dorset is never mentioned in the texts of the novels. Wessex is a unity of six counties – county boundaries are forgotten (Life, p. 127). To visit Hardy's Wessex we must not wander around Dorset, but read the books. Hardy's West Country is a 'daisy-and-buttercup land' ('Growth in May', CP, p. 626) – pastoral, idealized. But it is also a place where passions and terrors rage. In Hardy's mythopoeic world, love is tougher than Nature is. Love causes more suffering than Nature. Hardy's Wessex is more a lovescape than a landscape. The melodrama is played out on the spiritual and emotional plane as much as on the material one. So, the poet persuades us:

> Ache deep; but make no moans:
> Smile out; but stilly suffer:
> The paths of love are rougher
> Than thoroughfares of stones
> ('The End of the Episode', CP, p. 227)

Hardy did not suffer in silence – artists rarely do. The novels, the stories, the many poems – these are the records of his suffering.

At the heart of Thomas Hardy, in amongst the discourses of passion, despair, marriage, labour, landscape, religion, folklore and ethics, is a profound *ambiguity*. Hardy is ambiguous about his characters (Tess – pure or impure woman? Was it rape of 'seduction'?); his relation with his fiction is ambiguous; his views are ambiguous. He is ambivalent about most things. This makes him difficult, challenging and highly entertaining to read, The question is, what does this 'sexist male', who wrote a hundred or so years ago, in another place, in a different social climate, have to do with us today? Why is he so popular? Why do contemporary feminists think it so important to discuss this sexist, unsuccessfully-married, ideologically-dubious dead Victorian poet? There are many reasons for Hardy's enduring popularity. Now we can see a little more clearly what he's done – what's he's doing:

> I see what you are doing: you are leading me on
> To the spots we knew when we haunted here together.
> ('After a Journey', CP, p. 349)

One

John Cowper Powys in Context

And from T. Hardy I learnt, long long ago, to see all human feelings, gestures, actions, & everything else! – my own & everybody's– against the Inanimate Background of Nature, whether flat or mountainous or moorish or swampy & marshy or of desert sand.

John Cowper Powys[5]

---

5 Dec 14, 1955, Blaenau-Ffestiniog, Wales, Wil, p 338.

John Cowper Powys was influenced by writers from across the whole history of Western literature: from his beloved, much-read Homer, through Boethius and Milton, through the early Romantics to Hardy. Powys was an insatiable bookworm – he seems to have spent much of his life either reading or walking or writing. His multifaceted reading is reflected in his books. He admired Scott, Dickens, Dostoievsky, Balzac, Hardy, James, Poe, Arnold, Keats, Wordsworth, Pater, Rabelais, Hugo, Whitman, Heine and Goethe among many others. The list of authors discussed in an early collection of essays of 1916 includes: Byron, Blake, Voltaire, Pascal, France, Rousseau and Brontë. So by the time he came to write his quartet of Wessex novels, he had already written critical studies of books and writers. He had already lectured widely in America – Powys says that he wrote *Wolf Solent* while 'travelling through all the states of the United States except two.' (p. 11) He had been through the whole *Ur*-culture machine. He knew all the great names and landmarks of literature. He was steeped in the myths and legends of Greece and Arthurian Britain. He had a Victorian love of books and knowledge, like Thomas Hardy. For him books were objects of romance, enabling escape and dreaming. They were treasures in which lost worlds could be rediscovered.

Much of Powys's fictive world is driven by this slowburn of bookish lore. The novels are the product of someone who has *already* been a philosopher, a lecturer, a storyteller, a would-be magician, a rather mundane poet, an occultist and an eccentric. Powys is best described as a writer. That is, someone who loves writing, whether it be letters, essays, novels or philosophical commentaries. He is the great *amateur* – wholly in love with writing. This is clear from his many books, which include novels, philosophical essays, poetry, correspondence and literary criticism. Hardy too was an amateur, a self-educated soul. Both writers would agree with Carlyle who said: 'The true University these days is a collection of books.' (*Heroes and Hero-Worship*, V).

As a novelist, Powys stands on his own. He has most in common with Thomas Hardy and D.H. Lawrence. But even here there are more dissimilarities than similarities. He began writing in the age of Decadence and Symbolism (Wilde, Mallarmé, Beardsley). His early poetry (which is rather bad) reflects this era. He wrote the Wessex quartet in the modern age of Proust, Joyce, Eliot, Yeats and Lawrence. He continued to write well into our era of post-war fiction (the age of Beckett, Camus, Greene, Golding and Borges).

The lack of an easily applicable literary frame-of-reference for John Cowper Powys has surely contributed to his neglect by most critics. In appreciating Powys we have to go along with Wordsworth's famous dictum that 'every great and original writer... must himself create the taste by which he is to be relished.' (*Preface* to the *Lyrical Ballads*) Every writer creates their own world, but Powys's world stands apart from those of his contemporaries. He is an original – an English eccentric, in the style of Peake, Graves, Lawrence or Moorcock. G. Wilson Knight has called Powys 'perhaps the greatest of all novelists' (Knight, Neg, p. 191).

The writers John Cowper Powys most adores are the great storytellers of world literature: Homer, Cervantes, Melville, Hardy and Shakespeare. He likes the big, sweeping story, with larger-than-life characters and landscapes to match them. He is an enthusiast: his literary criticism abounds in superlatives. In an early book of criticism (*Suspended Judgements*, 1916) he writes of Brontë, in a typical passage:

> Emily Brontë, like Walt Whitman, sweeps us, by sheer force of inspired genius, into a realm where the mere animalism of sexuality, its voluptuousness, its lust, its lechery, are absolutely merged, lost, forgotten: fused by that burning flame of spiritual passion into something which is beyond all earthly desire. (SJ, p. 315)

This is criticism in the style of Pater and Ruskin – a great gushing torrent of lush adjectives and superlatives. Powys exalts content above style and form. He cared more for what was being said, rather than how it was said. The author who figures more than other in his work is probably Homer. Powys is certainly a Classic pagan rather than an apologetic Christian. So many times Powys refers to Homer, or paraphrases him. From Homer Powys gathers a love of mythology, magical events, and a simplicity of narration. Homer also gave Powys the significance of the mythic gesture. So much of Powys's sense of drama stems from the ordinary human gesture that is exaggerated up to the stature of a divine moment. This mythic exaggerating of life lies at the heart of Powys's poetic world.

John Cowper Powys hero-worshipped Hardy (*Letters to C. Benson Roberts*, p. 15). He was immensely excited when 'the greatest writer *then living on this earth*' came to visit the Powyses at Montacute (A, p. 229). For Powys, Hardy was a vital source of myth, history and poetry. Lawrence is closer to Powys's elemental sensualism, but Powys does not seem to have read Lawrence deeply. He acknowledged Lawrence's 'dark gods' (A, p. 376), but Hardy and Scott, with their sharp sense of historicity, were the writers for him.

John Cowper Powys said he felt 'deep and intense' about history (A, p. 393). He was immersed in history and historiography. The past impinges upon Powys as a physical presence. Continuity is essential – 'you must have *something* old in the background' he wrote (A, p. 436). He wanted living links with the Past. He wanted magnetic connections with Greece, Wales and prehistory. The direct experience of history, via his sensual lust, gave him an 'unforgettable psychic taste in my mouth' (A, p. 434). He loved Dorset and Wales more for their history than for their landscape. History is sensual for Powys, it permeates the soil of a place. He must have that physical presence.

Powys is very much a writer of the intense, Dionysian kind. Nietzsche wrote of the one 'who suffers from superabundance of life, who desire a Dionysian art and likewise a tragic view of an insight into life'.[6] In a similar vein, Schopenhauer wrote: 'Intellect is a magnitude of intensity' (*Essays*, p. 125).

Interesting to compare the two autobiographies, to see the ways in which Powys and Hardy manufactured their lives for the public. Powys's *Autobiography* is of course much longer than Hardy's *Life*. Powys is intense. He admits to many fetishes – for ankles, for sylphlike boy-girls, for his knees, for bread and tea. He is open about himself. A visit to a prostitute is eased by being compared to Dostoievsky (A, pp. 381-2). There are many instances of Powys's sensualism, many walks of ecstasy. Much of the *Autobiography* is highly idiosyncratic. Powys says 'My literary

---

[6] *A Nietzsche Reader*, p. 132.

likes and dislikes are physical' (p. 320). He liked writers for their bodies as much as for their art. Powys is full of such highly individual ideas.

Thomas Hardy is infinitely more protective. He tries to detach himself from his life. He tries to fill his autobiography with interesting anecdotes and literary asides. It is all so civilized, genteel, controlled. Hardy hides behind a literary persona, carefully carved from his life. He hides a great deal. He comes across as a thoughtful, liberal writer and thinker in retirement in Dorchester. Powys comes over as a very odd character, an erotomane who wanders about the planet with some unusual æsthetic principles. We might regret not having autobiographies by Lawrence, Beckett, Rimbaud and Durrell. We have to content ourselves with their letters and essays.

John Cowper Powys's fiction is freighted with *romance*. That is, the Victorian romance of history and literature, the romancing of the Past so popular in the Victorian era. It is also refers to the romance of ancient mythology and the romance of Romance – Romantic love and mediæval knightly Romances. Powys is the ultimate Romantic, in many ways. He is, like Graves, Durrell and Lawrence, one of the many of the 'Last Romantics'. His stance is life-affirming, life-indulging. He described himself once as a 'Pragmatist and Wish-fulfilmatist' (Wil, p. 189). The swooping and feverish force of Romantic poetry suffuses much of Powys's fiction. In the Wessex novels the reader is guided from one ecstasy to another (Faw, p. 150). These ecstasies form the core of the typical Powys novel. The language of the Powysian ecstasy is Romantic, deriving from Keats, Blake, Shelley, Goethe and Hölderlin, shot through with the sensuous melancholy of Baudelaire and Verlaine (SJ, pp. 207, 428).

John Cowper Powys is difficult to categorize. We place him (usually) with Lawrence, Peake, Graves, Blake and Hardy. At first glance, Powys seems to be working in the British nature-poetry tradition of Wordsworth and Edward Thomas. His immediate predecessors are Hardy and Lawrence. In Hardy (and Brontë) we have that fierce enmeshment of nature-mysticism and character. But Powys's novels wholly lack Hardy's narrative drive and feeling for drama and development. From Hardy, however, Powys learnt how to interrelate landscape and psychology in an authentic manner. Whereas Hardy is concerned with the furtherance of the dramatic story, Powys is more interested in the ex-static states of beingness. In this Powys has much in common with Lawrence. Both writers use the details found in nature as vehicles for their characters' feelings. Lawrence uses these musings to open up his text to wider issues of human emotions or politics. In Powys the movement in meditation is inward, downward and backward – into the worlds of history, mythology, and the claustrophia of the self. Again and again, it is clear that Powys's ultimate goal is not societal commentary or political polemic, but self-integration, self-awareness and self-transcendence.

One writer very close to Powys is Robert Graves. The mythical, Arthurian and legendary substructure of Britain fascinated writers such as John Cowper Powys and Graves, Lawrence, Yeats and Blake. Graves said that the Goddess has been 'banished to the wet woods'.[7] This is true of *Porius*, in which matriarchy has retreated into the rainy Welsh hills. Graves's poetry is full of references to Celtic and Greek mythology. He fills his poetry with trees, apples (relating to the Arthurian Avalon – 'apple island'), hills, seasons and other folkloric elements. For Graves, poetry creates a 'magic circle', a sacred space in which miracles of love can occur. Like Powys's heroes, Graves' aching poets are on knightly, mediæval Quests for the Goddess, for love, for the Past. Like Powys's characters, Graves' have to traverse difficult terrain. Like Powys, Graves delights in extreme states of consciousness, reflected in the landscape by such elemental furore as 'Lightning enclosed by a vast ring of mirrors'.[8]

Graves' favoured landscape is also, like Powys', wild. 'This is a wild land, country of my choice' he says in 'Rocky Acres' (p. 73), meaning the rugged hills around Harlech in North Wales. Created in Deya, Spain, Graves' poems never the;less nearly always describe a British landscape. Like Powys's world, Graves' green poetic realm is elemental, wild, magical and ancient. Its full resonance of meaning is dependent upon an in-depth knowledge of plants, folklore, seasons, Celtic and Greek myth and the tradition of English poetry. Graves' mythopoeic system is more fully refined than John Cowper Powys'. *The White Goddess* is certainly one of the richest sourcebooks of poetic lore published in modern times.

---

7 *Oxford Addresses on Poetry*, Cedric Chivers, Bath, 1974, p. 58
8 'Blackening Sky', *Collected Poems 1975*, p. 349.

Graves' *The White Goddess*, and its forerunner, Frazer's *The Golden Bough*, provide the best glozes on Powys's Celtic discourses.

Like John Cowper Powys, Graves loved Wales and Welsh mythology. He studied it throughout his life. Like Yeats, Graves was a Celtic dreamer, someone for whom myth was as real as everyday life. Graves' life-philosophy was based on his cult of the White Goddess, and this deity links up with Powys's use of Cerridwen, the Goddess of Wales. Welsh mythology is matriarchal, as is Powys's and Graves' philosophies. Both writers used the Welsh landscape, with its rocky hills and soaking rain, many times in their works. Graves' concept of the poetic trance, in which true poetry is written, has much in common with Powys's ecstasies. Both writers idenitified with the poet Taleissin; both writers adored the *Mabinogion*. Both writers had a cultic love of trees. Graves built up a complex system of tree-lore and language, which forms such a large part of his *The White Goddess*. Like Powys, Graves was trying to reach another realm of experience, symbolized by his Black Goddess figure. Graves was by far the better scholar, the better critic, and the better poet. His historical novels (*I, Claudius*, *The Golden Fleece* and others) have been highly praised. Graves' precise, economic prose states his ideas plainly, contrasting so powerfully with the elongated, meandering sentences of Powys. Both writers were regarded with suspicion (and disbelief) by the literary establishment (and they still are). Graves, after all, created a *Goddess*, no less, while Powys wrote of a multilayered cosmos of sadists, sylphs, magicians and giants. No wonder they are both still regarded as marginal writers, although Graves is firmly in the mainstream of 20th century British poetry. Graves is the poet's poet, but Powys is in no way a writer's writer like, say, Nabokov or Beckett or Borges. Not so strange, then, that Powys should hate Graves,[9] because Graves invaded Powys's secret sacred land too often. The landscape they took their inspirations from was very much the same. In both writers the Goddess Cerridwen and the genius-poet Taleissin feature strongly, as does the wildness of the Welsh mountain Cader Idris.

---

9 Garlick in Hum 72, p. 303.

Two

John Cowper Powys's Wessex Quartet

I...invent a long complicated story with a lot of characters and a host of incidents and exciting situations and elaborate and intricate disquisitions on the psychology of these entangled persons...

John Cowper Powys[10]

---

[10] Letter, 31 July 1956, in Wil, p. 371.

The Wessex quartet is John Cowper Powys's greatest achievement – in literature or philosophy. Set mainly in 1930s Dorset and Somerset, they are long and intense explorations of self-transcendence. They are *Wessex* novels, and that means they are written under the shadow of Thomas Hardy. Though Hardy is invoked many times, his presence is weak – it is swamped by John Cowper Powys's own overbearing personality. Wolf's mother says: 'I expect I've worked myself into a fuss by reading Thomas Hardy!' (WS, p. 411). Powys takes up many of Hardy's themes, but extends them in his own idiosyncratic fashion. He uses fictional place-names and real ones. Thus Sherborne becomes Ramsgard, while Dorchester retains its own name. Like Hardy's Wessexscape, Powys's land is filled with (often caricature) yokels and country folk, aristocrats, the working class and not a few outsiders. It is a nostalgic world, in which the Past often overwhelms the present. The typical Powysian anti-hero moves back into Dorset to regain his/ her childhood. The journey is back into the personal and the mythical Past. In Wessex, the characters are surrounded by the Past, by their mythical ancestors. One of Powys's chief characteristics is to go beyond the middle ages to a Roman or often prehistoric era. All these levels of Time enclose the present-day characters, just as in Hardy. The ruins of the Past, both emotional as well as architectural, are to be seen everywhere. Powys was a believer in the occult – in the 'television effect', for instance, in which ghosts continually haunt the same place. Powys's protagonists go back to Wessex to re-activate their relationship with these ghosts. It is often the opening thrust of the novels, this journey back towards the lost parents, the lost Past and the lost homeland. Powys's novels begin as a mythical homecoming. The search for the lost parents concerns the expiation of guilt. The Powys-man desires absolution. He wants to be shrived. He wants to wake up the old contacts. He wants, as Wolf does, to literally take up with the Past, with the parents again (as Wolf wants to touch his dead father's skull). The father is lascivious (in *Maiden Castle* and in *Wolf Solent*). In *Maiden Castle* the father is finally found – at the end of the Wessex quartet. The Powys-man, Dud, is both repulsed and fascinated. The father-figure is loved and hated. He is heavily sensual (like Geard and Uryen) and he is powerful (he can reach a Beyond which the Powys-son wants to grasp). Somehow, the father is in touch with things. He is the link to the ancestors, to the Past, to the old gods. The father is a god-figure himself. He is a magician – Geard, Sylvanus, Uryen – or a strange, twisted kind of intellectual – Teucer Wye, Urquhart, Dr Brush, Matt Dekker. The father is associated with paganism and occultism. One of the driving urges of Powys's fiction, then is this urge to confront the parents, to re-activate the œdipal drama.

The homecomings at the beginning of John Cowper Powys's novels were truly mythical – and they were for him too, being written in America before he returned to live in Britain. This small biographical detail – that the novels were written while Powys was lecturing and living in the States – contributes to their peculiar quality. For the towns and people in the books seem old-fashioned for the times in which they were written. There is a lack of verisimilitude, of social observation, of contemporary detail. Powys's Wessex is a phantastical one, so like the real Dorset, yet also terribly dream-like and isolated. Powys visits his world with his mind but not his body; he used maps to help re-create the places for him; his Wessex is a remembered, time-altered landscape. The journey each character makes at the beginning of each book echoes Powys's own yearning for his West Country homeland.

Powys's novels are part myth, part dream, part social commentary and part fairy tale. In a letter of 1956 he wrote:

> I am born an Inventor of Fairy Tales...To invent, that is my 1st gift, and to marshal a host of people my second gift, and to cunningly propitiate all sorts of invisible powers and forces, causing coincidents to help me with surprises, is my third gift. (Wil, pp. 371-2)

The pantheon of 'old Friar John's' fiction features few 'ordinary people', few people we might see in a contemporary soap opera. There is the John Cowper Powys-man (Wolf, Dud, Magnus, Crow); the fallen priests (Dekker, Valley); the enigmatic sylphs (Thuella, Curly, Persephone); earth-goddesses (Gerda, Wizzie, Perdita, Nell); ineffectual and marginal quasi-artists types (Athling, Jason, Brush, Gaul); crabby old men (Abel, Teucer, Loder); sadists (Brush, Evans); eccentric spinsters (Lucinda, Jennie, Elizabeth, Euphemia); obsequious political activists (Philip, Red, Wye, Cattistock); and magicians (Sylvanus, Uryen, Geard, Merlin).

John Cowper Powys sets his people against each other in classic configurations of pairs of opposites, reflecting the mythic model of the 'created world'. Characters gradually merge – Dud imagines himself becoming his father. True elemental fusion only occurs in Powys's passionate lovers and magicians (Sam and Nell, Perdita and the Jobber, Sylvanus, Merlin etc). Without passion there is dissolution (in Dud, Magnus, John) or a mixture of submission and escape (Wolf). Powys's cast of characters reveals his love of marginal, desperate souls. he cannot but see strangeness everywhere he looks. He turns 1930s Dorset into a vision of a mediæval Hell at times. He loves to mix the sensuous and the ascetic – the Godly and the excremental (in Sylvanus and his 'Caput-anus' ideology, for instance [Wey, p. 381]). Uryen is disfigured with the mark of the Crow of Bran on his chest. Powys's magicians are struggling to reconcile pain and ecstasy. Powys's magicians smell pungently. They are heavy with beingness – so heavy they stink. Here again sex and excrement fuse. His characters move towards an androgynous state of parthenogenesis (BH, p. 211). This 'Self-Birth of Psyche' from the Grail-Cauldron is a never-ending process – it continues after death.

Wolf Solent, 1929

Wolf Solent is John Cowper Powys's greatest novel, his greatest work. It is his most powerful and coherent. Unlike the other Wessex books, *Wolf Solent* is unified in its themes and motifs. It is written in Powys's sprawling style, but is sustained by an intensity of feeling far deeper than in any of Powys's other works.

It is the story of a selfish and often psychotically self-centred man who loses his life-illusion, which he calls his 'mythology'. He becomes disenchanted with people, God, love, ambition and society. It is a claustrophic, subjective novel, written in a stream of consciousness manner reminiscent more of Woolf's *To the Lighthouse* than Joyce's

Ulysses. The stuff of the novel is Wolf's thoughts and feelings, his ideas on all manner of subjects, his ecstasies and his despairs. The character and the book are bound up closely together. To hate Wolf the man is to hate *Wolf* the book. Wolf *is* the book, just as Ursula is most of *The Rainbow*.

The story begins with a classic device: the outsider returning to his/ her homeland. Thomas Hardy's novels open with a solitary traveller, walking, usually at twilight, on some country lane. John Cowper Powys begins his books with a Return – in *Wolf Solent* the journey is, as in *Jude the Obscure*, by train – for now the countryside is covered with a civilizing network of railways. Wolf is quickly introduced to a strange world of strange people. One of the delights of the Powys novel are the many odd characters he creates. So here we have a host of them: an incestuous old bookseller (Malakite), a homosexual antiquarian of Dorset (Urquhart), a bizarre Goethean poet (Jason) and a hideously ugly spinster (Selena Gaunt) among many others. Powys loves whatever is unusual, weird or even psychotic. He loves whatever and whoever lives on the edges of society. He languishes in the meticulous creation, for instance, of evil, of hatred, of ugliness, of ambiguity. He loves the in-between states of people, when they are both male and female, dead and alive, ecstatic and despairing. His characters are deliberately, self-consciously strange. He peoples his books with strays, runaway children, tramps, fallen priests, sinful women, violent men, bizarre artists. He is not in any way interested in 'ordinary people', if they even exist. His strange people seem more authentic for all their strangeness.

Apart from Wolf's many ecstasies, not much *happens* in the novel. Wolf returns to Dorset, a possessive mother, two lovers, a 'perverse' employer, and has other sheared encounters. As with most of Powys's protagonists, Wolf is not much changed at the end of the book. He fails to be mature, he fails to take on responsibilities, he remains an outsider, lost in his own dreamworld. He is profoundly self-deluded at times. How *mistaken* he is about reality! How Wolf *deludes* himself, veering off into mock-sublime but often ludicrous views on things. Of course, with such a melding of hero and book, we are not sure if it is Wolf or his world that is mad. Or maybe it is the author? A postmodernist analysis of Powys's books might explore his cultural position – his relation to contemporary writers and their influence on him, which may be, after all, slight. Powys allows more of his self to be revealed in his books than most other authors do. He lets himself be on display. Yet it is his achievement that we go along with all this self-delusion on Wolf's (and the author's) part.

Wolf Solent is an English provincial Goethean *Bildungsroman*. It recounts the journey towards self-realization of its anti-hero. But it fails to resolve many of its multitudinous themes and strands. The apocalyptic intimations never come to anything. The perversity of Urquhart is never satisfactorily clarified. The bizarre and the unreal are suggested but remain frustratingly unmanifest. Powys loves to build up a great atomic bomb of dramatic apprehension, but he never explodes it. He continually subverts the laws of narration. His is a different kind of discourse, focussing on ecstasy, not story.

We have had other self-absorbed books before, such as those of Goethe, Camus and Hamsun. But John Cowper Powys's is especially claustrophic. There's no way out of here! In some ways, Wolf is closest to Hamsun in his *Mysteries*. In these books an outsider infiltrates a calm provincial town, mixes with all the characters, but never makes a deep connection with any of them. There is the same detachment in Powys as there is in Hamsun or Sartre.

Wolf Solent is another outsider-novel. The Powysian anti-hero is not too different from Hamsun's Nagel, Camus' Mersault, Sartre's Rosquentin, Durrell's Gregory, Joyce's Stephen, Rilke's Malte, Huysman's Des Esseintes, Auster's Stillman, Huxley's Anthony Beavis, Forster's Rickie, Lawrence's Paul or Aaron, Hardy's Jude, Waugh's Ryder or Goethe's Werther. We have been here before, in this world of the European/ Western white young/ middle-aged pseudo-intellectual philosophizing male. The drifter, the outsider, the often aristocratic, disaffected man on the edge – it is familiar stuff to us now.

John Cowper Powys's Wolf is made in the same existentialist mould. Wolf is squeezed into a very tight ontological container. He is trapped in the connecting tube of some cosmic egg-timer, while all the sands of ecstasy pour down through his soul. Psychically, he is at war with himself. Superego (his mother, not father), *anima* (Christie), id (Gerda), shadow (Urquhart/ Jason) and ego (father) battle it out inside Wolf's mind. In *Wolf Solent* there is always a suggestion of vastness, but these intimations never materialize into something useful and practical. The infinity is inside, in Wolf's inner space. This is how Powys likes it. But it negates deep relationships with other people – Wolf's main problem. The book is verily a journal of 'mystical vignettes in the margin of an occult biography...' (*Wolf Solent*, hereafter as WS, p. 572). Powys's usual novelistic structure is to present us with an experience and then to move away from it. His characters are in the thick of things, but always seem to be moving away from them. Lawrence goes in closer, then closer still, then even closer still. Powys dances away. He is always in retreat. He retreats to Dorset, then to North Wales, then into his own ecstasies, then into the Past, then into the phantasies of the far side of the universe. His protagonists hide. They live in an interior, reptile world. Perhaps this is a reaction from the constant social exposure of his time teaching and lecturing. His people escape into shabby rooms, to mull over their experiences.

The quest of the Powys-man is to marry the inner and the outer worlds. There is so much interiorization in Powys books. His fiction is firmly 20th century, like Woolf and Joyce. But this inward-looking produces a lack of humanity, a lack of political awareness. The 'Other' is not another person, but the deeper self. Powys tries to make the secret, inner soul live. He tries to dredge up the deeper self, to bring it out into the open. Certainly his magician figures (Sylvanus, Uryen, Geard, Merlin) are all trying to do this. They want to expose their souls, to make them viable forces in the everyday world. Powys tries to rejuvenate a magical cult of sensations. It is not easy, because when the secret self is exposed it shrivels, like a deepsea fish. It hides, and cannot bear up too well to the harsh outer daylit life.

The Wessex novels are constructed, as is most drama, on a system of opposites, which conflict. Thus Wolf has his rival (as does his mother); there are two lovers, one earthy and one spiritual; there are two powerful local 'perverted' men (Urquhart and Malakite) and so on. This scenario instantly recalls Hardy's *Jude the Obscure*, with Gerda as Arabella and

Christie as Sue (even the names chime – Christie and Sue Bridehead – heavily ironic Christian names). There are subtle references to *Jude*. Gerda's father, for instance, is a stonemason (Jude as he might be thirty years on, perhaps). Wolf and Gerda live next to a pigsty, later on. Gerda, like Arabella, is associated with animals (though Hardy is fiercer than Powys: Gerda whistles like a bird, while Arabella cuts open a pig). Christie is a wraithlike spirit, and is, like Sue, strangely chaste, with a host of pagan and mythological connotations.

The other novel close to *Wolf Solent* is *Sons and Lovers*. Again, there are the two lovers, one intense and religious, the other heavy with sensuous flesh (both Gerda and Clara are sexualized through their breasts). Lawrence is far better at dealing with emotions between lovers, however. In *Wolf Solent* the love-affairs are curiously fudged. André Gide, in *Strait is the Gate*, also portrays the conflict between sensuous and spiritual love. He does in a short novel what it takes Powys (and Lawrence and Hardy) hundreds more pages to do.

In *Jude the Obscure* and *Wolf Solent* the journey is from the sensual to the spiritual woman; in *Sons and Lovers* is is the other way round. This is typical of Lawrence. For him, fulfilment must involve the whole of the body, not just the spirit. At the end of each novel each man (Jude, Wolf and Paul) is pretty much alone. Jude dies, while Paul and Wolf are left alone, wandering in nature, under vast skies. The struggle is the same: for self-integration, to become complete. In his *Study of Hardy* Lawrence wrote: 'The final aim of every living thing, creature, or being is the full achievement of itself.' (p. 12) And, as Lawrence says, it is the flower not the fruit that is the culmination. The journey, not the end, counts.

Thomas Hardy's *Jude the Obscure* tells the tale of the failure to become complete, to join together the sensual and the spiritual, the pagan and the Christian. In Lawrence's and Powys's *Bildungsroman* a kind of wholeness is achieved, but at a high price. The relations with other people are fractured. Hardy describes failure, while Lawrence, more positive, describes yearning coming upon yearning. Powys moves into a metaphysical stance of solitude, and finds consolation in the knowledge that cosmically, it doesn't matter – for *ripeness is all*.

Hardy's *Jude the Obscure* is structured around a complicated sequence of parallel events – external events mirroring the inner states of the characters – the classic way of the novel. Lawrence's and Powys's books are sequences of interior states. Powys has an amazing disregard for events going on outside of his anti-hero's mind.

While Hardy's and Lawrence's novels contain critiques of society, religion, ethics and love, Powys's are notoriously devoid of such discourse. Powys's anti-heroes are religiously irresponsible, like Camus' Meursault. Wolf doesn't *care* that much, and certainly not like Jude cares. Powys and Lawrence both modelled their spiritual women on Sue Bridehead. Sue is one the first examples of the 'modern woman' according to all the critics. Powys's Christie is closely based on Sue. In, for instance, her love of literature, paganism and philosophy; her association with pagan deities; her strange chaste form of love; her detachment and wayward intensity. Lawrence's Miriam is similarly drawn, though more intensely, and with more emphasis on the religious side of things.

Lawrence's *Sons and Lovers* is like a postscript to *Jude the Obscure*. But whereas Hardy always keeps his narrative driving along – he always has his eye on the characters – John Cowper Powys wanders off his track so many times. These are the joys of Powys, these wanderings, but they are also the source of many frustrations.

So much of *Jude the Obscure* is a rigorous discourse on Biblical and Classical learning, on theology, on education, on class and status, on paganism and Christianity, on traditional values versus modern ones, on the role of the individual in society, on labour, on ambition, on sexuality, on sexual politics, on domesticity, on spirituality, on love, on faith, on so many things in the culture. Powys's *Wolf* does not come up to this very high standard. Powys's novel's intentions are different. But, even so, *Wolf Solent* is not as successful as Hardy's bitingly accurate polemical text.

What distinguishes *Wolf Solent* from other similar novels is John Cowper Powys's tremendously powerful sense of nature and sensualism. It is intense, violent, vivid, eidetic and profound. Small objects are imbued with gigantic meanings. Feelings and organic details fuse in a new, visionary manner. Wolf's soul is invaded by the myriad mysteries of things (WS, p. 106). He exalts in a world of a 'series of disembodied sensations' (p. 224). He has ecstasies of beauty (p. 324), eroticism (p. 275), underlife (p. 442) and memory (p. 107). A typical example of Wolf's extraordinary raptures occurs on one of his many nocturnal walks:

> Gathering up all the spiritual strength he possessed, he flung his mind outwards, far over those silent reaches of meadow grass and fallow land. He imagined as vividly as he could all that was going on in that darkened margin of Blackmore. He followed the skulking of foxes under the hazels, the stirrings of hedgehogs in their hibernating quiescence, the crouching of birds on leafless boughs, the burrowing of moles under their hillocks, the breathing of cattle in their barns. He imagined all these things so intensely, one by one, that he began to feel that he shared those nocturnal movements – that he was no stranger among them, but himself a furtive, lonely earth-life among other earth-lives, drawing, as they did, some curative magnetism from the dark greenish-black hide of the great planetary body! (p. 442)

This is a standard Powysian ecstasy – with its attention to the minute elements of life that are part of the vaster aspects of things. It is classically Romantic, but shot through with Powys's own preoccupations. Powys likes to swoop down among all kinds of livings things, from birds in the sky, to the roots of trees far underground. Powys's brother, Llewelyn Powys, also wrote of nature in all its bewildering detail – in *Love and Death* he speaks of 'hot puffs of air, sweet with the perfume of banks of bedstraw', of 'budding willow-herbs, soft and damp to the touch' (*Love and Death*, 1939, p. 166).

Thomas Hardy's novels too are full of a loving attention to natural detail. In the opening paragraph of his early novel *Under the Greenwood Tree* he speaks of the individuality and significance of trees:

> To dwellers in a wood almost every species of tree has its voice as well as its feature. At the passing of the breeze the fir-trees sob and moan no less distinctly than they rock: the holly whistles as it battles with itself; the ash hisses amid its quivering; the beech rustles while its flat boughs rise and fall. And winter, which modifies the note of such trees as shed their leaves, does not destroy their individuality. (*Greenwood Tree*, p. 11).

Here Hardy describes the songs of the trees – a concept and experience both everyday and poetic. Hardy is clever – he hides his nature-mysticism under quite ordinary prose, weaving it skillfully into his narratives. Powys is more explicitly ecstatic. Another example of sudden, overwhelming ecstasy occurs again when Wolf is out walking (he seems to do this more than anything else in the novel):

> That incredible patch of blue seemed something into which he could plunge his hands and draw them forth again, filled like overflowing cups with the very ichor of happiness. Ah! That was the word. It was *pure happiness*, that blue patch! (p. 151)

A patch of blue sky – this is all the hyper-sensitive Romantic poet needs to launch him into ecstasy. Wolf loves simply walking and sinking into self-created trance-states. These times are what he lives for. He comes to realize this at the end of the novel. He decides to do without people, or things. A key passage, indicating clearly Wolf's philosophical stance, centres around the importance for Wolf of memories:

> They [memories] had to do with wild rain-drenched escapes beneath banks of sombre clouds, of escapes along old backwaters and by forsaken sea-estuaries, of escapes along wet, deserted moor-paths and by sighing pond-reeds; along melancholy quarry-pools and by quagmires of livid moss. Indescribable! Indescribable! But memories of this kind were – and he had long known it! – the very essence of his life. They were more important to him than any outward event. They were more sacred to him than any living person. They were his friends, his gods, his secret religion. (p. 107)

Ecstasy above other people – this is Wolf's outlook on life. He uses people as catalysts for his own self-absorbed phantasies. His daydreams are intense, and they overwhelm him. In this sense, Powys is truly a mystical novelist. His ecstasies have most of the hallmarks of the true ecstasy in authentic mysticism. It is not too much of a leap to compare Powys with St Teresa or Jan van Ruysbroeck. Wolf's ecstasies compare well with those of Joyce's Stephen:

> O what sweet music! His soul was all dewy wet... A spirit filled him, pure as the purest water, sweet as dew, moving as music. But how faintly it was inbreathed, how passionately, as if the seraphim

themselves were breathing upon him!'[11]

Unlike Joyce, Beckett, Rilke, Yeats, Lawrence or Green, Powys does not have the heavy weight of Christian/ Catholic intensity inside him. Their philosophies are formed out of the fervour of Catholicism – think of the pagan fever of André Gide which came out of his Puritan upbringing. Powys's ecstasies are refreshingly devoid of ecclesiastical piety and doctrine. Where Lawrence, Joyce and Rilke continually grapple with theological teaching (even when describing their pagan sensualities) Powys, like Rimbaud, lets his ecstasies fly free of all that institutionalized baggage. Powys is terrifically, joyously free of Christian, scriptural ethics. Unlike Hardy, who nearly get submerged and drowned under them in *Jude the Obscure*. Powys's ultimate reference-point is Classic Greece (Homer) and post-Roman Wales (Merlin, Taleissin, Ceriddwen) in Geoffrey of Monmouth, the *Mabinogion* and other Celtic/ Arthurian romances.

The language Powys uses when he moves into his ecstatic mode (not as refined or as intricate as Joyce's) is still the language of mysticism. As with all true mystics, Powys is searching in *Wolf Solent* for a suitable language for his ecstatic visions. The sense of experimentation and exploration, as with Lawrence's *The Rainbow*, makes the work so much more exciting.

As with the end of Lawrence's apocalyptic novel, Powys's *Wolf Solent* ends with a scene of symbolic, metaphysical ecstasy. Wolf wanders out into a meadow of golden buttercups – 'It was literally a floating sea of liquid, shining gold!' (WS, p. 629). He is drowned in Saturnian gold. He stares into the pagan sun. He realizes his life-illusion is dead. It is a crisis-time, a moment of renunciation and catharsis. This is the climax of the novel: Wolf sees the landscape as a god. He wants to pour the gold over all the people he knows. He has to realize that 'ripeness is all', and that he has to '*Endure or escape.*' (pp. 632-4)

It is a suitably intense ending to the novel, but is so much weaker than Ursula's vision of the rainbow. Powys aims to tie up all his characters and themes in this one extended symbolic scene. But we know that Wolf's life has in many ways ended: he continually sinks himself into the Past.

---

[11] *A Portrait of the Artist as a Young Man*, Penguin 1960, p. 216.

For Ursula, however, everything is beginning: she is throwing herself into the future, trembling with yearning, and Lawrence's ending is majestic.

John Cowper Powys, like Lawrence, has always had problems with endings. Nevertheless, the soul-alone ontology of *Wolf Solent* is Powys's own, and one of his clearest statements. For Wolf, the final equilibrium lies not with God or people or art or emotions or objects, but with the primæval elements.

Where the novel falters is in its depiction of Wolf's love-affairs. Gerda is treated sweetly enough in the blackbird-singing sequences, but later she is treated cruelly by both author and protagonist. She is also given a blandness more appropriate to Wolf. Christie is more sympathetically drawn. She is one of the white wand-like girls that Powys adored so much. She is a Sophia-figure, a wraithlike Lilith, beautiful but ethereal, erotic and untouchable. For Wolf Christie is the stuff of Arthurian legend. She is linked with the Somerset wetlands and Glastonbury (p. 327). She is Wolf's Life-Quest, his Grail, his Eternal Feminine, his *anima*, his Goddess.

When the time comes for Christie and Wolf to embrace, Powys cannot hide his misogyny. Just before they are about to make love in Christie's green bedroom, Wolf lapses into one of his erotic hallucinations. Christie is left out of it all. She tells Wolf he doesn't understand how other people feel (p. 466). Christie thinks she has been prevented from being loved sexually by the face Wolf saw at Waterloo Station. As in so much of literature, it is the woman who has to bear the brunt of the man's failure to love. Wolf is an emotional cripple, unable (and unwilling) to make a deep contact with another human being. Powys here defrauds his characters (and his readers) of a basic humanity, the 'pity' he so loved in Hardy (PL, p. 605). When Powys brings his mythic sensualism into contact with other people the result is fraught with difficulties. He cannot reconcile the two – love and sensual solitude. Only once or twice did he create a love-union than was authentically realized and not misogynistic – in Perdita and the Jobber in *Weymouth Sands*, and in Nell and Sam in *A Glastonbury Romance*.

The opening chapter of *Wolf Solent* is a good example of Powys's style and form. He opens the book with one of his famous long sentences (a six-liner). The sentence/ paragraph sites us in England, on a train from London to Dorset, in the company of someone who dislikes company. This character enjoys 'an orgy of concentrated thought' in which time spools out to become timelessness. Already, then, in the first sentence, Powys is giving us ecstasies.

He goes on to relate the anti-hero's love of sensuous detail (a crawling fly, smells from the window, colour). We are given a little history and background of the character, and why he is on this train. We find out about his possessive mother, and how he disgraced himself in a classroom. Powys's strange way of looking at the world is displayed in his use of odd phrases, such as 'a vivisected frog's-belly of a world' (p. 16). Another strange way of seeing, yet somehow wholly authentic and accurately observed, is when Wolf imagines a prehistoric giant leaping along beside the racing train. This works well, dealing as it does with someone simply staring out of a train-window in a brown study. The telegraph wires sinking up and down with the motion sounds authentic. More strangeness: Wolf imagines a 'long-drawn melancholy cry' echoing out over the West Country on a windy November evening – for no reason at all!' (p. 17) More history and observation follows. Then the real Wolf begins to come out. 'All I want is sensations!' he says (p. 19) This is a key line. Then follows the description of his 'mythology'' which is a 'sinking into his soul' (p. 19). The source of this 'mythology' is Weymouth, a place forever in Powys associated with a blissful childhood. Wolf's 'mythology' is secret, intense and of utmost importance to him. It is described in sensual, earthy imagery:

> He would have said that his magnetic impulses resembled the expanding of great vegetable leaves over a still pool – leaves nourished by hushed noons, by liquid, transparent nights, by all the movements of the elements...(p. 20)

More pedestrian yearnings follow, as Wolf aches for 'some girl who'll let me make love to her' (p. 21) The *passive* stance of the Powysian male in sexual relations is typical. A series of questions, aimed as much at the author as at his audience, ends the opening chapter. The author is thinking aloud here, as he embarks upon another voyage into the unknown – a novel. Intimations of infinity are counterbalanced by concrete realities – what is it going to be like, really like? Thus Powys introduces us to his phantastical Wessex world.

A Glastonbury Romance, 1932

A Glastonbury Romance is a great, big sprawling mess of a book. It is not a drama, nor a story, nor even a 'romance' in the loosest sense of the word. There is hardly any action, plot, development or resolution. It is far too long – each chapter is practically a short novel in itself. It would greatly benefit from being cut to a third of its present size. John Cowper Powys here goes against all the rules of conventional fiction, but his daring is more often failure than success.

In *A Glastonbury Romance* John Cowper Powys waffles, side-tracks, and drifts about like some decrepid Victorian machine on its last legs. He halts, looks about, goes off in another direction, has tea breaks, backtracks, runs, crawls, wobbles, flips over, twists, occasionally leaps of the ground, though all too often he just plods along regardless of the effects on his exasperated reader.

What a book! But how wonderful it might have been. For here we had the Arthurian and Grail legends, Britain's own and greatest collections of myths and folklore, interpreted by one of the few authors fully equipped to do them justice. Instead we get a flabby gargantuan of a book that flops along, structureless, formless, gormless – a beached whale of a book unable to regain the seas of mysticality, howling away to itself in pathetic incoherence on some melancholy strand.

Having said all this, Powys's neo-pagan extravaganza is far and away the best modern phantasy novel on Arthurian themes. *A Glastonbury Romance* is far better in many respects than the books of C.S. Lewis, Tolkien, Stewart, Tolstoy and a host of other science-fiction and sword-

and-sorcery writers. The main problem with the book is that it tries, so hard, to be all-inclusive, to be comprehensive and encyclopædical. It is written, as Wilson notes, 'from a God's eye point of view.' (*The Occult*, p. 65) But Powys makes as big a mess of his created world as God has made of our own.

In the book Powys lets himself run wild. Here Powys the mystic comes to the fore. Unfortunately, Powys did not excise the bad sections (as most writers do). He left them in, and they weigh the novel down terribly. The ramshackle nature of *A Glastonbury Romance* makes one appreciate even more the ruthless driving force of Hardy's *Jude*, or the concentrated passion of Gide's *Strait is the Gate*. Powys is like Henry Miller: both writers love to overwrite, to let themselves explode into torrents of words. Not for them the acerb concision of Forster or Raymond Carver. Powys gushes. He is a waterfall of emotions and words. He goes down to the roots of things, and far up into space, beyond the sky, to the First Cause which dwells in the sun and at the edge of the cosmos. It is an expansive vision of things, in which Powys aims for to grasp the stars. It is this tension between the tiny and the vast, between the utterly ordinary and the mytho-cosmic that makes *A Glastonbury Romance* such a confused novel. The interstellar viewpoint is at odds with the human one, and the human viewpoint is confused enough.

The political, social and ideological themes are badly wrought. We cannot take John Cowper Powys seriously in his creation of capitalist and communist and socialist characters. Powys's people in *A Glastonbury Romance* are like puppets, mere vehicles for political and sexual discourses. The sexuality is all too loosely handled. Powys delights in creating homosexual, lesbian and possessive sexuality, but he does not know what to do with it once he's suggested it. He is vague just where he needs to be precise. The book reflects his uncertainties – both in terms of form and of philosophy.

The sadism is unconvincing – it centres around an 'evil' picture in a book which haunts the lonely Mr Evans. Out of an image of an iron bar bearing down upon someone's head Powys constructs a cult of intense evil. It is simply not believable. Mr Evans' psychosis is, but not its source (even though Powys rightly associates Evans with St Paul, another anally neurotic sadist). The rain-god in *Wolf Solent*, and the bedpost in *Maiden Castle*, are also similarly vague. They are meant to be symbols of immense evil – of godlike, suprahuman evil – but they fail to convince us.

A Glastonbury Romance is a book made up of a series of events and characters only loosely united by the main theme. *A Glastonbury Romance* is good in parts, but not as a whole. This is usual in Powys's works. The theme – the re-establishment of a mystical religion of Christianized paganism in the twentieth century – is only really dealt with in the characters of Sam, Dekker and Geard. Geard's new cult affects the whole town, and it is only the fact that all of Powys's characters live in the same town that unities them together. The book, after all, is the *Glastonbury Romance*, not the Geard or the Dekker Romance. It is a novel of place and nature as much as of people and events.

The new mystical cult of the Grail forms the core of the book. Robert Graves has said that the Arthurian legends together constitute a Bible for the British. They are Britain's very own mythologies, even if they have been imported in part from France, Norway, Germany and much of Europe. John Geard, the vatic mouthpiece of this new cult, is the first of Powys's great magician-figures. He is sensuous, fleshly, and curiously ignorant of the source of his powers. He is a grand (though flawed) creation. Powys fills him with a vitality and humour that contrasts so effectively with John Crow's spiteful vapidity. One of the best scenes in the book is where Geard dreams he has been visited by Merlin's enchantress, Ninue. Powys's fascination with Arthurian legend culminated in the later *Porius*. It is absolutely fitting that Powys should be more intrigued by Merlin and Ninue, rather than by Arthur and Guinevere.

It is Sam who is the hero of the book, in the traditional sense. He is granted the vision of the Grail, which John Cowper Powys regarded as the 'heroine' of the tale (pxiii). The Grail-vision is one of Powys's best sequences – certainly his most mystical. It blends all his main ecstatic motifs: light, water, Celtic myth, anal sexuality, verticality, biting realism and cosmic eroticism. Powys carefully describes the subtle changes that such ecstasies bring about: Sam moves from feeling bleeding darkness through a theological disquisition to a sense of humility and renunciation.

Powys is ruthless in his story of Sam. He demonstrates how during the inrushing of timelessness equilibrium-of-self is destroyed, and he fails (like Jude) both his lovers (Nell and Crummie).

Perhaps the best of the seemingly interminable scenes and chapters is when Nell and Sam make love. Here Powys delicately captures the thoughts of two people preparing for and dreaming about their night together. It is a marvellously sustained and *cogent* piece of writing. We would certainly like to see more of this sort of writing. It is so much better than those confused interior scenes teeming with characters and their feelings, such as the silver bowl tasting, or the Christening parlour conversation. Powys's description of the tense build-up to the love-making rings deep and true.

With the big crowd scenes, John Cowper Powys's control weakens. The chapter 'The Pageant', intended to be a fitting climax to Part One of the book, is an immense failure. It centres around the mock-crucifixion of Mr Evans, but Powys tries to add weight to the spectacle by putting his commentary on the event into the dialogues of the many onlookers. Artistically it might have worked, but instead we get a hopelessly confused description of a complex scene. How annoying Powys is when he fudges such scenes, such as the battles in *Porius*, or some of the confrontations in *Owen Glendower*. Powys attempts at verisimilitude fall flat (pp.xi,xiv). He is far better with characters adrift in their solitude, such as in the genuinely præternatural night in 'Mark's Court'.

Real drama and tension is provided in the novel, however, in the Sam–Mat son–father relationship. This provides the true heart of *A Glastonbury Romance*. The elder Dekker is one of Powys's best creations: a brutal but wholly sympathetic rendition of a man torn to the depths of his being between carefree sexuality and chaste Christianity. Powys handles the hypocrisy and schizophrenia of Dekker brilliantly. Gradually Powys teases out the irony and double-standards of the situation, the age-old sex–sin–death equations sited at the powerbase of Christianity. Sam's renunciation of Nell, and his taking up of the Grail Quest are superb demonstrations of patriarchy-in-motion. Sam chooses to follow in his father's footsteps, moving away from the Goddess into an ascetic, arid, all-male world. This tension is of course ever-present in Hardy (and Gide, Joyce, Proust and many others). The age-old question for these Christianized writers is how to reconcile individual sexuality with mass religion. The marriage of sex and spirit can only be resolved by the individual, in the self. This is what Hardy's and Powys's characters have to learn. Often they learn too late.

In John Cowper Powys sexuality is spiritual, while his sense of spirituality is very erotic. He does, like Freud, sexualize the universe. Powys's magician-figures embody this unifying of sensuality and spirituality. Geard is a heavy, sensual man. Powys says through the character of Geard that any new religion must embrace the flesh as well as the spirit. It is, as Lawrence said, essential to include the body in the rebirthing of the spirit. Powys is like many twentieth century artists in this goal of soul–body/ sex–spirit union (think of Picasso, Gill, Chagall, Schiele among painters, for instance). He was unusual, though, in his inclusion of the whole planet and the cosmos in his eroticization of the spiritual.

A Glastonbury Romance is Powys's gigantic attempt to move into the epic realms of Tolstoy, Homer, Dante and Cervantes. It is his most ambitious work, but he over-reached himself. Powys's effort is self-consciously heroic. But at least it is also often comic. His street-urchins are lots of fun, though Red, Abel and Legge are hollow caricatures of stereotypes. Philip and Mary Crow, too, despite having their own sort of raptures, are cardboard characters. Much more interesting are the dispassionate Zoyland and the sylphlike, yearning Persephone. They make love in a strangely detached, dreamlike fashion which fits in with their personalities.

The final Flood sequence is confused in its symbolism and meaning. It is too obvious, too awkwardly handled, too much like join-the-dots poetry. It has potential, of course: the ancient Isle of Avalon asserting itself once again, surrounded by water. But as usual in this book Powys fluffs his chances of making something great out of it.

In its invocation of 'the great goddess Cybele' he book ends as badly as it began. There are few beginnings as bad as that to *A Glastonbury*

Romance. Powys intones his mythic rhetoric in a solemn, grandiose tone – literary Mannerism at its worst. He references Rome, Stonehenge, and Jerusalem, hoping for the big, wide perspective. But the symbolism is fragmented. Everything changes, says Powys; the Timeless remains; humankind is forgotten; Powys moves gently into his beloved 'Unknown Dimension'.

The Goddess yet abides, however. Here John Cowper Powys has much in common with Graves. Both writers look towards Wales, Celtic lore and a former, glorious matriarchy. The Mother overwhelms them. After the Flood from the Goddess's womb at Glastonbury, the soul retires into a pagan twilit world. The ending is a Return-to-the-Mother, after the breaking of the waters, as happens just before a birth. Powys spirits himself away to the Source of the Grail-cauldron's power – the Goddess. Here, as Cybele, She is the One that makes life. She is a Corn-Goddess. Powys is at the height of his powers, in the midst of the Wessex quartet. In the next book the floodwater at the end of *A Glastonbury Romance* expands to become the great shimmering ocean at the heart of *Weymouth Sands*.

Weymouth Sands, 1934

Weymouth Sands is the most lyrical of the Dorset books. The sea and the soft ecstasies it induces form the core of the novel. Everything in this book flows from the sea. The sea dominates the story. The dichotomy of the wet sand and the dry sand is one of the primary themes. Despite the loneliness and eternal dissatisfactions of the characters, *Weymouth Sands* is one of Powys's happiest works. Certainly it contains Powys's most luminous pieces of prose. These are centred on the ocean (see pp. 171, 324, 392, 455f). Powys deeply relished re-creating what he called the 'air of real West-Country exclusiveness about *Weymouth Sands*' (p. 457). The sea features prominently, as an actuality and an all-inclusive symbol, in key chapters, such as 'The Sea-Serpent' and 'Punch and Judy'. The second main theme is the ebb and flow of love. Love in *Weymouth Sands* is tidal: the high tides of love's water stain the wet sands of childhood and youth, but draw back from the dry sands of adulthood and death. You are either on the wet or the dry sand. The children always play on the wet sand. Sylvanus 'seemed to worship, not poetically but *really* the sun, the sun, and the sky'. He has a 'superstitious acknowledgement of the divinity of the sea.' (p. 324) Powys's water-symbolism is clear enough here: you have to get wet to get alive – you have to dive in to the waters of life, whatever the risk.

> That shivering dance of reflected light from the heart of our planetary universe had a more mystical effect upon him [Sylvanus] than any other phenomenon between earth and sky. The only thing superior to it in its power to stir him was the dazzling glitter of the sun on the sea. Sunlight and water – whether the water were salt or fresh – always struck Sylvanus as being the nearest revelation of the Ultimate Being that man could attain. (p. 392)

Weymouth Sands is a ragbag of scenes thrown together in an impressionistic way. They are coalesced (again, as in *A Glastonbury Romance*) primarily by the sense of place (never stronger than here in this shabby seaside town). None of the characters really connect with one another. It is a town of drifters. The locals are all yearning for something, but they have difficulty articulating it. They are united through living their life among the elements. Powys conjoins them, with his Godlike vision, with his ability to sweep up storms. In the fervour of the elements, out in the open air or cuddled up in bed, all people are one. Powys squeezes them all together with his visions of apocalyptic weather conditions and attention to the tiniest natural details.

There are no grand statements in the book, and nothing is definitively resolved. Life is never that simple in Powys: he goes for the 'complex vision'. It is a novel of disaffected souls, of neurosis and ambivalence, of misunderstanding and fear, of yearning and covert violence. Disappointing though it is in many respects, *Weymouth Sands* transcends itself through Powys's intense feeling for the personally heroic and the mythically poetic. The place resonates within Powys at the deepest level. He re-creates the glamoured innocence of childhood. His ecstasy shows.

There is again the regular pantheon of Powysian figures – Magnus, the disaffected semi-intellectuial alone, Sylvanus, a humane magician-figure, various ambivalent boy-girls (Curly, Peg), and surly men of action – the Jobber, Cattistock, etc. There are also the intriguing figures of Gypsy May and her sidekick, Larry Zed, as well as the romantically named 'Punch-and-Judy girl', Marret. There are some marvellous characters in Hardy and Powys – Diggory Venn, Grandfer Cantle, Susan Nansuch, Tim Tangs, Gabriel Oak, Tess, Sue, Jude, Marty, Uryen, Sylvanus, Elphin Cantle, Nell, Geard, Merlin, Bacon, etc. They are all memorable – the minor characters as much as the major ones. Powys took Hardy's Greek chorus and exaggerated them to become his now-familiar waifs, urchins, spinsters and old codgers. The cast list of favourites continues with Mother Legge, Euphemia Drew, Lobbie Torp, Funky, the Punch-and-Judy girl and Selina Gaunt. Who could resist Grandfer Cantle in *The Return of the Native* when he says: 'I'd be very glad to ask her in wedlock, if she'd hae me, and take the risk of her wild dark eyes ill-wishing me.' (p. 101) Or Timothy Fairway later on in *Return* talking about dancing:

> You be bound to dance at Christmas because 'tis the time o' year; you must dance at weddings because 'tis the time o' life. At Christenings folk will even smuggle in a reel or two, if 'tis no further than the first or second chiel... For my part I like a good hearty funeral as well as anything. You've as splendid victuals and drinks as at other parties, and even better. And it doesn't wear your legs to stumps in talking over a poor fellow's ways as it do to stand up in hornpipes. (p. 72-73)

The tone is just right, the language-register and vocabulary spot-on – and the subject is the genial discussion of the high-points of life: birth, death and love, and their celebrations in christenings, funerals and weddings. There aren't enough of these celebrations of being alive – they have been seriously eroded in this post-everything age. These rustic types certainly enjoy themselves when they go visiting. Hardy captures delicately the right balance between innocence and world-weariness, between simple happiness and nostalgic melancholy.

Larry Zed is the best of John Cowper Powys's urchins. He is plucked straight from early Thomas Hardy and touched in with Dickensian eccentricities. He is fully realized and filled with humour and pathos. The red-headed half-wit enjoys Powysian sensual feelings (Wey, p. 134). He gets them from simple things such as cowsheds, eel-heads, sunsets and seaweed. He has a scrapbook of seaweed. The chapter 'Lodmoor', with the its spiritual ravishment of Perdita by Larry, is one of Powys's best scenes. It includes the Tarot-reading scene and some humorous Dorset dialogue. Larry mutters to himself about his 'Nothing-Girl', a dream-figure of his masturbatory phantasies that visits him like a beneficent wraith from mythology: 'There be a wondrous soft place between the Nothing-Girl's titties where she lets I lie...' he says (p. 133).

The 'Nothing-Girl' is one of Powys's odd but successful creations. The Larry — Perdita scene is delicately handled. It is a psychic seduction. She lies on Larry's bed in the barn, thinking of other things (such as her lover, the Jobber). Larry, meanwhile, is ecstatic to have a woman lying on his bed. He keeps repeating to himself: 'I've got a girl on me bed!' (p. 169). It is heavily romanticized, this scene, but is redeemed by its genuine humour. Using the most simple language Powys describes the fervid erotic consummation brought about by the two youths' hypnotized eyes.:

> Larry's whole soul gleamed in his green eyes as he hung over her. His brain felt dizzy; but it seemed to him as though touching her so, and while she lay there prone and still beneath him, that a veritable consummation of his desire was already taking place. To his fervid imagination it was enough that their eyes clung together and that she knew he was ravishing her in his thought. Her bare hand, round which his fingers burned, was to him then her whole body. (p. 173)

This is a spiritual rape ('ravish' comes from the same root as rape). It is redeemed from seeming like a rape by John Cowper Powys's idiosyncratic idea of ethereal love. This hand-clasped occult contact recalls the tender moment in *Return*, when Charley gets to hold Eustacia's hand in return for a favour: 'Charley took it [her hand] in both his own with a tenderness beyond description' (p. 183) Powys's scene replays Hardy's, but extends it, and adds to it his elemental sensualism. *Jude the Obscure* also records a spiritual, ætheric love-affair. Jude idealizes Sue, seeing in her photograph an angelic, haloed personage (*Jude*, p. 124). As his love-from-afar for her increases (the *amor lonh* of the troubadours) Jude is worried by his sexual feelings (p. 146). He sees 'in her almost a divinity' (p. 199). Their consummation, played out against a background of increasingly modernized and secularized towns, is fraught with problems.

In Powys's *Weymouth Sands* it is the unintellectual poverty-stricken characters that make the book work. The others – Cattistock, Dr Brush, Lucinda and the dancing girls are not convincing. The Jobber has some of the quality of Heathcliffe. He is half-caricature. But as Perdita's dæmonic 'sea-lover' (p. 171) he attains more emotional plausibility. Their love-affair and love-making on the wind-swept Portland rock, is marked with genuine passion. The symbols – the earthmagic/ phallic stone Skald carries, and the boulder (reminiscent of an Eric Gill stone-carving) are all too obvious. Yet their night in the storm at the Sea-Serpent's Head is vividly portrayed, and elevates the text.

The other love-story, between Sylvanus and Marret, is told with a deft poignancy. Like Powys's other mages, Sylvanus is a solitary character. He has a mixed-up anal–ecstatic cult. He is a follower of Tantric sex magic. He is painted in soft but luminous colours. Powys creates a tender farewell at dawn for his characters. He introduces piquant metaphors. As Sylvanus watches his lover and Larry Zed moving over the brow of the hill at dawn he is 'aware of a sensation in the pit of his stomach as if there were an umbrella inside him that was blowing inside out.' (p. 518)

Weymouth is still as Powys described the place, just as much of Dorset is still as it was in Hardy's time. There is still a sense of space, of fresh air, of openness, in Weymouth, despite the tacky shops, stinking cars and hordes of tourists. It still has that old seaside holiday flavour to it, and the curve of low Dorset hills to the east is majestic. Powys's novel is a pæan to this once-secluded spot. His Weymouth is both the real town in Dorset and a highly mythologized paradise.

Maiden Castle, 1936

Maiden Castle is the most disappointing of the Wessex books. John Cowper Powys seems to have exhausted himself, his environment and his themes. Gone are the ecstasies, the lyrical visions and the vivid characters of the earlier books. Even less happens in *Maiden Castle* than in *Weymouth Sands*. The books muddles along, with only one really good scene – Uryen and Dud No-Man on Mai-Dun Castle itself. (The novel was abridged on publication in 1936, and has since been repaired).

Maiden Castle is a novel of dry, sterile love. It has a dry, sterile Powysian anti-hero, Dud. Spiritually, the landscape of *Maiden Castle* is a desert. A chilly, supernatural wind blows through it. It is arid and barren, despite being set in Dorchester, a county town surrounded by crystal clear streams and rivers. The town is presented like some second-hand cast-off from an early Hardy short story. It is a loose, frustrating, unresolved book, a novel of impotence and failure. The sense of failure – Powys is really at the end of some cycle here – is not redeemed as it is in the other West Country books by Powys's lyricism. It is interesting to note that the first three Wessex books were written in America, while *Maiden Castle* was written in Dorchester and Wales. Ironically after living in the UK Powys seemed to move further away from his subject and landscape. Much of the earlier glamour has gone. *Maiden Castle* is literally a skeletal novel – not at all the ripe fruit of *Wolf Solent*.

Three figures keep the book together – the most impressive is another of John Cowper Powys's magicians, Enoch 'Uryen' Qurim. He is messy, sombre, noble, massive, gaunt, malefic, a denizen of an earlier, magical age (p. 242). His presence gives the novel real power. Without him the book would be so much more fractured. For it is not, like Wolf, held together by its anti-hero, Dud, but by Uryen.

Second is Wizzie, the circus-girl, another of Powys's sylphs, placed against Thuella Wye. Wizzie's berrating of her aged rapist, Old Funky, has much in common with Tess's demolishing of Alec (before she murders him in the boarding-house). It is however highly improbable that a girl like Wizzie would stay with a man like Dud No-Man. He is the ubiquitous Powysian failed artist, failed liver of life. He lives through books, in the

Past. Like Wolf, Dud has many odd and annoying personal habits. He is often as autistic as Wolf. He wilfully ignores the needs of other people.

The relationship between Dud and Wizzie is indeed strange. He is extraordinarily insensitive to her desires and her soul. He practises a 'cerebral sensuality' (p. 184). Their love-making is sterile. This trinity of strange beings is like an ill-starred trine of astrological air-signs. Wizzie, the independent, free-dancing Aquarian sprite; Dud the non-committal Libra; and Uryen, a schizophrenic Gemini with Saturn and the other planets deeply embedded in Capricorn, living in the half-world of pre-Celtic mythology. Significantly, Powys switches over the central commentary of the book to Wizzie halfway through. Her prophesied union with Uryen could have made the novel much greater than it actually is. That could have been a profound union of souls. But, as with all the other relationships in the book, this potentially magical one is thwarted.

The other characters also in exist in a nervous, restless relation to each other. Teucer Wye, with his copies of Plato in each pocket, is another Powysian loathed old man. Thuella's relation to the novel and to her creator is as ambiguous as her æsthete sexuality. She is the archetypal Powysian wand-like girl. She is all frustration. The political ciphers (of Fascism and Communism) are hardly touched in at all. Always on the edge, the characters in *Maiden Castle* never really connect with each other. Their fragmented emotional liaisons reflect the fractured structure of the novel. Only Uryen and Wizzie push their passion through to some sort of completion. It is verily a novel of Eliotian sterility, a waste land world full of the 'thoughts of a dry brain in a dry seasons'('Gerontion')

As it is set in Dorchester, one might expect the spirit of the old Wessex poet to suffuse the novel. But he is a pale ghost, only referred to obliquely. Powys must have been very conscious of this – of setting his novel in the town of Hardy's great story of *The Decline and Fall of the Mayor of Casterbridge*. But *Maiden Castle* is vastly overshadowed by Hardy's *Mayor*. There are references to Hardy in Powys's 'Dorchester Romance' (Wil, p. 26), but on the whole Hardy's book is immensely superior. Dud 'buys' Wizzie near the beginning, inverting ironically Hardy's famous opening of *The Mayor of Casterbridge*. But whereas Hardy's town is lovingly and so fully realized, Powys's Romano-British settlement is merely another background element in Dud's socio-historic dreamworld.

When Dud approaches *Maiden Castle* with Uryen there are echoes of Thomas Hardy's short story *A Tryst at an Ancient Earthwork*. Much is made in John Cowper Powys's narrative of the 'profile of the whole stupendous ruin' (*Short Stories*, p. 385). As in Hardy's story, there in *Maiden Castle* an evocation of mytho-history, a strange conversation upon the earthwork, and the finding of an archæological object. Mai-Dun is the setting (how could it be otherwise?) for the central confrontation of the novel.

History, both personal and mythical, forms the structural underpinning of the book. Hardy was always conscious of the various layers of history built into Dorchester, and Powys teases these layers out into the open. Wizzie is thus the 'Stone-Age girl' (like Perdita); Dud relates to the Roman era and the Mary Channing hanging; Uryen goes back furthest, to the old gods, to Saturn, Cronos, Bran and Time. He is a forerunner of Merlin in *Porius*. Although the Welsh magic is garbled (Powys was still forming it in his mind) it is powerful enough. The basic idea is that only 'love turned to hate' can create enough 'spiritual magic' to 'break through' into the Beyond (p. 236). This passionate message is delivered poorly by Powys's hulking mouthpiece. Powys seems to be unsure of his direction. Occasionally, Uryen's sermon on the mound is articulated as well as those of Geard or Sylvanus: 'Stir up sex till it would put out the sun and then keep it sterile! That's the trick. That's the grand trick of all spiritual life.' (p. 240) It is a powerfully realized scene, though, with its sunlight and wind and empty grassland. As Uryen summarizes his beliefs again, to the two girls, it is clear that Powys was already drifting off into the Cymric transcendence of *Owen Glendower* and *Porius*.

Maiden Castle is the most unsatisfactory segment of the Wessex quartet. It lacks the intense lyricism and ecstasy of the former novels. It suffers from John Cowper Powys's indecision. The Hardyan element is weakly integrated into the book. Uryen's earthmagic, Wizzie's fight for freedom, Thuella's yearning – they are all dealt with too swiftly. There is not enough depth and real grappling with problems. Thuella yearns, just like Eustacia Vye, for Something More Than This, but Powys founders. He makes Something happen. swiftly, as when Uryen grabs the girls and rushes through the fire. This scene, heavy in symbolism, is soon forgotten – it is not developed, and is not referred to again in the novel.

Maiden Castle is a sad, rather undernourished leavetaking of the Wessex landscape so beloved of Powys. In comparison, *Wolf Solent* is violent in its nature-loving lyricism. *Wolf* has most in common with *Maiden Castle*, and is by far the better creation. The sense of place, so important for Powys, is noticeably absent in *Maiden Castle*. The Glymes is a grotesque creation, but the town itself is seen through dusty grey glass. Everything is obscured, shifted, misted-over. Rarely are things brought into sharp focus. This is not an eidetic novel, like Wolf. As he moved the site of his books closer to the centre of the West Country, moving closer to the capital of it all, Powys seemed to drift further away. He is not all there in *Maiden Castle*. His heart is elsewhere. The Hell of ordinary life to which Dud and the others are condemned, like Sue, Clym, Grace, Bathsheba and Angel in Hardy's novels, is particularly grim in *Maiden Castle*. The magicians die heroically or ignominiously, but Powys's heroes are remarkably unchanged, but not unscathed. Dud, certainly, has not changed much by the end of the book. *Maiden Castle* should have been a great rounding-off of the Wessex quartet, but unfortunately it was not to be.

We might conclude this discussion of Powys's Wessex novels with some spoof versions of possible additions to the West Country books:

Cerne Giant

by John Cowper Powys

JOSH MAPPOWDER COMES to Cerne Abbas in Dorset from Norfolk to research a history of the famous ithyphallic Giant. He stays with a strange aunt, Mrs Creech, in Abbey Street. He is soon hypnotized by a haunting, sylph-like girl whom he finds drawing the statue of the Virgin Mary in the church. Through her he discovers that some bizarre rituals are taking place on the Giant, presided over by the local communist, Sydney Stalbridge. Scenes might include midnight trysts under the arch of the Abbey porch; a rainstorm which washes away the turf outlines of the Cerne Giant (curiously leaving the phallus intact); and on one grey twilight evening Josh finds the lusty shape of the Giant painted in lilac on his favourite patch of moss on the wall of the Tithe barn.

The Avebury Circle

by John Cowper Powys

AUBREY KNIGHT, EXILED from a preaching tour of America due to a scandal involving a pearly dryad from Georgia, returns to his roots in the ancient village of Avebury. He discovers that his dead parents were not after all married in the local church, but only 'lived together'. Reeling from this shock to his secret life-illusion and fiercely Puritan nature,

Aubrey becomes besotted with Alice Keiran. She is the daughter of the Herculean archæologist, Paul Kieran, who is currently excavating the Avebury stone circle.

After two or three hundred pages we are introduced to Mr Abel Taleissin, known locally as 'the Goat', on account of his face (and nearby goat-farm). Aubrey meets Mr Taleissin the night before Hallowe'en. In a strange, protracted and somewhat unbelievable scene of confused visions, Mr Taleissin steals Aubrey's walking stick and breaks it over his knee. Aubrey is stunned. Mr Taleissin expounds his new religion of Cerridwen, the Welsh Goddess. Aubrey, meanwhile, wonders if this strange man from Wales could be his real father...

Other scenes might include a Christmas picnic in the snow on Silbury Hill; an ætheric love-making in the nearby Avenue of stones; and the startling discovery in West Kennet Barrow of a goat's skull next to an ancient book containing illustrations of immense evil...

The Winchester Romance

by John Cowper Powys

SIMON SWITHIN IS INVITED to the ancient capital of Winchester by the antiquarian priest Edward Bedevere. The task is to investigate the Arthurian legends behind Winchester. In the fields beside the River Itchen Swithun is mesmerized by the beauty of Charlotte de Blois, afloat in state (or so it seems) with her hair streaming around her like the Lady of Shalott. Only the next day (it happens to be April 30th), Swithun meets another 'gairl', Mel Morshead. She is a runaway from her tyrannous gypsy father of Plush Bottom, Dorset. She sets fire to Swithun's soul as she queues up for a loaf of bread in the Butter Cross. Charlotte haunts his nightly walks around the Cathedral, but Mel it is who comes to live with him in his dingy rooms near the Great Hall.

Serle Templar, a prominent and energetic socialist counsellor, is trying to re-activate a cult of the Round Table. Tristram, a local butcher's son and lover of Gregorian chant, is being groomed by Templar for the position of Arthur. The miraculous appearance of Mervin Williams, a circus magician, during a midsummer bonfire party on St Giles Hill startles everyone. The decayed figure seems to walk through the flames and survive! Swithun is wracked with a cosmically deep jealousy when Mervin takes Charlotte as a lover,. Everything is set for a reunion of a company of neo-Arthurian souls, except they are lacking a suitable Grail. Beanbag, the local mad boy with an evil streak in him that seems almost sublime, digs up a beautiful chalice on St Catherine's Hill after being given an enema by Doctor Rufus at the nearby animal testing laboratory. Things begin to hot up when Tristram spends a night with Mel while Swithun is out walking (he is astonished and loses his ability to sink into sensuality) and Mervin Williams disappears with Charlotte. They are last seen before a power-cut during an Arthurian pageant in the town's theatre...

Three

The Wessex of Thomas Hardy and John Cowper Powys

...for hours I would sit up reading The Return of the Native *or* Far From the Madding Crowd *or* The Woodlanders *or* Jude the Obscure...*till by degrees as I listened to the wind in the chimney the genius of Hardy would drive my demon away and some formidable Spirit from Stonehenge would come rushing out of the Magic West into this dark house and my whole inner being would change.*

John Cowper Powys, *Autobiography* (p. 309)

The Wessex of John Cowper Powys is based on a recognisable, real country, but is also the product of a vivid imagination. Soil and soul deliquesce into one another. It is sited very firmly on the actual landscape and topography of southern England. But it is also a very 'private country', a personal sort of place, far away from crowds and cities and technological revolutions.

John Cowper Powys's Wessex, like that of Hardy, is a creation of love. Both writers were deeply in love with their geographies. Their Wessex are landscapes of the soul, border countries, psychic maps. Hardy's Wessex remains the more impressive – his Wessex is fully imagined, meticulously researched, and based on many visits, walks, cycle rides and historical surveys. Powys's Wessex, however, was recreated from the other side of the Atlantic Ocean. His is a long-distance product, mediated by memory and Time. Powys creates the Wessex of his boyhood, not of the contemporary world (of the 1930s). Hardy, too, kept referencing the realm of his childhood. While Hardy was steeped in his Wessex, Powys was always looking at his terrain from a great distance (both temporally and spatially). Hardy's Wessexscape is the more authentic (or rather closer to the real place). Hardy lived in his landscape fully. But Powys's interiorized Wessexworld is more suited to his concerns. His Wessex is suited to his themes of interiorization and psychology. Hardy is the naturalistic writer, somewhere between Zola and Dickens, a documentor of his surroundings. Powys is always transforming his environment into (often) metaphysical speculation (like D.H. Lawrence).

Hardy's verisimilitude is more convincing, too. He gives us a good, all-round picture of the lanes, the hills, the villages – the layout of the land. Powys concentrates on the big atmospheric conditions – of the skies, of huge tracts of Somerset fenlands, or, more usually, on tiny objects – plants and animals, or on smells and tastes. Powys uses the landscape as a springboard for more personal, intense thoughts. Hardy's region fuses with his characters, but he is always concerned with people, with narrative, with development, with motive and outcome.

A tour of Powys's Alternative Wessex would not mean an excursion around Dorset and Somerset, but a journey into the mind of the writer. It is the same with Hardy. Hardy's Wessex is an imaginative construct, an act of poetic invention. Hardy does not imitate – he makes his landscape anew. He re-creates, re-builds. His Wessex is a 'partly real, partly dream-country' (Preface to *Far From the Madding Crowd*, in Per p. 9). King Lear, 'that traditionary king of Wessex' presides over Hardy's poetic region (Preface to *Return* in ib., p. 13).In his 'General Preface to the Novels and Poems' [1912] Hardy wrote:

> I considered that our magnificent heritage from the Greeks in dramatic literature, found sufficient room for a large proportion of its action in an extent of their country not much larger than the half-dozen counties here re-united under the old name of Wessex, that the domestic emotions have throbbed in Wessex nooks with as much intensity as in the palaces of Europe, and that, anyhow, there was quite enough human nature in Wessex for one man's literary purpose. (Per, p. 45)

From the provincial English rural novel to the Classic Greek tragedy, from the local to the universal – this is Hardy's aspiration in the creation of his Wessex which, he claimed, was nevertheless 'done from the real' (ib, p. 46).

Thomas Hardy's Wessex is a place of spirit. It is a 'landscape of the soul'. Wessex is his sacred space, his 'bliss-space', his mythic Centre. The vertical axis around which Wessex spins is Dorchester. Casterbridge is the social Centre, while Egdon Heath is the wild, spiritual Centre. Between the two lies the birthplace, the homeland – Stinsford and Bockhampton. The creation of Wessex enabled Hardy to control time and space. Despite its foundation in history, Wessex moves towards the condition of timelessness. The novels and poems are prayers and hymns which help keep Wessex the Centre of the world. At the mythopoeic Centre Hardy plants the Greenwood Tree. His Wessex is what Eliade called 'the religious valorization of space' (*A History of Religious Ideas*, p. 42). Hardy uses Wessex to unify his sense of space and time, emotion and history. The Wessex writing is Hardy's own 'song of the universe'. He fills his Wessexworld with a range of sacred sites – temples (the many churches), sacred groves (the many woods), holy mountains (the Wessex heights of Pilsdon Pen, Hambledon Hill, etc), streams, rivers and oceans, and the many human centres, some holy – Melchester, Christminster, Sherton

Abbas – others secular – Weatherbury, Budmouth, Havenpool.

Hardy does not create a 'provincial' world. The city is not the Centre. His country is not 'out of town'. He is 'regional' and 'local' certainly, and he writes in a modernist version of a Romantic topographical sublime. There is no mistake about it: Wessex is the Centre of the cosmos for Hardy.

Far deeper than the topographical map of Wessex is the emotional web of relationships. Wessex is an overlay, a palimpsest of history and emotion, but it is the emotional pattern that Thomas Hardy spends most of his time weaving. Surveying the landscape of Hardy's (and Powys') Wessex, you soon realize that the contours, outlines and details you're seeing lie on the emotional, not the physical plane. Mapping Hardy means charting his mind and the soul of his region. The pattern that emerges is one founded in personal experience, in suffering, in longing and disappointment. The weft and warp of Hardy's Wessex-tapestry is woven tightly. To extract one strand would unravel the rest. Hardy's Wessex is solidly unified. Notions of class, character, labour, ambition and place are packed in tightly together. This is why any study of Hardy must discuss so many issues, and also why he is such an enduring writer. He is no provincial, relegated to some inferior position critically. He is at the forefront of literary criticism, and rightly so.

Dorchester is the social capital of Wessex, while Salisbury, Winchester and Oxford are the Christian centres. Just as important for Hardy are the pagan centres – Maiden Castle, Cerne Abbas, Cross-in-Hand, the hill-forts, Stonehenge. As for Powys, Dorchester combines the prehistoric, the Roman, the mediæval and the present day. All these time-scales are embodied in Maumbury Rings. Enter Dorchester now and you see a much-changed town from Powys's and Hardy's day. Despite the new by-pass, traffic still thunders along the High Street. In the main shopping street, Cornhill, there are chain stores that can be found anywhere in 21st century Britain – Boots, Marks and Spencer, Superdrug, Waterstone's. etc.

Dorset County Council headquarters offices dominate Colliton Park – these are vast, bland buildings, reflecting the hundreds of po-faced business people who work there. This is not authentic Dorchester, neither is the new hospital on the Bridport Road, the garages, the Tutankhamun and Dinosaur Museums, the shopping arcades, big supermarkets and car parks. Supermarkets and their car parks particularly create huge areas of concrete and wasteland. They are not built for people, but for cars – not for local inhabitants but for those bourgeoisie who drive in and out as fast as possible. The new by-pass makes the water-meadows surrounding Dorchester so noisy. It is the same story throughout Britain – whole towns destroyed by the 'great car economy'.

Where is, then, the authentic Dorchester? It is there in the Walks, particularly the West Walks which run beside a park. Go down to the Hangman's Cottage – there is peace and quiet. Beyond, along the footpath, at the blue bridge, you stand at the meeting-point of five waterways. Here at least is the essence of Dorchester – and of Dorset: lush green, clear water and blue clouds.

Elsewhere in Dorset Hardy's and Powys's Wessex is easier to regain: on Golden Cap, on Chesil Beach, in the pulpit rock of Portland, at Anvil Point by the lighthouse, on Hod Hill, in Sherborne Abbey, at Sandbanks or in Knowlton Stone Circle. Here, in these places, is the real Wessex. The more off-the-beaten-track, the better. Don't go to the picnic spot at the Hardy Monument, but to St Catherine's Chapel at Abbotsbury. Eggardon Hill at sunset is pretty unbeatable. These are the sites where the spirit can soar. Because Hardy's Wessex is so much a soul-space, you need to visit these out-of-the-way places, if you must visit Wessex at all. Hardy's success was not so much the mythologization of his environment, as the poetic targetting of love and tragedy.

Much easier to find the real Dorset than the 'real Hardy'. Wessex lies somewhere between the two. Easier to disagree about the nature of Thomas Hardy's Wessex than to define his true artistic province. Hardy's poetic realm 'is an imaginative Wessex only' filled with 'visionary places'.[12]

The influence on both Hardy and John Cowper Powys is 'the Dorset man' William Barnes, who aimed for an obsessive precision in the use of language, and who tried to keep Dorset dialect as authentic to the region as possible. How touching is Barnes' attempt to re-name 'photographs' as *sun-prints*, or 'vocabulary' as word-stock. Hardy used dialect (*dumble-*

---

12 Hardy in *Countryman*, 13, July 1936.

dores, heart-wrings, coll) – but he is freer with it. He outgrew Barnes' provincialism, always aiming for a universal outlook.

Hardy's use of the vernacular is also much better than John Cowper Powys', whose folky lingo is funny, but not convincing. His Dorset dialect does not ring true. Thus: 'Dummy Skald had zummat to zay to Master Ca'Stock, us have heard tell, afore this little job can be car'd out!' says a Portland voice in *Weymouth Sands* (p. 414). When Powys's cosy chorus of rustic types is put there for comedy, the result is OK. Otherwise, his vernacular falls too often into self-parody. Hardy also goes for the comic touch, but his Dorset dialect is more accurate, reflecting regional differences, and the penetrating influence of William Barnes. Thus Henery, in *Far From the Madding Crowd*, says: 'I look round upon life quite cool. Do you heed me, neighbours? My words, though made as simple as I can, mid be rather deep for some heads.' (p. 133)

There is more humour in Powys, but more humanity in Thomas Hardy. Hardy sympathizes with other people more, while Powys takes us deeper into the soul. Powys's vision is optimistic, while Hardy's is more pragmatic and realist. Lawrence's use of dialect is interesting to compare with that of Powys. It began authentically enough in *Sons and Lovers*, intensified in *The Rainbow*, but fell into pastiche by the time of *Lady Chatterley's Lover*. Mellors comes out with some ridiculous phrases, that have since become prime targets for parody:

> 'Say: Lift up your heads o' ye gates, that the king of glory may come in. Ay, th' cheek on thee! Cunt, that's what tha're after. Tell Lady Jane tha wants cunt. John Thomas, an' th' cunt o' Lady Jane!' (*Lady Chatterley's Lover*, p. 219)

In Lawrence, though, nothing is so simple. Lawrence's use of dialect is bound up with his rigorous investigations of class, status and sexual politics. His use of dialect is a narrative weapon, used to bludgeon his many targets of hypocrisy. In Hardy and Powys the methods are altogether much softer.

Lawrence is not afraid, either, of severely criticizing his world. He lays into his Nottinghamshire in many books – they reflect his love and hatred of the place. He writes: 'ugly winter-grey of houses [that look] like a vision of hell that is cold and angular.' (*Women in Love*, p. 450) Lawrence describes our modern world of suburban vapidity, while Hardy's is a much rosier vision (except perhaps in *Jude the Obscure*). Hardy chooses isolated spaces, such as the enclosed village of *The Woodlanders*:

> one of those sequestered spots outside the gates of the world where may usually be found more meditation than action, and more listlessness than meditation...yet where, from time to time, dramas of a grandeur and unity truly Sophoclean are enacted in the real (p. 44)

Hardy's great talent was to produce from such listless places extraordinary dramas and passions. Out of the soil of Wessex he creates marvellous stories of ecstasy and despair. He set his tales in backwater towns, and then proceeded to turn them into sites of magnificent drama. Yet all the narratives of Hardy's major novels are wholly authentic. He manages to make us believe in these people and these places.

John Cowper Powys's places, on the other hand, are formulated by the fracturing mechanisms of memory. Like Proust and Cavafy, Powys is a re-creator, a poet of remembrances. The lack of contemporary real-life detail in his Wessex books is counterbalanced by an astonishing exaggeration of natural details. Powys brings the Romantic cult of the primitive and the eidetic into the 20th century. While Hardy and Lawrence were concerned with the decline of the old values, Powys was content to place his narratives in landscapes of the soul only loosely based on the real world. Hardy's novels move towards the landscape of the city, as do Lawrence's (symbolized in *Jude* by those many railway journeys – that sense of alienating displacement). Lawrence and Hardy also revolt against this modernist drive towards the urban way of life. Hardy's Jude is in love with the city, although in Hardy's trenchantly ironic story, the city is a nostalghically imagined place. The reality turns out to be hard and unyielding. The more one thinks about *Jude the Obscure*, the more one realizes just how many important themes he combined in just one narrative. A whole range of social, political, religious and ethical issues feature in the book. *Jude the Obscure* is astonishing. It is really, really astonishing.

No book of Powys's measures up to *Jude the Obscure*. But Powys's concerns are somewhat different. Powys deals with individual states of consciousness, not the towns (Sherborne, Weymouth, Glastonbury, Dorchester) which fade away under the bright descriptions of people's states of mind. Powys loves the solitary, mental life, above the outside, social life. He is something of an anachronism in the 20th century, producing rural pastiches and phantasies while Baudelaire's 'ant-seething city' has taken over as the premier site of the modern novel (Durrell's Alexandria, Huxley's London, Joyce's Dublin, Miller's and Gide's Paris and so on).

In his evocation of scenes in which people and nature fuse, Powys was moving into a new realm, ruled over by his peculiar way of seeing. In Hardy we have vividly rendered scenes, as sharp as Dutch still-life paintings. But they are set in a traditional mould. The language concentrates on description, not invention, as it does in the 20th century novel. In Beckett, in Lawrence and Joyce, language is part of this invention. Beckett's prose is a major element in the whole artwork. In Hardy, a certain realism still prevails. Hardy is not unreal. In *The Return of the Native* we have some memorable scenes where Nature dominates the characters – in the moonlit Maydance, for example, where Eustacia 'floated round and round on Wildeve's arm, her face rapt and statuesque; her soul had passed away from and forgotten her features' (p. 322). In *The Woodlanders*, during another Maytime revel, the supernatural appears (the Devil is hinted as being a possible 'demon lover' for the village girls). Hardy cleverly has Fitzpiers step in to fulfil this role. In Powys, the powerful elements of the world conjure up ecstasies and the præternatural. In a ritualistic scene, the midsummer picnic on Mai-Dun Castle, the sun seems to suck up all the life from the revellers' bonfire. Powys moves in close to focus on the flames: all the 'life-lust' becomes 'spiritualized and etherealized' (MC, p. 371). This is always the way in Powys. The elements are always threatening to expand the narrative away from the characters. The characters are (often) so airy, so delicately rooted to the earth, that they are always about to fly off. The elements, whether they be the sun, wind, water or whatever, are so strong that they can spirit away the characters. The characters' hold on life is tenuous.

Thus Wolf is so easily tripped off into another dimension. Dud can phantasize freely, using only a bit of moss on a wall as a catalyst. Powys's people are like artists, like Leonardo da Vinci, who could happily stare at a wall. Or like Zen monks, who can meditate on the tiniest and most insignificant objects. *Satori, samadhi*, rapture, possession, trance, illumination, union, *ananda, dhikr, kensho*, beatification – they are just a breath away. All you have to do is to open yourself up to such experiences.

Writers like Powys, Hardy, Whitman, Gide, Heine and Lawrence are so finely tuned in to details, to Nature, to being outside in the world, they can have ecstasies from the smallest of things. How many times do the characters in Lawrence's *The White Peacock* rush out to look at some newly born flower! Oh Gosh, it's all so wonderful, so exquisitely delicate, so divinely pastoral! Powys too is like this. In *Lady Chatterley's Lover*, there are some marvellous descriptions of people being carried away by the beauty of simple things. There is such mystery there, in Lawrence's description of Connie in the woods:

> The wood was silent, still and secret in the evening drizzle of rain, full of the mystery of eggs and half-open buds, half-unsheathed flowers.

Connie feels the silent but surging life in the trees:

> Today she could almost feel it in her own body, the huge heave of the sap in the massive trees, upwards, up, up to the bud-tips, there to push into little flamey oak-leaves, bronze as blood. It was like a tide running turgid upward, and spreading on the sky. (*Lady Chatterley's Lover*, pp. 126-7)

The sweeping tidal metaphor, the feeling of the surge of life in things, is what brings Powys and Lawrence together. They are the Whitmans, the Shelleys and the Verlaines of the modern novel.

The mysticism of the trees – the presence of the trees. This is common to Thomas Hardy as well as Lawrence and John Cowper Powys. Lawrence said he would like to be a tree for a while. And Blake noted the power of trees to move some people to 'tears of joy'.[13] What a dreary place the world would be without trees. Trees have such mystery, such presence.

---

[13] W. Blake, *The Letters of William Blake*, ed. A.G.B. Russell, 1906, p. 62.

You don't need to know about the vast accumulation of ritual, religion, folklore, magic and symbolism surrounding trees to experience them fully. The Cosmic Tree, the World Tree, the Moon-Tree, the magic Tree of Life – the tree is one of the basic symbols – like the egg, snake and moon. Trees have real majesty – no wonder they feature so prominently in nature writing. Chuang-tzu wrote of the Tree of Idleness (Durrell's term):

> You have a great tree and are worried about its uselessness. Why not plant it in the realm of Nothingness in the expanse of Infinitude? Then you might sit by its side in actionless activity and lie under it in blissful Rest.[14]

Connie feels the *'inwardness'* of the trees: 'They seemed a very power of silence, and yet a vital presence.' (ib, p. 67) Hardy is rarely as mystical as this. He is concerned, like Austen or James, with the furtherance of the narrative, with a certain kind of realism. But in *The Woodlanders*, and most marvellously in *Tess*, Hardy created many scenes where people fuse with Nature, and with trees. But what in Hardy is Gothic fancy, in Powys is hard reality – a mental reality, but none the less concrete for all that. In Powys the elements and Nature are powerful presences. Much of *A Glastonbury Romance*, for example, is made up of passages in which characters' thoughts spin out wider to include the beingness of nightwinds, or the feelings of distant suns and First Causes. Hardy too brings in a First Cause (or Fate, or Watcher, or whatever). But his most powerful evocation of a Natural Presence is Egdon Heath. Lawrence recognized in this wild tract of land in south Dorset the major character in *The Return of the Native*. Lawrence calls the Heath 'primitive, primal earth...strong and fecund...the deep black source' (*Study of Thomas Hardy*, p. 25). The earth of Powys's Wessexscape is similar. Like Lawrence and Hardy (and Durrell) Powys had a strong sense of the qualities of the deep, magnetic, nourishing soil. Powys's Wessex is deep, full of historical, emotional and elemental depth. The earth features highly in Powys's art, whether it is the wetlands of Sedgemoor, the wooded rainswelled valleys of North Wales, the flatlands of Norfolk, or the wild landscapes of Dorset.

Of Hardy Lawrence wrote: 'This is the constant revelation in Hardy's

---

14 Chuang-tzu in W. Tale Bary, ed. *Sources of Chinese Tradition*, Columbia 1960.

novels: that there exists a great background, vital and vivid, which matters more than the people who move upon it.' (*Study*, p. 28) The same can be said for John Cowper Powys's West Country, or Durrell's Egypt, or Gide's and Camus' North Africa, or Brontë's Yorkshire, or Naipaul's Wiltshire. In his first poem, 'Domicilium' Hardy wrote: 'Behind, the scene is wilder.' (CP, p. 3) This is true: behind, beneath, beyond the scenes, the passions, the revelations and the rages are much wilder. Hardy sets his narratives against what he called 'the blind profound' (in 'Night-Time in Mid-Fall', ib., p. 73). He sets his stories on metaphorical islands adrift in raging seas. The earth slips from under the feet of the Hardyan self: the spirit stumbles: Hardy records the falls. Rage, rebellion and unreality flood in to the natural Hardyan world. Wessex is overturned. Hardy sets up the world at the beginning of each novel carefully – set up so it can be knocked down. Hardy loves the catharsis that religious destruction brings. He wants a revelation of the human spirit of Apocalyptic proportions. In *Tess* and *Jude the Obscure* his rage is immense. His rage powers these two novels along, accelerating them up into the 'great novel' class, and rightly so.

In Powys's world the earth is strong and infuses the characters with a particular radiance. *Porius* could only be set in Wales, could only have been written after many years soaking up the rainfilled darkness of that truly wild country. In Powys the elements rise up and rush through the characters – such as when Cordelia in *A Glastonbury Romance* hears the wind moaning amongst two giant trees. Or in *Porius*, when the hero sees the clouds as 'powerful Beings' and, in his ecstatic reverie he muses: 'It was as if the grey earth had become the mystery of time, and the grey sky had become the mystery of space' (P, p. 562).

The king of this feeling for the spirit of place is D.H. Lawrence. In *Kangaroo*, for example, when Somers experiences the terrifying nature of Australia: 'Something big and aware and hidden!' (p. 19) In Powys, as in Hardy and Lawrence, there is something bigger, and darker, and stronger, and deeper than whatever is on the surface. Beyond people, behind their emotions, deeper than their souls, is the great spirit of the landscape. Lawrence's characters typically found this dark presence in Australia, or Italy, or Mexico. Thus Kate in *The Plumed Serpent* experiences 'the dark undertone' of Mexico (p. 82).

The dark presence, whether a passionate Nature in Hardy, a cunning city in Durrell, the dark gods in Lawrence, or the powerful elements in Powys, does not always reside in foreign places. There are still places 'where the spirit of aboriginal England still lingers, the old savage England'.[15] In places as ordinary as the South Downs, the spirit of 'savage England' still lingers.[16] It is in the forests of England, in the sacred groves of the ancient tree-worshipping cults that the real spirit still survives. Tree-worship and tree-lore goes back a long way, as Graves notes in his *The White Goddess*, and Frazer in his *The Golden Bough*. Tree-worship (and stone-worship) is one of the authentic British cults, quite understandable in an island once densely populated by trees. Lawrence calls this feeling 'the space of grey old oaks, making the everlasting silence of Britain.' (*John Thomas and Lady Jane*, p. 101)

John Cowper Powys's own stance in nature-mysticism is expounded in *Wolf Solent* by Christie. She internalizes Wolf's own musings, regarding philosophy (Hegel, Leibniz, etc) as a 'particular country, in which I can go about' (p. 91). This is Powys in a nutshell. His books are the records of travels in countries of the mind. He wanders among perspectives of philosophers, pagans, gods and magicians, in the same way that Hardy roams in the company of passionately yearning lovers. Powys loves to saunter about in the shires of the soul, in the sunlit lands the mind creates, like the painters Claude Lorrain or Corot. Powys is the inner spaceman, happy in his inward-looking visions. Christie explains what Wolf has been feeling all along. She is verily his own soul, his inner self, his *anima*, his desire for wish-fulfilment. She describes this philosophical Grand Tour thus:

> When you get a sudden feeling of life going on outside…far away from where you sit…over wide tracts of country…as if you were driving in a carriage and all the things you passed were…life itself… (WS, p. 91)

This is poetry, daydreaming, meditation, drugs, sex, art – travelling without moving. It is armchair voyaging, holidays in the mind. Television

---

[15] Lawrence in *St Mawr*, *Complete Short Novels*, p. 335.
[16] Lawrence in *England, My England, Collected Short Stories*, p. 286.

has taken over this self-hypnotic role now. Instead of losing oneself in books, or in art, or drugs, or sex, we now have television. At least with books there is the initial effort of reading. Television on the other hand is languidly passive for the reader of the text.

Wessex now is not vastly different from the days of Hardy, Barnes and Powys. There is still a sense of space, and history – around Dorset and Wiltshire in particular. Darby and Finn define the three types of landscape in Dorset: 'the down, the vale, and the heath' (Darby & Finn, p. 127). The ocean must be added to this list, for the sea gives Dorset a special atmosphere, making it quite different from other inland spots of 'exceptional beauty', such as the Lake District, or Snowdonia. The coastline gives Dorset sudden vast prospects – a sense of open air and space. You never get quite the same experience of spaciousness inland. Dorset is small, but the variety of landscape, and the infinities of the ocean beyond makes it seem vast. Thus Hardy in *Tess*:

> To persons of limited spheres, miles are as geographical digress, parishes as countries, counties as provinces and kingdoms. (p. 151)

For country people, even in this age of cars and trains and commuters who travel hundreds of miles to and from work, counties are still like mini-nations. Some rural people will not have been to Dorchester from Loders, even though the two places are only a few miles apart. Similarly, people living in Hereford will travel down to Cardiff, the Capital of Wales, to do their shopping, instead of, say, going to Birmingham or Worcester, because they still regard themselves as Welsh.

A typical Dorset day has fresh wind blowing in from the south-west. Shadows move slowly across the landscape. There is a deep tone to the shadows, and real brightness in the lights. The main colour in Dorset is green – there is green everywhere. Dorset light is more Flemish than Impressionist, more like a Ruisdael than a Monet. It is definitely Turner, not Constable. On a good Dorset day, everything gleams, everything glistens, as if it is pristine – newly minted. Wessex is the perfect place for a sense of the pastoral sublime – from the lushness of Fordington's fields, to the wilderness of the high West Dorset cliffs.

Only a few painters have fully captured that sense of light and space experienced on a sunny and cloudy day. The typical 'Dorset Day' is filled with the shadows of low finely-sculpted cumulus clouds moving across the landscape driven by the south-west wind. How few landscape painters – from Giorgione through Claude to Constable – have managed to render this sense of space and motion and light. Turner caught this light, perhaps because he studied carefully the Dutch School – van der Velde, Ruisdael, Vernet. The light in the British landscape tradition – of Wilson, Cozens, Girtin *et al* – seems so flat in comparison with, say, Rembrandt's *The Three Trees*[17] or Ruisdael's *Wheatfields*.[18] The latter picture, like those of Vermeer, de Hooch and Hobbema, capture the effect of light on the landscape, of sunlight travelling across it. Only much later did painters such as Corot, Millet, Delacroix and the Impressionists render natural light and shadow so richly.

Dorset is a magical place. It sucks light and magic into it. There is something about the earth here that is enriching. It is a refreshing combination of air, skies, winds, countryside, history and soil. There is a temperate openness about the place, and a great variety of vistas – from the many tumuli, to the lagoons around Poole harbour, to the Wessex heights and hills, to the little villages, from the unusual geology of Chesil Beach to the high town of Shaftesbury, from the secret dewy vales of Marshwood to the wild cliffs around Lulworth, from the gaunt, prehistoric forts such as Maiden Castle and Eggardon Hill, to the ancient forests around Cranborne Chase. It is an out-of-the-way country. There are spaces here that seem very secret, very cut off from the crowds and the cities.

John Cowper Powys's love of walking is understandable: walking is certainly the best way to see Wessex, and Dorsetshire in particular. Walking takes you into yourself, as well as into the landscape. Only when walking do you feel the earth truly and fully – the scents, the feel of the wind, the immensity of the skies and the hills. West Dorset is particularly wild – around Eype Mouth, for example. The Isle of Purbeck, too, has a prehistoric loneliness (something like Cornwall or Wales). Dorchester is

---

17 1643, etching, 8 x 11in, National Gallery of Art, Washington.
18 Oil, 40 x 51in, Metropolitan Museum of Art, New York.

noisy – it is full of cars. But there is still a poetry of the streets there. In the evening, in May, around six o'clock, when everyone has driven home, there is a tranquil solitude about the town. It returns to being the sleepy country town, a county capital retaining much of its past history. It is a mystery that Dorchester is still surrounded by water and streams – streams as clear as Tibetan mysticism. And one can walk out of the town centre into the countryside within minutes. The High Street, too, the scene of so much of Hardy's life and fiction, is pretty much intact. No great leaps of the imagination are needed to transport the mind back to the Victorian era, or before that to mediæval times.

The sea at Weymouth is as Turner and John Cowper Powys described it – brilliant blue, or sometimes an incredibly deep turquoise. The cliffs to the east are superb, and the stones and wet sands are still there. Even when inundated with hordes of tourists, Weymouth retains its Victorian air. True, much of it has been rebuilt – there are endless housing estates north and west. The holiday industry creates many 'tacky' structures. But they all add to the atmosphere, in summer, when the sun is beating down. Upwey is a secluded spot – the magical wishing well is unchanged. Stinsford churchyard, the burial place of Hardy's heart, is still as it was (although you can hear the obnoxious noise of the new bypass there). Towns such as Wareham, Wimbourne and Blandford have grown massively since Hardy's time. Yet in The Square in Wimbourne, for instance, you still feel in touch with an older, more human-scale way of living. The undulating panoramas of West Dorset, with its cliffs, beaches, hidden woods and huge earthworks, still looks like dragon country. Here you can imagine that dragons and witches exist quite easily. Chesil Beach remains vast and spectacular. Portland is as roughly-hewn as ever. There are a host of other Wessex places that retain their ancient magic. Abbotsbury, Shaftesbury, Durlston Head, Stonehenge, Salisbury, Winchester, Lyme Regis and so on. Sherborne, too, has been much changed by the onslaught of materialism. But it survives as an elegant, intimate town. It has the Cathedral of Dorset, Sherborne Abbey, with the tombs of two English Kings (now discounted as authentic). The fan-vaulting in the Abbey is intricate and soaring. The town is cohered by its warm, yellowy Ham Hill stone. The sunlight on the golden stone reminds one of Italy. The scale is human – it is small-scale. Despite the weight of the architecture and stone the feeling is of lightness. The town retains its deep sense of history, which features so much in *Wolf Solent*. It is easy to imagine, too, Giles with his apple-branch looking like a corn-god in *The Woodlanders*, beside the Conduit.

Yeovil is pleasant enough around Princes Street, the High Street and the church, but there are now massive shopping developments which ruin the rest of the town centre. It hardly now accords with Powys's description of it in *Wolf Solent*. But Powys's Wessex was always highly artificial, always mediated through a pageant of sheared consciousnesses, despite being, like Hardy's, 'done from the real'.

History permeates Wessex. The levels of history are everywhere to be seen – in the earthworks, the later mediæval structures, in the fossils and the decayed vegetation. Thomas Hardy's and Powys's Wessex is steeped in history. Not just human history – of lives led fully in so many corners of the terrain – but also pre-history, and the history of plants, hills and fields. This idea of history soaking into a landscape is nowhere better explored than in V.S. Naipaul's beautiful book *The Enigma of Arrival*. Naipaul investigates at a graceful, contemplative pace, the spaces and histories of the Wiltshire Plain. His North Wessex is a tract of decay and change. Houses have successive occupants; fences, once-new, fall apart; memories of old, long-gone characters fade; time moves in waves. It is a kind of stasis and flux which Naipaul so elegantly describes – a record of travels outward and journeys homeward. He writes:

> As much as any comparable area of Egypt or India, the region (once a vast burial place) was full of sacred sites: the circles of wood or stone, the great burial mounds, the medieval cathedrals and abbeys, and the churches that were often no less grand.'[19]

Naipaul is the poetic successor to Hardy and Powys and the whole British nature tradition in literature. He is extremely sensitive to place, and to humanity. He is penetratingly accurate in his observations of people. He gently teases out their characteristics through their strange habits. He does in a short novel what it takes Powys much longer to do. He

---

19 *The Enigma of Arrival*, Penguin 1987, p. 270.

extends time, explodes space (but softly), and delivers a multitude of insights, all modelled in the quietest, most simple and unobtrusive, and unself-conscious prose.

Naipaul is a chronicler of country ways and human lives in the manner of Hardy. He has that same gentle sense of poignant observation as Hardy – it is an unegoistic vision. He is, like Powys and Hardy, impressionistic, not didactic. He does not force the reader to swallow some polemic, which Hardy also disliked (see the Preface to *Tess*, in *Personal Writings*, p. 27)

Wolf Solent is the great novel of Powysian nature-mysticism. *Wolf Solent* marks the full-blown full-bloodied return to the Wessex homeland. In *Wolf Solent* the Powysian vision congeals and unifies its integration of self and nature, of the excremental and the ecstatic. There is a genuine joy in Powys's descriptions of Sherborne and Yeovil and the Dorset–Somerset borderland. But soon the Wessexscape in *Wolf Solent* becomes a dreamscape, a Powyscape, an inscape. Wolf the character begins to sink deeper into himself. He absorbs the 'Sap-sweet emanations from the leafy recesses of all the Dorset woods' (p. 226).

As with Hardy, the places in John Cowper Powys attain a mythical quality. Powys recites place-names like a litany, He constantly reassures himself of the sacrality of his favourite part of the world. In *A Glastonbury Romance* Powys constantly reminds us of the Tor, the Abbey, Chalice-Hill and Queen's Sedgemoor. Often it is all too obvious that Powys is reading names off a map, unlike Thomas Hardy who could visit a zone of Dorset and write about it the next day. In *Weymouth* each place has a special significance for Powys, being the sites of his childhood. There is much of the child in Powys. He loves to invoke Chesil Beach, the Nothe, Portland and the Clock in Weymouth. These are ordinary spots, quite ordinary parts of the world. But in Powys they are infused with magic.

At key moments in his texts John Cowper Powys will pull back from the plot to remind us of his holy niches. It is as if he is riffling some sacred picture-book in his mind. Powys's West Country books are clearly meant to be the Bibles of those places. Powys could never, though, displace Hardy's *Tess*, *Mayor*, *Return* and *Jude the Obscure* from their position as the Wessex novels.

By the time of *Maiden Castle*, Powys's litany of Wessex spaces had lost much of its holy power. Two places only retain the energy of Powys's animism – Dorchester and Maiden Castle. But even these are obscurely evoked. Maiden Castle itself is vast, windblown and immensely impressive, with an all-round view of central Dorset. But this is not shown in Powys's novel. Neither is the langour of the town described, or the oddly-shaped faces of the inhabitants, so different from other parts of Britain. Powys was losing his touch in *Maiden Castle*. In *Weymouth Sands*, though, he really excels in his poetic evocations of the landscape. The intensity clearly cannot be kept up for years. Lawrence lost his intensity after *Women in Love*, as Hardy did after *Tess*. *The Well-Beloved* is awful, by comparison. How weak and misogynist and vaguely imagined it is compared to the full-blown creation of *Tess*.

As we have parodied John Cowper Powys, it is only fair that we spoof Hardy too:

A Graveyard Romance

by Thomas Hardy

A MAN, JOSEPH RIPERS, is walking at dusk from Po'sham to Abbotsea. Before entering the Cock and Hen Inn for the night, he hears a sobbing sound coming from the nearby churchyard. Creeping up, he espies a lovelorn maid lying stricken by grief upon a freshly-laid grave. It transpires her only love drowned off Chesil Bank, working for her step-father, Parson Chaldon. Emma Chaldon is informally engaged to the small-time landowner, Frank Lytchett. Ripers begins to visit Abbotsea for late-night trysts with Emma beside the former suitor's grave. The drama is forced to its tragic end by the unannounced arrival from Budmouth of Louise

Pentridge, who had'known' Ripers when he was garrisoned at Casterbridge. She brings a new-born child with her. Unable to deal with such hypocrisy, Frank Lytchett stalks Emma and Ripers at Abbotsea churchyard. From his house on the Port Bredy Road, the Parson one night hears a shot and dashes forth to discover the awful truth...

Too Late For Lovers

by Thomas Hardy

Thomas Toller lives in his deceased uncle's cottage at Estminster. He works in the markets of Ivell. An orphan, the local Conjuror acts as a surrogate father to him. A chance errand takes Toller to Sherton Abbas where by the Conduit in the autumn halflight he saves the beautiful Helen Swansong from the clutches of evil William Matravers. Back in Estminster, Toller's betrothed, Alice Hope, is not pleased by his new infatuation. She leaves Toller's aunts' farm to work for the Clares in Emminster vicarage. Matravers pursues Toller and Helen across Wessex, to Lulstead Cove. They try to find refuge with Helen's old schoolteacher, Jack Haddock. After a week of verbal abuse, Helen gives in to Matravers, and goes back with him to Sherton Abbas.

Meanwhile, Matravers has blackened Toller's name among the market people, and Toller can't find work. Desperate, he walks barefoot along iced-up roads to Emminster, to ask for Alice's hand in marriage once more. Too late! She has eloped with his best friend. They left for France in a boat piloted by Haddock's son, Bumptious. Like Lancelot, Toller finds solace in the church, and lives for ten years at Middleton Abbey (though he has not believed in God ever since, aged seven, he saw the roof of Wellbridge Church collapse on the kneeling congregation – he had been playing truant with Flossy Stickles at the time). On a mission to the Abbey at Sherton, Toller meets Helen Swansong. She is now a widow in black. Her wizened arm clutches him in the Lady Chapel. He turns: 'Too late beloved' he hisses. Her dead faint brings on instant consumption. She dies.

Four

The Ecstasy of Landscape

At such times, how ardently my heart embraced it all: I felt as if I had been made a god in that overwhelming abundance, and the glorious forms of infinite Creation moved in my soul, giving it life.

Johann Wolfgang von Goethe, *The Sorrows of Young Werther* (p. 65)

John Cowper Powys's vast descriptions of landscape takes us back to the period of Goethe, Wordsworth, Heine and High Romanticism. The big, sweeping vision of the Romantic Sublime, epitomized in painting by Turner, is found in Powys's and Thomas Hardy's Wessex novels. Both writers like to define landscape in the terms of the euphorias of the German Idealist Romantics (Heine, Goethe, Novalis, Hölderlin). Both writers have a vast vision of Nature (with a capital 'N'). Both writers use lonely souls wandering through a vast Otherness.

The beginning of Hardy's novels feature this Romantic aspiration of the soul alone amid infinite Nature. Hardy goes for this Romantic vision in the opening of *The Return of the Native*. Powys is unusual because he is like this *all the time*! Gabriel Oak gazes at the stars in *Madding Crowd*, and *Tess*, the eternal victim, also happily stargazes, but the Powys's souls do it continuously. Hardy's figures amidst Nature are mostly more active than hose of Powys. So Tess struggles through the country, and Jude feeds (or does not feed) the birds. Giles climbs up trees, or goes to market, or plants trees with Marty. Eustacia stalks the Heath. But in Powys Nature is mediated through lazy males who do not seem to work, or do much, except analyze themselves endlessly (Angus Wilson noted this aspect of Powys's characters in his Introduction to *Weymouth Sands*, p. 13).

Hardy's individuals are driven by the British Protestant work-ethic: you must work to live (only being paid for labour valorizes life). But the existential anti-heroes of John Cowper Powys's fiction (and of Gide, Camus and the late Lawrence) do not work. They are middle-class people, with nice financial allowances. Wolf, Dud and Magnus don't seem to do much, but they experience a lot. The difference is (surely) that Hardy's people are genuinely working class Lawrence's people began as proletarian, but his later modern characters became typical 20th century angst-ridden drifters (Kate, Connie, Aaron, Somers). While a poet like Pasolini deals with the sub-proletariat, and makes powerful, polemical, political art, Hardy and Lawrence use the working-class as the vehicles for essentially bourgeois notions (of rebellion, of ethics and æsthetics). Powys also uses working-class characters, but his heroes are definitely middle-class alienated wanderers. Powys was concerned with politics, but never made his political themes as powerful Hardy's, and Hardy's ideological discourse was never as polemical or as extraordinary as that of Lawrence.

Powys melded the visionary prose of High Romanticism with the existential discourse of the modern novel. His Wolf feels Nature like Lawrence's Paul:

> The beauty of the night made him want to shout. A half-moon, dusky gold, was sinking behind the black sycamore at the end of the garden, making the sky purple with its glow. (*Sons and Lovers*, p. 55)

This passage compares well with the Powys-man's many night-time revelations, such as Wolf's when he 'stretched out his arms into that darkness' (WS, p. 136) Many of Thomas Hardy's characters stalk the infinity of the night (Tess making her bed in the wood; Jude atop the ladder, mesmerized by Christminster; Marty alone by moonlight in that superb ending to *The Woodlanders*; or the many astronomical trysts of Viviette and Swithin in which 'human life at its highest excitement was beating within the dark and isolated tower' (*Two on a Tower*, p. 126)

Passion in the night reaches its height in Hardy in the doomed figure of Eustacia Vye, with her 'Pagan eyes, full of nocturnal mysteries' (*Return*, p. 118), an image straight out of Baudelaire, Moreau or Rops. Eustacia is a magnificent figure. Nowhere in Powys is there a character of the resonance and stature of Tess, Jude, Henchard or Eustacia. But Powys did use Hardy's vast spaces and sense of the præternatural in his Wessex quartet. In *Maiden Castle* there is the powerful description of the 'ghost-wind' at the Glymes house. It is here, in the meeting-point of the ordinary and the occult, that Powys is successful:

> When he first caught it, it came to him, faint and muted as it was, with the kind of shock that our animal nature receives when it touches the Unknown. (MC, p. 146)

How different is John Cowper Powys's descriptions of landscape from that of another lover of the spirit of place, Lawrence Durrell. Hardy and Powys are awkward and archaic in their phraseology. They are stuck in the lingo of mid-Victorian magazines – they use polite but confused sentences and phrases. Hardy blocks the flow of his prose with really annoying turns of phrase – often hackneyed maxims that jar the ear and ruin the sense. Powys too used cliches, but his worst fault is the long sentence. How much better is the style of Lawrence – those intense passages of rhythmic writing, using repetition and one of the strongest feelings for sound amongst any poet or writer. Or compare Hardy and Powys with the highly stylized prose of Durrell, in his *Avignon Quintet*:

> The calm happiness and beauty conferred by tutelary water nymphs or river Gods – and indeed the Rhone was once such a God. Then the silky air, the ambient cool air. The quiet folded-away quality of chalk and limestone valleys with their sectors of violet dust and red – the signs of a soil rich in bauxite some wiseacre tells me.[20]

How rich, languid, fresh yet ruthlessly precise is Durrell's prose-style, so different from the prolixity and prosopopoeia of Powys, with his endless *longueurs*. Powys is a first-draft writer, he has to get it all down in wordy flood – a Pollock of the novel. Durrell refines, constantly – re-writing, clipping, shaping, squeezing his voice ever narrower and tighter. Durrell's wordstock is massive – he swallows dictionaries whole. Powys clings (like Hardy) to archaic terms. He is always more concerned with content – not style or form.

Even tighter, yet no less illuminating, is Beckett's prose:

> A winter night, without moon or stars, but light, he sees his body, all night, this impossible body, it's me in him remembering, remembering the true night, dreaming of the night with then the day, the same as he managed yesterday to endure yesterday.[21]

Beckett must be the modern master of the long sentence. Such mordant control he has, such Steinian precision. He shows how to orchestrate sound, sense and pauses. Most of his *The Unnameable* is a single sentence, stretching out over pages and pages. Beckett has the most sophisticated sense of rhythm in modern writing. No one can match him for hypnotic rhythmic prose, which nevertheless always makes sense, is always

---
20 *Monsieur*, Faber 1976, p. 209.
21 *Texts for Nothing*, XII, *Collected Short Prose 1945-80*, Calder 1984, p. 111.

meticulously constructed. Beckett has made the use of the comma, the pause, mystical. He has taken Stein's metaphysics of language to its extreme, and succeeded.

Powys, on the other hand, is struggling with a multitude of sensations, trying to lock them down into a conventional prose-structure. Powys's prose aims to circumscribe his mythos of sensualism using orthodox means. Powys's literature is in a state of flux. It is tidal, always trying to burst its banks, to flood over into the unknown world beyond. But all these writers who were trying to find a new expression-language for the novel – Woolf, Joyce, Nin, Lawrence, Beckett – they are the really fascinating artists.

How do Thomas Hardy and Powys compare with Beckett? Hardy is traditional: there is little breakdown of expression in his prose. He still maintains a certain solidity of language, a certain belief in the power of language to communicate. *Under the Greenwood* and *Far from the Madding Crowd* contain many sequences of simple description. Hardy is (on the whole) content to descant, to narrate, to tell stories. In *Tess* and *Jude the Obscure*, the break-up of the narrative discourse becomes apparent. John Cowper Powys, meanwhile, is a modernist in terms of his historical context, but a traditionalist in terms of his art. His wordplay is conventional, but he is trying to particularize mystical ecstasies. His books are full of 'raids on the inarticulate'. His characters' speeches sometimes decay into... masses... of... disjointed... sentences... such as this... Compare this passage from *Rodmoor* with the above Beckett quote:

> There began to fall upon the place where they sat, upon the cobble-stones of the little quay, upon the wharf steps, slimy with green sea-weed, upon the harbour mud and the tarred gunwales of the gently rocking barges, upon the pallid tide flowing inland with gurglings and suckings and lapping and long-drawn sighs, that indescribable sense of the coming of night at a river's mouth, which is like nothing else in the world. (R, p. 203)

Powys ends up by *listing* his multitudinous sensations. His sentences begin well, but end up as an index of experiences. He tries to incorporate this sight, that smell, this memory, that foresight. The result is bound to be confused. Beckett does not crowd out his prose. He is clear. So much of his meaning is in the rhythm of his prose, the musicality of his language – 'to endure tomorrow...to endure yesterday' and so on. Beckett carefully modulates his words to suit his ever-changing narrative. Powys tries for rhythm sometimes, as does Lawrence, while Hardy is content to narrate in a plain (if often affected) manner.

Powys tries to incorporate everything in one swoop. He tries to condense Wordsworthian visions into a tiny space. But he is not poetic, he does not have the fine musical sense of Beckett or Valéry or Durrell. Powys's control is weak – he is perissologic, jumbled, maundering. He is still caught up in the frenzy of speaking with tongues. He has not sat back and analyzed his ecstasies. Woolf is closest to Powys in this respect – in her recording of multiple sensations as they are experienced by the individual consciousness. Woolf is confusing to read too. In Woolf's *To the Lighthouse*, we are placed in one character's mind, then someone else's, with no change in the lingual register. The result is a confused stream of multiple consciousness. It is challenging to read, more challenging to digest fully. Woolf and Powys (and Joyce) are not easy meals. Durrell, on the other hand, is a fabulous feast, with each dish clearly marked and presented and easily digested. In Woolf, though, there is always a tight control on the mental stream of information, so that she can throw out lines of real insight and piquancy: 'So that is marriage, Lily thought, a man and a woman looking at a girl throwing a ball.'[22]

The passage from *Rodmoor* illustrates Powys's spirit in writing: the tidal momentum, the inertia of heavy masses of water swelling up to overflow onto the land. Thus Powys builds up his long sentences to form huge tracts of prose. Not for him the great plains of Proust, or the shimmering rivers of Lawrence, but the depths of a mystical ocean of writing. The Powys-man is on a harbour wall, watching the onrushing mass of ecstasy and vision approach him. The swelling of the tides describes most appositely Powys's style. In *Wood and Stone* Powys speaks of a 'tidal wave of fertility [pouring] over the whole valley' (Wood, p. 295).

---

22 *To the Lighthouse*, Grafton 1977, p. 69.

Hardy is full of amazing scenes of people amongst Nature. The settings in his novels are vitally important – they are no mere backdrops, they are not tacked on to titillate the town-dweller with a little rural beauty. Think of the Christmas carol-singing in *Greenwood Tree,* or in *Madding Crowd* Oak and Bathsheba atop the ricks in the storm, the sheep-shearing, the sword-display, the sheep-fair; or in *Return* those bonfires, and the Maypole dance (when 'All the dancing girls felt the symptoms, but Eustacia most of all' [p. 332]). The dance-scene is so fully and sensuously realized, in that bewitching half-light. Then we have Elizabeth and her mother coming into Casterbridge in *Mayor* – and Henchard on the bridge. Marty and Giles planting trees in the early morning (Marty saying "How they [the trees] sigh directly we put 'em upright" (*The Woodlanders*, p. 106); Giles looking and smelling 'like Autumn's very brother' (p. 261); Grace and Giles in the wood at night, when she calls to him 'Come to me, dearest!' (p. 375). Or there is the moaning of the sea merging with the cries of a woman giving birth in *The Well-Beloved* (p. 133). Tess and her brother on the cart; Tess and Angel at dawn at Talbothays, like Adam and Eve – 'they met in that strange and solemn interval, the twilight of the morning' amid 'spectral, half-compounded, aqueous light', alone in those midsummer dawns, for other people (always the enemies of lovers) 'were nowhere' (*Tess*, pp. 186-7); Tess alone at night, outdoors; the sleep-walking; Tess working in the snowbound fields; Tess walking to Emminster; Tess and Angel at Stonehenge. Lastly, Jude, eternally attached to the top of the ladder by the Brown House, looking for and finding 'the new Jerusalem' (*Jude*, p. 62).

Thomas Hardy abounds with nature-mysticism. He creates an unsurpassed paradise out of the English countryside. It is an extraordinary achievement. In his poem 'To Thomas Hardy' Powys eulogized the old poet:

O Master of human smiles and human moon,
Of strange soul-searchings, raptures, agonies...
O master, thine a special need of praise
From me whose heart is all thy sweet West's own. (Poems, p. 19)

Hardy's Wessex is so full of life, so keenly observed, so lovingly recreated. It is a fiction, a piece of nostalgia (very much so) but it also rings true and clear. Hardy's Wessex is an authentic part of the world. He is accurate in his characterization – of people and of the landscape. It is this deep sense of psychology, this insight into the workings of the emotions and the landscape, that gives Hardy the edge over most other British novelists.

Nature is worshipped mystically in both Thomas Hardy's and John Cowper Powys's fiction. Powys is much more extreme than Hardy. Among British artists, Powys is one of the most extreme of all. Elements in Hardy's and Powys's nature-mysticism link them to mystics such as Spinoza, Novalis, Rumi, Ruysbroeck, Heraclitus, Plato, Hui-Neng, Eckhart, Boehme, Plotinus, Chuang-tzu, as well as the British nature-poetry or rural tradition (which includes Vaughan, Traherne, Blake, Wordsworth, Jefferies and John Smith) and the American poets (Whitman, Emerson, Thoreau). The key elements in mysticism are all found in nature-mysticism at some point, mystery, identification, unity, ecstasy, timelessness. In all nature-mysticism there is a sacred kind of identification, a *participation mystique* with nature. We find this in Powys's sensualisms, or in Hardy's evocations of Egdon Heath or Talbothays. Tess is a mystic – she thinks that nature embodies her feelings. Hardy's and Powys's players are contemplatives – they are mystics meditating on nature, on being, on mortality. Sometimes Hardy is very subjective, seeing external Nature as part of internal human feelings: 'Nature is Imagination itself' says William Blake.[23]

Thomas Hardy and John Cowper Powys are God-soaked writers. They are not, then, pantheists, still less are they monotheists. There is something of pantheism in their philosophies, but it is more useful to apply Zaehner's term of 'pan-en-heinsm' to them (R. Zaehner, pp. 28, 50). Though both writers' life-views contain elements of Gnosticism and neo-Platonism, they do not usually believe that, ultimately, 'all is One'. They move instead to a Lawrencean belief in a holy kind of singularity in life. Nature must remain a Total Other, ultimately. Though Hardy often personifies Nature, anthropomorphizes Nature (as in *A Pair of Blue Eyes*, p. 210) he acknowledges that Nature is an entirely separate entity from humanity

---

[23] *Letters*, ed. A.G.B. Russell, 1906, p. 111.

(even though humanity thrives on Nature and is born from it). Both Hardy and Powys are fiercely elemental writers. They are poets, intuitives, and basically pagan in their outlook. Hardy and Powys make Nature dæmonic, cruel, violent, pastoral, infinite, but not a vehicle for God-driven intentions. Divinities do move through their landscapes, but they are fickle and cruel ones such as First Causes. Nature in Hardy and Powys is mythic, vast, menacing, playful, nourishing, but, ultimately, no matter how much humanity works it and controls it, Nature transcends all of humanity. Gabriel Oak realizes this on Norcombe Hill.

Nature is holy, for Thomas Hardy and John Cowper Powys, but answerable to none, whether man, woman, animal or god. Hence the trend in Hardy and Powys and much rural fiction to a sacral solitude. Hardy wanted both love and solitude – that mythic secret place away from all other people and influences. But it is an escape with the right lover, at the right time. John Clare put it thus in his sonnet 'Love and Solitude': 'Take all the world away – and leave me still/ The mirth and music of a woman's voice,/ That bids the heart be happy and rejoice'.[24]

Powys is violent in his desires. His nature-mysticism is exuberant and copious. He includes stones,m bits of moss, as well as the Wordsworthian clouds and essences. Powys's nature-mysticism excludes other people. His is a mysticism of the self-alone, in the sense of Thoreau, Emerson and Richard Jefferies. In *The Story of My Heart* Jefferies wrote:

> I was utterly alone with the sun and the earth. Lying down on the grass, I spoke in my soul to the earth, the sun, the air, and the distant sea far beyond light...Now is eternity; now is the immortal life. Here this moment, by this tumulus, on earth, now; I exist in it...To the soul there is no past, no future; all is and will be ever, in now.[25]

This pastoral ecstasy is much like John Cowper Powys's sensualism. These nature-mystical experiences all centre around the Western concept of the soul. They approximate to Hardy's definition of Turner's art: *landscape plus soul*. The soul is at work in Hardy and Powys, as it is in Lawrence, Eckhart, Vaughan, Plotinus and Plato. Powys goes farther than Hardy, and the identification of the self with Nature is deeper. The Powys-

---
24 In Wright, ed., p. 258.
25 In Happold, ed., pp. 386-90.

man dwells for a time actually within bits of moss, or in stones, or in winds. Hardy is more concerned with humanity, with how Nature relates to people. So when the Hardy protagonist has an ecstatic nature-mystical experience – Oak on Norcombe Hill, Eustacia on Egdon, Jude at the Brown House – they always move back into the world of people and communities. While one suspects that Powys's characters would really like to disappear into the very essence of a stone or a lake, one knows that Hardy realized that such mystical escapes were impractical, as well as being near-impossible to achieve even momentarily.

The soil in Thomas Hardy, though, is mystical. It is full of pagan and pastoral elements. Hardy's Wessex is a country of rich soil as well as rich soul. His sense of the Wessexian soil is deeply humanized. History permeates it. Human actions shape the landscape. Wessex is drenched in history – in all Hardy's fiction landscape has a strong and deep historical dimension. Hardy's Wessex is a 'palimpsest of successive strata' as Urquhart says in *Wolf Solent* (p. 45). Hardy's Wessex is richly stratified historically as Dorset is rich in geological stratification. Both Hardy and Powys delve deep down through successive layers of human history in order to reach the underground lakes and rivers of prehistory and ancient passion. While Hardy's Wessexians crawl across the surface of the landscape, silhouetted against the open darkling sky, Powys's Wessex-folk sink deeper into themselves in back alleys, wood-paths, and dim sitting-rooms. Powys aims to write of 'mystery and passion of secret despairs and occult ecstasies of strange renunciations and stranger triumphs' (Visions, p. 191). Powys writes of the instability of forms. He tries to describe shape-shifting and skin-changing.

Thomas Hardy's drama typically contrasts Nature and culture, landscape and civilization, the unconscious and the social conscience, the red of human blood and fire with Nature's harmonizing greens and browns, the tiny male crawling over the body of the Great Mother Planet.

Hardy prefers the borderlands – psychically and physically. He writes of people on the very edge, moving towards madness. Hardy's landscape are darkening at the edges – night is coming on, the hills are abandoned for the wild woods, stones grow out of the Earth, out of the Past, churches and trees loom up menacingly, the moon is on the wane, the sky fills with the bruise-greys of Turner's late cloudscapes, and the night-creatures crawl out of the thickets and caves – witches, giants, færies. Hardy's characters move out of the civilized circles of light, into the psychic darkness beyond the safety of the hearthfire. The poetry, like the fiction, is full of Gothic graveyards, ghostlore, hauntings, nightmares, all kinds of deceptive phenomena. His spaces are borderlands, the crumbling edges, and the interzones where anything might happen.

Lawrence sets his scenes beside potent rivers, while Hardy (and John Cowper Powys) has ponds and forests and prehistoric mounds. Hardy's world is an abandoned England, a country of disrepair and half-remembered customs. His sense of Nature is of a magical, feminine realm. He descends into it – not much ascension in his works, not many hill-top views, or wide-open vistas. His characters *go out* into the night, but really they are sinking deeper into themselves. Hardy's nature-mysticism is self-communion. His people go out to go in. They sink deeper into themselves. Hardy is full of countrified, Englished versions of spiritual Night Journeys, those Dark Nights of the Soul such as were undertaken by Mohammed and St John of the Cross.

Hardy tends to retreat from light. His is not a bright, pastoral, Arcadian world. It is not the world of early mythology. Turner intensifies light, while Hardy intensifies darkness. There is a complex mysticism of darkness, traditionally, as there is of light. Vaughan, Dionysius, Ruysbroeck and the Sufis use darkness in their mysticisms. At its most extreme in *Jude the Obscure,* Hardy's dark vision is nourishing – in the negative sense of the Oriental Void. Hardy is moving in *Jude* towards one of the basic precepts of Jungian psychology: where opposites meet and fuse, and where the opposite of a statement is also true.

In Lawrence too there are many extraordinary scenes where people and Nature merge at a deep level. In *The Rainbow*, the scene where Anna and Will put up the sheaves of corn by moonlight is one of the most gorgeous and authentic descriptions of courtship and love in literature – 'he was drawing near and she must turn again. And there was the flaring moon laying bare her bosom again, making her drift and ebb like a wave.' (*The Rainbow*, p. 160). When at last they meet, and embrace, after this long dance of desire, Lawrence unleashes his startling, rhythmic, ecstatic language:

> And he drew near, and she drew near.
> 'Anna,' he said, in wonder and birthpain of love.
> 'My love,' she said, her voice growing rapturous. And they kissed on the mouth, in rapture and surprise, long, real kisses. The kiss lasted, there among the moonlight. He kissed her again, and she kissed him. And again they were kissing together.

How utterly *right* this is, how delicate yet also how strong this prose is. It has a Biblical simplicity and grandeur, rarely attained in literature. Lawrence uses the simplest words, that sound childish in their mouthing separate from their context – love, kiss, moonlight. But he manages to imbue them with a tremendous poetic weight, with such a rapturous density, they become religious.

It is rare for any writer to achieve this kind of passionate intensity. Lawrence, more than Hardy and John Cowper Powys, could create these scenes of bodies and souls fusing with Nature so well. They are vividly realized scenes – Ursula and Anton kissing by the Trent in the darkness, or Ursula prowling in the foam, crying 'I want to go!' (*The Rainbow*, p. 531). This scene of the most intense yearning is not only one of the highest points in literature, it also captures a moment in which life is burning at its brightest, its deepest, its most intense. Ursula throws her soul out into the universe, knowing that no one and no thing is big enough to contain it. There is a wealth of emotion and insight in that scene.

At night Powys has the wind, Hardy has the stars, but Lawrence claims the moon. There are many communions with the moon in Lawrence's fiction – Clara and Paul making love beside the river; Mrs Morel in the moonlight; or Paul and Miriam on the shore in the evening:

> The country was black and still. From behind the sandhills came the whisper of the sea. Paul and Miriam walked in silence. Suddenly he started. The whole of his blood seemed to burst into flame, and he could scarcely breathe. An enormous orange moon was staring at them from the rim of the sandhills. He stood still, looking at it. (*Sons and Lovers*, p. 229)

Paul here is clearly an early version of Wolf. The moon makes Paul want to shout, or it freezes him. He is hypersensitive, like the Powys-man. Lawrence moves his nature-scenes further onward than Powys. Powys's scenes seem to stop with the individual's consciousness. Lawrence's always spring out further, to the connection, the relation, with other people. Lawrence moves outwards, Powys sinks inwards. Like Lawrence, though, Powys uses nature-mysticism to counterpoint his stories. Like Lawrence, Powys moves towards using night-scenes more and more. Lawrence's nature-scenes are about the relations between people (Birkin smashing the moon's reflection in *Women in Love* relates to his affair with Ursula). Powys rarely brings in other souls into his mythic sensualisms. Lawrence describes revolts against the society or the self, while Powys describes the self and nothing much else. Lawrence's scenes of the self alone are piquant because of the character's relation to other people. Thus Aaron in the yard looking in at his family, or Somers on the coasts of Australia, or Kate drifting on the sperm-like lake in Mexico. These compare favourably with Wolf beside Lenty Pond, or Sam walking beside the river, or Dud on his walks. Powys uses Nature as a background to love too, most notably in *Wolf Solent* with Wolf and Gerda on Poll Camp. How different, though, is Powys's detached, rather mean and selfish concept of romance compared to Lawrence's – Lawrence has Connie and Parkin running in the rain. Such exuberance is out of place in both Hardy and Powys.

What distinguishes John Cowper Powys from Thomas Hardy, Lawrence, and the whole tradition of rural literature, is his peculiar perceptions of nature. Powys's fiction is one long pathetic fallacy – he is full of total animism. In *Porius* Powys speaks of 'the secretive psycho-sensuous trick of ravishing the four elements with the five senses' (p. 506). This is a later version of the Powysian 'mythology' or 'life-illusion'. In Powys the elements assume grand proportions. He makes personifications out of his elements as the ancients did. He has tumultuous floods, sorcerous winds, hyperphysical plants, beatific clouds and transcendent geologies. His elements have their own essences which become enmeshed with the consciousnesses of his characters. Powys's elements are impersonal – they are manifestations of a 'Total Other' (yet this Otherness is always self-referential, always refers ultimately to the soul of the observer, the Powys-man). The wind in Powys does not simply blow over a character, it *penetrates* her/ him. This profound sense of elementalism turns Powys's sensualism into something ardent and consuming.

Each of the four Wessex novels can be viewed as portraying one of the four elements: air, the wind, blows throughout *Maiden Castle*; earth is represented by the Jobber's stone, by Portland and by the sands of *Weymouth Sands*; water floods *A Glastonbury ROmance*, and in it swims the mystical Christ-Fish; fire is the element of the alchemical book *Wolf Solent*. Powys's favourite elements are water and stone. For him the tidal ebb and flow of things is the deepest law of the universe.

Wolf Solent burns with fire – the fever of the novel ends with Wolf's vision of the Saturnian gold. For John Cowper Powys fire is a Heraclitean element of destruction and regeneration. He was aware of the pagan aspect of fire, and of the old fire-festivals, when he had Uryen grab the two girls and run through the bonfire in *Maiden Castle*. In *Wolf Solent* fire symbolizes the end of the Quest upon which the Powys-man has embarked. Air feeds fire, and all Powys's fiction is elevated by the power of the wind. The wind in Powys is certainly fertile – he conjures up magical zephyrs and tempests that can transform people. Air was a favourite element of Nietzsche. Dud is a wind-worshiper (MC, p. 245), for him the breeze is Welsh and bewitching – it is a 'cold, slippery, invisible Being' (ib). Powys's wind is connected to his Homeric æther, and to all things supernatural. His sense of the ærodynamic is mystical. In the poem 'Earth-Worship' Powys wrote: 'I want no more than exultant air' (Poems, p. 32). In *A Glastonbury Romance* the wind breathes through the town at night and links all the characters together. In this way, using the elements, Powys raises his uneventful books towards greatness.

Water features strongest in *A Glastonbury Romance*. The novel is all about the creation of a new mystical cult of the Grail. Like the poet Taleissin, Christ the Fish is to be re-Born out of the Grail-cauldron. The movement is from the water-sign Pisces into the new age of water-bearing Aquarius. John Cowper Powys was aware of this idea long before the hippies in the 60s got hold of it. Glastonbury is called a fishtank, and indeed reading Powys is sometimes like seeing everything through the distorting elements of water and glass and potted plants. The townscape of Glastonbury is seen as a bizarre fishtank with a floor cluttered with miniature plants, spires and stones. The waters of mysticality flow through Powys's fiction, but what a pity he fudged that potentially great scene in *Porius* where the phallic lance is plunged into the Grail-like lake.

Weymouth Sands is a rock-ridden novel, but over the stone flows the ocean. Sylvanus *really* worships the sun, sky and sea (Wey, p. 324). He revels in the stark simplicity and supra-human divinity of sunshine and water: 'Sunlight and water...always struck Sylvanus as being the nearest revelation of the Ultimate Being that man could attain.' (p. 392) The elements, then, are not the Ultimate in themselves, but only revelations of it. The revelation is in the flow, the livingness of it all. Powys contemplates Nature's life, not her beauty (Cul, p. 180). Nature is no abstraction for him, but a force, a presence. In *Weymouth Sands* water and stone are present from the deepest levels upwards. Water stains the sand (p. 455) where the children play. The dry sands connote adulthood and death (sterility). The wet sands throb with life, with children. Mysticality flows from wetness, as in *A Glastonbury Romance* (in which blood and water feature so strongly). Powys naturally leans towards earth and water imagery. The one floods over the other, but stone lies under everything. This points towards a duality, one of Powys's great failings as a philosopher. His duality is at odds with his Heraclitean Oneness. He calls himself a Taoist, but no Taoist acknowledges dualities. Taoism adores water, though, as one of its primary metaphors for the way of things. In *Weymouth Sands* John Cowper Powys speaks of:

> that fatally double sound of the sea...systole, diastole, centripetal, contrifugal, flow-in, ebb-out, the long planetary rise-fall, up-down, pendulum swing of this self-contradictory universe. (p. 464)

This passage displays the basic trait of Powys when he is in his elemental mode: to expand his metaphors up to the mythical, the cosmic, the gigantic. He can't resist it. Thus the 'planetary' connection. He makes these connections poetically, intuitively, like any poet. Thus in *A Glastonbury Romance* links are made between water, the mystical Christ-

Fish, the fish-tank of Glastonbury, the Island of Avalon, the womb and the foetus and the Goddess Cerridwen. Powys loves to move up to the mythical plane, as did Hardy and Lawrence. Lawrence, indeed, deals with mythical, metaphysical, philosophical issues all the time. The big difference is that in Hardy and Lawrence and most other novelists these discourses stem from one's relation with other people. In Powys they stem from the contemplation of inanimate objects, plants, walls, animals and the elements. Richard Storm in *After My Fashion* 'exults in the huge grotesqueness of the gigantic advertisements, in the yells of the truck drivers, in the flapping clothes lines, in the piled-up garbage, in the hideous and vociferous children' (p. 185). This is a wild, excremental vision of America that looks forward to Henry Miller. Powys wants everything in excess. In his crazed dextrality, he moves into overload mode more rapidly even than Miller. He wants everything at once – to embrace all of creation.

Five

The Mythology of Sensualism

What people regard as fantastic and lacking in universality, I hold to be the inmost essence of truth.

Fyodor Dostoievsky (letter, 1869)[26]

Deep pools there are, pools quiet and still,
Far off, where none of them guess...

John Cowper Powys, from the poem 'Escape'[27]

---

26 In Allnott, ed, p. 68.
27 In *Mandragora*, p. 20.

Like many poets before him, John Cowper Powys loved to immerse himself in the essence of nature. Powys's ancestors in this realm are Blake, Traherne, Vaughan, Novalis and Donne. Powys's vision is indeed in the grand tradition of Metaphysical and Romantic art. Underneath Powys's mannered Georgian poetic style lies a sense of wonder like Henry Vaughan's: 'with what flowers,/ And shoots of glory, my soul breaks, and buds!' ('The Morning Watch'). Powys combines this nature-mysticism with a Whitmanesque love of wildness and some of the more melancholy reveries of Edward Thomas. In Heine (and Novalis, Schiller, Hölderlin and Goethe) we find the prototype of the Powysian soul alone. This is from Heine:

Und meine Brust schwoll auf wie das Meer,
Und sehnend ergriff mich ein tiefes Heimweh
Nach dir, du holdes Bild...
[And my breast heaved like the sea, and yearning gripped me, a deep home-sickness for you, you charming image][28]

This is where it begins, the cult of the existential hero alone in the vastness of Nature – in Romanticism. In his own poetry Powys speaks of particular places where his soul raved endlessly: 'Come to the mossy places' he begged (in *Mandragora*, p. 113)

Wolf Solent marks the beginning of the full-blown Powysian mythic sensualism. Wolf's 'mythology' is his 'real life' (p. 21); he aims for a merging ecstasy which demands nothing in return (p. 153); it is deep (p. 20); and he will lose it by making love with Christie (p. 536). 'Stripped of it, there would be nothing left but a stoical endurance.'(p. 450). So Wolf has to grow up, to outgrow his sensualism. He has to leave behind his shamanic visions.

Powys's sensualism has much in common with traditional mystical experiences, with vertical meditation, with the altered states produced by drugs, sex, art and so on. The ecstatic passages in Powys'' fiction are amongst his best, and his most enjoyable. It is the same with Lawrence. Most of the characters in Powys have ecstasies, whether they be the typical Powysian anti-hero (Dud, Wolf, Porius), or the wonderful urchin, Larry Zed:

---
28 H. Heine's *The North Sea*, tr. V. Watkins, Faber, 1955, pp. 26-27.

But as if they boy had been hypnotized into making a leap forward over some time-gulf, he suddenly realized, without catching Nature at her conjuring trick, that the whole eastern sky, and the whole horizon of the sea, too, had lost its crimson and become shining gold. (*Weymouth Sands*, p. 137)

John Cowper Powys wants to be panoramic. He wants to include all kinds of experiences. He advocated multiplicity – a 'multiverse'. His sensualism is not pantheism, neither is it monotheic or monoscopic. It is often claustrophic, and self-centred. Sometimes he goes too far. In *A Glastonbury Romance* he included the thoughts of a 'First Cause', and of the sun. Here he made some really terrible fiction. How wonderful is Lawrence, though, with his sun-symbolism – in the story *Sun*, and in his *The Plumed Serpent*.

Powys was intoxicated by metaphysics sensually, not intellectually. For him philosophy was erotic. He viewed metaphysics voyeuristically, as he viewed women (A, p. 478-9). Powys aches to include everything – the occult, the vegetal, the elemental, the psychological. Powys exalts all kinds of consciousness and beingness. He loves the essence of stones and the fury of cyclones. All have a place in his multiverse. The characters Squeak, in *All or Nothing* (pp. 66-7) cries out for an expansive universe populated by 'a beautiful teeming, blossoming, bread-bearing, rose-tinted galaxy of stars, full of exultant living creatures{, a world of love and desire and ecstasy. His vision is not a sexualized one, but it is very erotic, as Fawkner has noted (p. 77). It is the identification that Powys's characters have with the world that is erotic, as it is in Lawrence. We only have to think of Connie in the wood to show this. In Powys there is a hierarchy of sensations, from the haptic up through the æsthetic, to the divine. The connections Powys makes, like Robert Graves, are poetic, intuitive. There is no system as such, just a heightened poetic sensibility (which is trusted wholly, over and above scientific ways of thinking).

In John Cowper Powys everyday things become the stuff of art – as in the views of Dostoievsky and Virginia Woolf. Woolf wrote: 'The mind receives a myriad impressions – trivial, fantastic, evanescent, or engraved with the sharpness of steel. From all sides they come, an incessant show of innumerate atoms' (*The Common Reader*, 1925). Powys, like Woolf, and, later, Beckett, aims to record these 'myriad impressions'. So the Ultimate Novel, if the Woolfian writer were truly free, would contain 'no plot, no comedy, no tragedy, no love interest or catastrophe in the accepted style' (ib.). This is the aim of Gide, Flaubert, Proust, Beckett, Joyce and Durrell, as well as Woolf and Powys. *Wolf Solent* is close to this Ideal, though not as close as *To the Lighthouse*. The trivial becomes universal, as in Proust. The aim is to grasp 'life as it really is'.[29] So in Powys's world, a Kafkaesque beetle crawling along can become a cosmic act.

André Gide, like Verlaine, Rimbaud, Blake, Lawrence, Petrarch and Ronsard, had an intensely heightened poetic sensibility. The luminous sensuality of his *Fruits of the Earth* is propounded with total authority and is utterly convincing. In his letters Gide wrote: 'Sensuality...consists simply in considering as an end and not as a means the present object and the present minute'.[30] Gide, likes Powys, creates a cult, a religion out of sensuality. Gide is full of a rich, luxuriant sensualism that is built on lazy wanderings, eroticism, intensity and eidetic apperception.

As in traditional mysticism, John Cowper Powys's characters have their ecstasies by sinking down into the essence of things. The poet Talesin, in *Porius*, strives 'for a particular magic of measured metre'so that he could 'sink into the essence of the thing' (p. 416) In the same way the sculptor Brancusi said he was 'within the essence of things themselves'. In Powys we find stones that feel, suns that think, and vast mythical gestures made by beetles and leaves.

The four books of non-fiction written in the 1930s – *In Defence of Sensuality, A Philosophy of Solitude, Autobiography* and *The Art of Happiness* – constitute a quartet of philosophical commentary which compliments the Wessex quartet. These four books of popular philosophy reveal Powys trying to deal with the themes of his novels. His approach is highly individual. It is as if he is trying to convince nobody but himself of his ideas on philosophy. He is immensely repetitive – he goes over the same points again and again. He only has one or two main points in each book, but he spins them out laboriously. Powys's philosophy is supremely

---

[29] *Le Temps Retrouve*, Random House, New York 1932.
[30] 'Lettres a Angele X', *œuvres completes*, vol 3, p. 220.

amateurish – he has none of the depth of perception of Russell, or the insight into epistemology of Wittgenstein. He is very much a novelist philosophizing. Lawrence is so much better: Lawrence moves through ideas very rapidly but usually in great depth. Lawrence does overwrite (and overthink) but he can apply himself to so many different kinds of situations. Powys is much more limited. His philosophical books are really supports for the novels. They are notebooks, sourcebooks. He will convince no one of his ideas – they are so personalized. He says all of this in the novels. But then, he is not a writer who tries to slip in his ideas unnoticed, in the Stendhalian sense.

The basic ideas are as follows:

It is a philosophy of *solitude*. The male self alone. Everything flows from this first law of Powys's vision. Powys's is a Romantic cult of solitude – of Emerson, Goethe, Thoreau, Rousseau, Wordsworth. R.W. Emerson wrote:

> The lover of nature is he whose inward and outward senses are still truly adjusted to each other...His intercourse with heaven and earth becomes part of his daily food. In the presence of nature a wild delight runs through the man in spite of real sorrows.[31]

This is true of the Powys-man, this immersion in Nature is self-sustaining. The contemplation of Nature becomes one's daily food – physically as well as soulfully. Nature feeds the spirit – let the body take care of itself with cups of tea and a walking stick. Powys's is a cheap nature-mysticism – no hardware is needed, apart from an oak stick. Powys hates crowds, preferring a mystical aloneness to everything else. Happiness comes from solitude, not from friends. Powys's is the ultimate existential life-view, in which the essential, social nature of the human animal is subverted. Already Powys's philosophy is inauthentic, for as Weston La Barre has rightly said: 'Man is the culture-bearing animal, who never is and never can be alone and still remain human.' (*The Ghost Dance*, p. xv) Powys's life-philosophy is automatically a failure in modern post-psychoanalytical terms. Its anti-social, anti-altruistic, anti-emotional, anti-feminine stance also makes it wrong in the eyes of the modern world. Any philosophy that does not take Marxism, psycho-

---

[31] *Nature*, 1836, in H. Hugo, ed., pp. 386-.

analysis, Einsteinian physics or many other ideologies into account is instantly made void. Powys is the ultimate Outsider, wanting nothing from society, except modern lavatories, electricity for tea-making, and lighting for reading. All the Powys-man needs is a patch of moss on a wall and his walking-stick! It is a cheap philosophy, asking not to change the world, or even really to get to grips with it, or with people or issues or societies. All Powys wants is, as Merlin says, to be left alone.

So in *A Philosophy of Solitude* John Cowper Powys writes: 'Only when the soul is alone can the magic of the universe flow through it.' (p. 56) One must become like a stone – hard, cold and enduring (Sol, p. 49). Powys's is a philosophy that does not want any intrusion from other people or ideas. It wants total solitude, just time and space enough to work on himself and his relation to the world. It is the ultimate egoist, autistic life-view. Cobbled together from other highly individual philosophies – the *Tao Te Ching*, Heraclitus, Hegel, Plato, Nietzsche, Spinoza – Powys's vision is really a fanatically defended excuse for non-involvement and self-absorption. It is a 'life-*illusion*' – and all illusions are made to be shattered. Although it is non-religious, non-institutionalized, Powys's philosophy is defended like the Christian faith is defended by multitudes of theologians and apologists. It is not, like other philosophies of the same era (Freud, James, Russell, Lawrence) a positive one: it is a submission and embracement of the world, but not a call for changing it. While Russell grapples with the hideousnesses of society, and Lawrence thinks always of the future, and how to make it better, Powys is content to discuss ways of living alone and in serenity with one's own thoughts.

The individual must slow himself down, must become ichthysaurian (Def, p. 11). Loneliness is happiness (p. 10). The self is supreme. When you've achieve the impossible – that is, got rid of everyone in your life – you are nearly ready to begin on the prime Powysian activity: walking. But first you must have a walking stick. All Powys's people have them: they are utterly essential. The Powys-man is like a Noah or a Biblical patriarch in the wilderness – they must have their staff, for support. The stick must be of oak. It will be like a sword to you (A, p. 101). The Powys walking-stick is of course phallic (the oakwood supports this). It is one's (masturbatory) companion, triumphing where others (women) have failed. The stick itself may be the instrument of an ecstasy, as when Sir Mort thrusts his into the ground in *The Brazen Head*.

Then comes The Walk. Most of Powys's people have a series of favourite walks. Walking is the way in which the Powys-man perceives and experiences the world. Walking is preferrable to any other activity in Powys's art. As Powys says: 'the real point about walking is that it isolates you in the midst of the Cosmos' (p. 148). You are now free to absorb anything that comes your way. You are utterly alone. It is a voluptuous attitude.

Then come The Experiences.

These are, primarily, sensual and elemental in nature. In them space and time are changed. Memory becomes exaggerated. The Past becomes as real as the present. Prophecies occur. The elements speak. And, in these vegetal-reptilian-animal-godlike ecstasies, the Powysian philosophy of solitude is affirmed.

The John Cowper Powys ecstasy begins by contemplating some tiny part of nature. On your walk you're bound to come across a wall. Look at it: let yourself sink into it. Let the greenness of the moss excite you and spin you away from yourself, and also of course deeper into yourself. It is not an æsthetic experience, but an elemental one. It is the All-and-Everything of that particular moment. Before time and the Past are actualized, simply revel in the beauty and extraordinary nature of that piece of green moss! Thus Powys in his *Autobiography*:

> 'I am looking at a patch of moss on a greenish marbly rock and I am aware of a deep sensual pleasure.' (p. 41) And in Cambridge: 'certain patches of grass and green moss' transported him 'into a sort of Seventh Heaven.' (p. 199)

So here's the Powys-man in the fiction: Sam in *A Glastonbury Romance*: 'What he felt was a strange and singular reciprocity between his soul and every little fragment of masonry, of stony ground, of mossy ground...' (p. 926). And Dud in *Maiden Castle* who, when he comes 'on a patch of green moss on a grey wall' he gets 'a sensation that's more important than what you call 'love', or anything else, nearer the secret of things too!' (p. 353) Lacrima in *Wood and Stone* feels the 'insidious sensuality' of the landscape

(Wood, p. 371). There are many many other examples – a multitude of them in *Wolf Solent*. For Porius it is called 'cavoseniargizing', a trick of isolating and uniting with things (P, p. 84). For Evans, it is more of 'an orgasm of egocentric contemplation' (GR, p. 812). You sensualize according to your nature. It is basically the same, though, with each Powysian character.

Ordinary things can be the sources of this ecstasy. From the sun on a wall one can have a 'Beatific Vision' (Def, p. 104) Or from tea (as in *Wolf Solent*). Thus far, John Cowper Powys's sensualism is not far from the pastoral view of life, as created in Theocritus, Virgil, Spenser and Hardy. The Elizabethan poet Sidney wrote: 'O sweet woods, the delight of solitariness!'.[32] Powys too loves the solitude of the woods. Marlowe sings: *Come live with me and be my love*, as does Thomas Hardy Powys instead says: *Come let me live alone*. There is no Other, no separate not-self Other up to the high standards of the Powysian solitary ego! Instead, Powys writes (in *Wolf's Bane*): 'Out into the cool air/ Where love, and music, dies behind us!' (*Poems*, p. 69). As in bucolic verse, Powys too populates his stories with satyrs, sylphs, Pan-figures, tramps and magicians. Powys is the god presiding over these characters, over this pageant this masquerade, like Pan presiding over a bacchanale. But they are all puppets for him, for the self-alone, for the saurian ego, extensions of his soul, his elemental feelings.

As in traditional nature-mysticism, in Powys's sensualism there is a *participation mystique* with the object of contemplation. Powys's sensualism, like Lawrence's, is the product of *relationship*. But Powys is more concerned, ultimately, with the self alone. And this is perhaps why is marginalized so often. He speaks of the 'ichthian act' (Hap, p. 24), a 'sinking-down', a 'psycho-sensuous ecstasy' that is '*a direct embrace of life*' (Def, p. 169). It is a sacramental experience – essentially one of a sacralization of life and living things. It is like the Australian Bushmen's *alchuringa* experience, the mystical participation with the earth and with life. There is nothing new about this – people have felt a mystic solidarity with the earth and with vegetation for millennia.

What is it then about John Cowper Powys's sensualism that

---

[32] From *The Countess of Pembroke's Arcadia*, in Geoffrey G. Miller, ed: *Poems of the Elizabethan Age*, Methuen 1977, p. 215.

distinguishes it from the nature-mysticism of Lawrence, Whitman, Thoreau, Heine, Goethe and Hardy? It is, surely, his extremism, which makes him speak of dead leaves in fox holes (*Ducdame*, p. 136), or of 'the bitter smell of the old hero's scrotum' (*Atlantis*, p. 284), or of a chilly vapourish landscape which suggests 'the slippery motions of great cold-bodied eels in the wet mud, with the sense in every direction of thousands of inert wintry marsh-plants invisible in the mist'(Weymouth, p. 134) It is this aspect of Powys's visionary sense that distinguishes him from other novelists. He sends his mind out into the crevices of the landscape, into secret corners and hidden holes. This, the tiny, saurian, small-scale slowed-down ego-contemplation, is where Powys excels most. When it is combined with the opposite, the other extreme, the infinity-reaching 'Saintly' dimension, the results can be miraculous. Suddenly the Powysverse opens out, from claustrophia to infinity. Most often it is the hyperspiritual wind which does this opening-out. The wind blasts in, and carries away the souls of the characters, scattering them far and wide. Thus in *Maiden Castle*, Dud's question to his father, Uryen, on top of the great earthwork

> was carried by the wind as it swept over tussocks of grass, over hoof-marks of horses, over windings of sheep-tracks. It was carried sighing and swishing over the heads of daisies, it was carried sobbing and soughing between the stalks of last year's thistles; it was carried sliding and slithering along narrow rabbit-runs; it was carried with faint elfin screams through the curves of snail-shells, it made sorties from mole-hill to mole-hill; it whistled over the thresholds of shrew-mice. (p. 246)

Archetypal Powys this – the small and the large, the infinitesimally tiny and the vast landscape working together. The wind here being the activator. More than a little magic is suggested by the fairy references (and also to Pan in the hoof-marks). The non-human is always stressed in John Cowper Powys's sensualism. He wants gods and magicians and sylphs and madmen, but not ordinary people. Of the three levels of his elementalism – vegetation, animals and the elements – he uses mostly the elements. Animals do appear – often odd choices of beasts, such as the water-rat that provides the *mise-en-scène* for Wolf and Gerda's courtship.

The cow, says Powys, is 'the most divine of all animals.' Creatures are not glorified, as in Lawrence. There are not mythical Lawrencean peacocks or horses in Powys. Animals are presented in all their basic animality – not as symbols or forces, but as themselves.

Perhaps the best scene involving animal elementalism, and one of the very best of all Powys's scenes – if not *the* best, for its raw magic – is when Merlin appears to Rhun and Porius:

> [they hear] flutterings and screams above their heads, and the scamperings and snorting and patterings and scufflings in the bushes and bracken around them had increased perceptibly, while the splashes in the water below became more frequent, one following another in rapid succession as if a large shoal of fish had been moving up the river in the darkness. (Porius, p. 57)

This is what Tolkien wanted with his Merlin-figure, Gandalf, but he never achieved this kind of Powysian intensity. This elemental, primitive, ugly wizard has recently been revived in Graeme Fife's radio drama *Arthur* on BBC Radio Four (broadcast December 1990), in which Merlin was 'up to his knees in snow' amid a forest of moonlight and howling wolves. How satisfying is Powys's primæval, Saturnian Merlin when compared with the recent attempts of Mary Stewart, Count Tolstoi, Bradley, Cooper, White and others.

The shoal of fish moving upstream in the darkness is a powerful image. It has all the supernatural as well as the formally natural aspects of true mystery. Robert Graves said that the mystery of the Goddess could be present in something as commonplace as the wind in the trees at night. Powys's scene has a similar spine-tingling effect. It brings with it a sizeable helping of the Unknown, as well as being a quite ordinary occurrence. This blending of the strange and the everyday is typical of the horror, science-fiction, fantasy and Gothic genres. J.G. Ballard writes in this exaggerated mode. His spatial metaphors are the postmodern equivalent of Powys's naturalistic ones:

> Later, the sexual act between them became a hasty eucharist of the angular dimensions of the appartment. [...] By contrast, Xero was an archangel, a figure of galvanic energy and uncertainty. As he moved

across the abandoned landscape near the flyover, the very perspectives of the air seemed to invert behind him.[33]

Ballard circumscribes the decayed postmodern post-everything urbanscape which is the decimated remnants of Hardy's pastoral 19th century vision. The image 'the very perspective of the air seemed to invert behind him' is extraordinary. It is highly idiosyncratic, so peculiar to Ballard, yet so right, so perfectly matched to its subject and context. In Ballard, as in Powys, Golding, Lawrence and Borges, the outside world reflects the dynamics of the inner self. The world becomes a map of tormented psychology. Ballard's figures collapse the contours of the world behind them as they move through it. And Powys's magicians (forerunners of Ballard's doctors and scientists) energize the animals and the plants around them, as they work.

This expansion – from the self-alone towards the surrounding landscape and plantlife and animals and elements – is the dynamic movement of John Cowper Powys's sensualism. The self in its heightened states actualizes the landscape. Powys's sensualism is not, however, occult, psychological or mystical (Wolf, p. 113). It is natural. It is bedrock naturalism, in which all aspects of nature speak as themselves, of themselves. The soul afloat in this world merely intercepts these emanations. The self is a filter, a *vehicle* for these impressions. Powys's sensualism is impersonal.– a sensation taken to its extreme (Com, p. 46). It is deeper than physical or mental or sexual phenomena: it is simply the flow of life (ib, p. 363). Powys's people simply intercept it, open themselves to it, embrace it (as in Taoism). The Powys-self has to *feel* philosophy, not simply read it (Cul, p. 8). It is usual for the Powysian sensual ecstasy to be experienced alone, but there are instances of more than one person feeling philosophy in the real: Rook and Lexie seeing the swan; John and Mary in the rowing boat; Lil-Umbra and Peleg at the stone-circle. A joint-ecstasy outside of love is unusual in most literature. In *A Glastonbury Romance* of course Powys tried to create many scenes of mass ecstasy – fitting for a novel about the rebirth of a cult of the Holy Grail. Much more difficult, as well, to make it work.

---

33 *The Atrocity Exhibition*, Panther 1979, pp. 13, 39.

On the face of it, Powys's sensualism is merely another type of an inrushing ecstasy quite common in mysticism and literature. In Gide's *Strait is the Gate*, for example, Jerome feels 'another joy, pure, seraphic, mystic' which he imagines as a violin's songs, a 'flickering flame in which his and his beloved's heart are melted together' (p. 21). This is a standard personification of love – a conceit going back to Petrarch and his *Canzoniere*. We hear these none-too-subtle metaphors in modern popsongs, which wail 'my baby's left me / I walk in the rain.' For the abused baby subjectivist, if the ego has been hurt, then the world must reflect some of this pain. If the dejected lover weeps inside, then outside it must be raining.

In Hardy, as in most rural literature, the personifications of emotions are depicted at the elemental level of being. Hardy turns his Egdon Heath into a 'Titanic form', a kind of Lawrencean dark god with more than a touch of Sophocles about it. Hardy is sensitive, also, to the presences of things. In the bad novel *A Pair of Blue Eyes* a cliff has a presence – a 'horrid personality' says Elfride (p. 202).

In John Cowper Powys's art the nature-loving sensation-seeking view extends to include all livings and all things inanimate too. If they are ugly, slimy, tiny or blind, even better. Powys (tries to) embrace all things. Powys extends his love of all things up to the universe itself. Somewhere in his *Avignon Quintet* Durrell says: 'The universe is a big hug with no arms!' You just have to know how to embrace it. You have to let the universe hug you. You have to get your 'angle of inclination to the universe' just right.

Here John Cowper Powys is a Taoist. Behind everything in Powys is his multiverse. It is a realm of multiplicity, not a hierarchy. His 'philosophy of Elementalism' stems from a 'particular kind of lonely happiness' (Sol, p. 172). The earth and air and sea give us this happiness. They are Powysian angels, carrying messages of ecstasy-in-solitude. Time is destroyed. In *Owen Glendower*, for instance, when 'the infinite duration of time crumpled itself up into a little round bell.' (p. 96)

The aim of John Cowper Powys's sensualism? Happiness. 'Lonely happiness' (Def, p. 172) but happiness nevertheless. Powys is hedonistic – pleasure-seeking. It is escapist, but Powys also believes that this lonely happiness should be the norm, not the exception. Sometimes it is to be where one is not (Sol, p. 186) But mostly it is about being there, and enjoying it. As with painters, the Powys self must be able to enjoy itself by simply looking at sunlight on a wall. Sunlight creates joy, for Powys (Hap, p. 188). The aim is to attain a secret, saurian kind of beingness, to be fully immersed in Nature. As Friedrich Schiller wrote: 'The poet will, therefore, be the expression of nature itself'.[34]

Powys's sensualism comes in various modes. There is the simple experience of the vast elements, or of a swooping mind flying over the landscape (as in *Wolf Solent*, p. 120). Then of the minutiæ, or of animals. This is direct sensualism. But there is also "imaginative sensuality' (A, p. 7) where Time, the Past, history and memory come to the fore. Here the John Cowper Powys-man will muse upon the many ancestors s/he might have, or of the people who lived in a particular place, or of the many tribes that inhabited a certain piece of land. Powys moved towards historicity in the later books. In *A Glastonbury Romance* we have the race-memory of the tribe of the Sedgemoor wetlands, and of course the many Arthurian characters. In *Maiden Castle* Powys travels back further; by the time of *Porius*, he had gone back to the beginning of Time in his Saturn-Cronos-Merlin figure. The immediate, direct ecstasy, such as feeling oneself flying over Dorset from afar (such as in the *Autobiography*, p. 138) furthers the narrative in the novels in a conventional manner. Generally, Powys's sensual apprehensions are physical – he likes people physically as much as emotionally (A, p. 177). He talks about seeing through to people's skeletons.

The ancestral, temporal, memory-laden ecstasies are more complex. In the, Powys binds his concerns with literary, poetic, historical and societal issues. Wales rushes in (A, p. 291) and has incantatory power (A, p. 334). Anything Welsh feverishly excited Powys, as anything Greek thrilled Gide and Durrell. In his fervent mode, Powys becomes intense, religious. Powys's phrase for this mood is 'sensual lust' He feels sensual lust when contemplating Nature – 'a definite psyhic sensuality...more than the physical sensation of eating and drinking' (A, p. 414). Like Proust, Powys makes much of the transports that smell and taste can produce (A, p. 434).

---

[34] *On Simple and Sentimental Poetry*, Bohn Library 1875.

His novels are full of the essence of the Past, of the resurrection of personal and race memory. His fiction reinvents the Past (as all fiction does). Powys loves memory, loves the transformative powers of memory, like Cavafy, Durrell, Hardy, Shelley and Verlaine. Again and again Hardy haunts the graves of his old beloveds in his poetry – 'Would that I lay there / And she were housed here!' ('Rain on a Grave' (CP, p. 341). In Hardy, when he's in the midst of a love-affair, it is as if he were throwing himself into the future, imagining with a morbid voluptuousness his midnight vigils at the graveside. He seems to gloat, as Emily Brontë does, over dead lovers, fancying himself, perhaps, as some latter-day grieving Isis, fluttering over some mythical lover. Hardy breathes life back into love through the magic of poetry.

Memory is stirred up, as the dead leaves of Autumn are stirred up, by the wind. For Powys the wind is a 'miraculous phenomenon' (Sol, p. 108). The wind rushes in, like the imaginative twilit Cymru, to stir up the multiple layers of memory. As Dud approaches Mai-Dun Castle he is very aware of its history. Maumbury Rings plays a similar role in *The Mayor of Casterbridge*. The amphitheatre forms a link between the present day world and the ages of prehistoric people, the Romans, mediæval and Reformation times. For Dud Maumbury Rings represents his connection with the wider world of history and culture. Through the site he dreams of the far reaches of the Roman Empire. Dud explains: 'It isn't just sensations that I live for…It's something that has behind it more than you – the feelings of our race for thousands of years.' (p. 326) The weight and poetry of history permeates Powys's fiction, as it does with Hardy and Durrell. Hardy was always aware of the human history of a place. In *Jude the Obscure* he speaks of Carfax, the meeting of four roads in Oxford:

> It had more history than the oldest college in the city. It was literally teeming, stratified, with shades of human groups, who had met there for tragedy, comedy, farce; real enactments of the intensest kind. At Fourways men had stood and talked of Napoleon, the loss of America, the execution of King Charles, the burning of the Martyrs, the Crusades, the Norman Conquest, possibly of the arrival of Caesar. Here the two sexes had met for loving, hating, coupling, parting; had waited, had suffered, for each other; had triumphed over each other; cursed each other in jealousy, blessed each other in forgiveness. (*Jude the Obscure*, p.

Here Thomas Hardy comes close to Durrell's concept in *The Alexandria Quartet* of a palimpsest, in which histories are thrown down one upon the other. Thomas Hardy sees history as 'stratified' – as layered, the bottom levels of course dimmer than the top, newer ones. History here is poetically seen, and the feeling flows from the spirit of the place.

Powys's love of history formed itself from reading books. But it is brought to the forefront of his experience. His characters live as much in a dreamworld of history as in the present. Sylvanus is aware of the 'old, biblical, mediæval appellations, how they hung about the world!' (Wey, p. 510). Christie and Wolf love the histories behind words (WS, p. 354).

There is as much mythology and history as there is elementalism in Powys's sensualism. Powys has that Victorian respect for the Past, for history. He is nostalgic. His mythic sense has much in common with the eternal dream-time of the Australian Bushmen, in which the initiate is 'brought in touch with the invisible things of the world of the past, present and future'.35 Psychologists call it the 'total impingement of past human lives on the individual person.'36 Powys is deeply affected by this 'total impingement of past human lives' upon himself, as is Hardy, Rilke, Schopenhauer and Naipaul. The Australian dreamtime corresponds to the universal myth of the former Golden Age, that time, *il illo tempore, ab origine*, when things were paradisal. *Porius* explores this myth in greater depth than the Wessex books. Merlin is Cronos, Time itself. Writing for Powys was thus a means of actualizing this early Golden Age. He could make it real through the methodololgies of fiction.

Artists are makers of myths – they are *poets* (from the Greek, meaning 'makers'). Myths tells us what really went on in the world. Myths reveal 'the multiple modalities of being in the world'.37 Myths reveal ontologies – modes of beingness. For Powys, writing stories was not writing *about* something, it was that something in itself. It was life. The artist makes the myth, but s/he also *is* the myth. Through this self-creation, this re-valorization and re-sacralization of themselves and the world, the artist

---

35 A.P. Elkin, *The Australian Aborigines*, Doubleday, New York 1964, p. 171.
36 Weston La Barre, *Muelos*, p. 8.
37 Mircea Eliade, *Myths, Dreams and Mysteries*, p. 15.

re-affirms life. Living becomes sacred again. Mythology does not therefore live life in the Past, but re-vitalizes life in the present. Every artist re-makes themselves, and their lives. In this way the artist can recover the Mythic Centre (as Thomas Merton notes). It is a process of re-birth, as always.

In John Cowper Powys this process is structured around an inward-sinking journey which corresponds with an outward-looking motion. Powys aims always to open things out, as well as turn oneself inward. For his characters, the opening-out and the going-in merge.

The mythic subtext of Powys's fiction is part of his complex stratification of existence. He aims in his fiction, as Joyce did, to actualize as many levels of experience as possible. There is a deep sense of yearning in Powys's art – for Wales, for ancient times, or particular races. Like Joyce, Pound, Eliot, Yeats and Graves, Powys drew heavily on myth in his art. He loved legends, though he never explored folklore as thoroughly as Hardy or Graves. Powys gravitates towards the phantastical. He enjoyed putting *Porius* together because the Dark Ages was a time when '*anything might happen!*' (Hum 72, p. 345).

Like Lawrence, Powys was a great advocate of *potential* – of emotional and spiritual potential. He realized too the necessity for multiplicity. As with the existential stance of Sartre and Camus, Powys wants a world in which the individual's potential can be realized. 'The human imagination must never be robbed of its power to tell itself other stories, and thus create a different future' he wrote in *Porius* (p. 44). The concept of a rigid, linear, patriarchal world is always hateful to an artist. Hardy showed how destructive this monomanic machine-system is in his novels. *Jude the Obscure* is the record of a society's condemnation of two people who simply try to live in a slightly different way from the average citizen. They are not child-abusers or pimps or activitists or terrorists – they are simply two people who choose not to be married. Powys's characters have already escaped – they have already given up, socially. Hardy tried so hard to integrate the two – society and the individual – teasing out remorselessly the problems the individual encounters along this road towards integration.

John Cowper Powys advocates a pluralist world (in the manner of

William James). Let stones talk, let trees breathe, let the sky impress you with its power – this is what Powys says. John Crow in *A Glastonbury Romance* reckons that a stone was worshipped '*simply because it's a stone!*' (p. 98). Powys tries to give back to Nature some of its dignity and presence. He wants everything to be left alone, so it can live.

In drawing together various time-zones (Greek, Welsh, Roman, mediæval) Powys was moving towards the state of timelessness, or multi-time. While composing *A Glastonbury Romance* Powys was aware of the key concept of Time: 'I can shuffle time, like you shuffle snow...I can let time fall, freeze, and thaw'.[38] Powys in his urge to manipulate time moves towards Pursewarden's concept of the *n*-dimensional novel, in Durrell's *The Alexandria Quartet*. Powys tries to view things from the inside as well as from the outside. He tries to get inside plants as well as people. His viewpoint moves towards the state of New Physics, with its quanta and quasars. Powys wants a new type of narrative that can embrace all these different types of viewpoint.

Timelessness is one of the hallmarks of the authentic mystical experience. It is an experience common in much of poetry and mysticism. Hardy's characters feel it – Tess, Jude, Eustacia, Gabriel, Giles. Hardy would never, though, concentrate on a mystical experience exclusively. He was always conscious of the driving motion of his story. Hardy rarely sidetracks, unlike Lawrence and Powys. Tess becomes a mystic, though. She has the ability of losing her body and slipping away into space, up to the stars. Jude too forgets his body as the stares at Christminster. Eustacia is very wraith-like as she stalks Egdon Heath. She can control time and space, with her telescope and timer.

Powys often stops the narrative in his books to have a closer look at something that has attracted his attention. He moves easily into timelessness, feeling quite at home among mysticisms visualized in the flat planes of Piero della Francesca's paintings, or in the brush-and-ink drawings of China. These painterly correspondences help to clarify the Powysian ecstasy. If early Hardy is like a Flemish interior, Powys is like one of these paintings studied with a magnifying glass. Some of Powys's interiors are the most painstakingly described in literature. In Powys's

---

38 Letter, 10 February 1931, in Hum 72, p. 326.

frugal mind-space a bed, a tree, a pail of water can be the catalyst for some rapture or other. His self-luminous quietism talks about 'that delicious, dream-creating, contemplative sensuality which is the purpose of intelligent life.' (p. 190) In the slowed-down state of the Powysian saurian ego, interiors acquire a new significance. Powys's dim, sparse rooms with their sensualizing characters remind one of Beckett's people in their dark rooms, or Des Esseintes in Huysmans' *Against Nature*. This is also the state, of course, of the writer – sitting alone, quiet, dreaming. While Hardy's characters tear around Wessex, Powys's sit and contemplate little statues. Even when Powys's characters walk these states are more like dreams. The extreme of this self-induced altered state is the sensory-deprivation tanks of the 1960s. This kind of behaviour is also highly irresponsible, shirking as it does all personal, societal, familial and domestic duties.

The ultimate sensualist in literature has to be Des Esseintes. In his aristocratic retreat, he tries a multitude of sensual stimulants, indulging in a Baudelairean series of occult 'correspondances': bejewelled tortoises, flowers, perfumes, animals. All this set in a claustrophic world of apathy and despair. Powys is literally a breath of fresh air compared with Huysmans' alienated world. At least Powys's people move about under the sky, in the open air. Powys's cult of solitude has something in common with Lawrence's belief in the fundamental *separateness* of the human animal. Psychologists, behaviourists, sociologists, historians, feminists, politicians and theologians would challenge this belief in the aloneness of people. But Powys was very much a writer who lived in his own world. The experience of ecstasy and timelessness, too, is usually not shared. Powys exploited this sensual solitude to the full.

Poets have long known that you can have an ecstatic experience to last a lifetime from the most commonplace things. The ecstasy might only last a few seconds of real, everyday time, but it expands and becomes timeless as far as the experiencer is concerned. A kiss can last forever. The poetry of Shakespeare, Hardy and Graves records the frustrating of this yearning by social circumstance and the vicissitudes of personality. Shakespeare sought immortality in art, but he knew that 'Love's not Time's fool'. Hardy and Powys, ever more romantic than a realist such as Shakespeare, ached for a timelessness through love. The Jobber, in *Weymouth Sands*, realizes that

> you could walk with a strange girl for no more than a quarter of an hour along the sea's edge, only to discover that nothing else henceforth to the end of your days, no person, no thing, no cause, no idea, can ever be, in your inmost, secretest feelings, as important as this brief experience. (p. 204)

In *A Glastonbury Romance*, Powys allows his lovers (Nell and Sam) to drown in a cascading torrent of blissful poetry culled in tone from *Lady Chatterley's Lover*:

> The 'reality' of that moment – of that infinite series of moments – was what they felt; and what they felt was beyond all human symbolism. What they felt was more rapturous than a rain of blinding, dazzling meteors falling through eternity. (GR, p. 311)

Ecstatic poetry is marked by repetition of key phrases, or of any phrase. It is a form of self-hypnotism. Here the repetition is 'what they felt'. This is pretty over the top – a 'rain of blinding, dazzling meteors' – it is archetypal love-poetry.

When Porius and Morfyyd make love for the second time he experiences ecstasies of light and mist, while she meanwhile yields all – except her inner self, her 'I am I' (P, p. 638). Lawrence's men and women too retain their sense of self. Lawrence rejoiced in a certain kind of insularity in love. Only once or twice in Powys is a true love-union achieved. Timeless and ecstasy experienced alone is more common. At the end of their stories, Wolf, Dud and Magnus resign themselves to a 'stoical endurance'. As long as they have their walking stick and a piece of ground to ramble over, they know they might be happy. Timelessness could still rush in at any moment.

The ending of each Powys's book is significant. Lawrence goes for the apocalyptic ending (in *The Rainbow*) or the stolid endurance in separateness (*Women in Love*) or the tenderness that comes from fucking a 'flame into being' (*Lady Chatterley's Lover*). Hardy's endings are more contrived, more laboured than Lawrence's – think of *The Return of the*

Native. His *The Mayor of Casterbridge* and *Jude the Obscure* end superbly, however. They end logically, following the downward curve of their tragic men to the bitter end. Powys's Wessex books end on odd notes. Wolf finds ecstasy in 'a cup of tea'; Skald's stone stops 'the Philosophy of Representation from blowing away!'; Dud moves back to the centre, to his everyday life '[he] went to meet Nance'; while the last words of *A Glastonbury Romance* are prophetic (and also a former title of the book): 'Never or always.' In the urge towards timeless ecstasy, it is always All or Nothing.

Mortal Strife, Powys's anti-war book of 1942, sums up his sensualism neatly. In the ecstasy 'your past's poetical essences' are revitalized (p. 147). Memory adds to the intensification of the moment. What happened in the past impinges on the present. These sensations occur in all the five senses, all at once (as in Rimbaudian synæsthesia [p. 148]). Powys rightly notes how the sound of seagulls can conjure the whole of the ocean (p. 148). He speaks of a religion's 'living presence, its touch, its taste, its smell' (p. 43). Like Nietzsche, Powys re-vivifies the sensuousness of religion. He is highly individual, talking about the *smell* of a religion. But it is there, just as in Aldous Huxley in his *Eyeless in Gaza* speaks of the foods that each religion eats (Christianity with its bloody wine and meats, Buddhism with its water and vegetables). Proust is another novelist who delights in fragrances, as in *Swann's Way*, when the scent of a hawthorn-blossom in a church gives the narrator a feeling of 'intense vitality'.[39] Heightened senses of smell bind up with Powys's hungry protagonists, who are always sniffing places out, yearning for that Something-Other-Than-This. The breeze, the primary Powysian element, of course is the carrier of odours. Smell intoxicates and, as in Proust, many of Powys's ecstasies stem from inhalations. Powys's landscapes are often described in terms of smell as much as vision. In this Powys become truly Rimbaudian – occult. Rimbaud is the poet who thought of vowels in terms of colours, who saw Eternity in the mixture of the sea and sun (in *A Season in Hell*), and who rapturously wrote in his *Illuminations*:

> Tout roule avec des mysteres revoltants
> De campagnes d'anciens temps

---
[39] *Swann's Way* I, Chatto & Windus 1966, p. 153.

([Everything flows with the repulsive mysteries of ancient landscapes.][40]

All gods, saints and martyrs are contained in the soul: 'All souls contain all.' (MS, p. 62) One is connected with one's ancestors (p. 147), and this feeling can be extended to include the whole planet. John Cowper Powys likes the big, sweeping visions of Wells and Gibbon. All this can begin from a simple phenomena, such as a train whistle. The train whistle takes the place in the city of the supernatural hissing of tress by night in the country. Instead of trees hissing, or seagulls crying, the trains whistle. Distant whistling trains takes us to the dream of a decayed urban America caught sharply in Edward Hopper's melancholy paintings and in the dusty rooms and desultory sex in William Burroughs' novels. Burroughs writes:

> sad train whistles cross a distant sky blue magic of all movies...in remembered kid standing there face luminous at the attic window[41]

> rectums merging a few seconds after blue movies and other sex acts with flicker ghosts shifting back and forth orgasms of the world...soft luminous spurts of memory riding the wind.[42]

Burroughs' precise folded-in polemic is about as far away from Powys olde worlde cosy armchair style as you can get, but some of the sentiments chime: the implication of the whole planet in individual acts (the whole planet can scream or shiver in both Powys and Burroughs); a folding-in of personal and race/ historical memory; a nostalgic view of childhood; a love of run-down provincial towns, and so on.

Powys also concentrates on certain words, such as *Ninue, esplumeoir, Caer Sidi* and *the Questing Beast*. Bertie Lawrence too has his favourite words, such as *fecund, loins, bowels* and *river of blood*. Drawn mainly from Welsh, Arthurian and Greek legend, Powys's words are magical: they haunt his characters. Objects too haunt the characters – there is Dud's hideous bedpost in *Maiden Castle* or Jason's rain-god in *Wolf Solent*. These

---
[40] *Complete Works*, University Press of Chicago 1966, pp. 121, 130-1, 199.
[41] *The Soft Machine*, Corgi, 1970, p. 110.
[42] *The Ticket That Exploded*, Paladin 1987, pp. 57, 98.

objects are charmed, enchanted, imbued with what Robert Graves termed *baraka* – blessedness. Powys is supremely superstitious. His Powys-men go through all kinds of peculiar rituals. Their eccentric habits make them people with whom one would not wish to live. Powys writes of rivers as goddesses, of sacred circles, magic mountains and ancient forests. He is like Graves in this, ever seeking the magical in the landscape. But with Powys it is just as much the physical as much as the symbolic aspects of these objects that fascinate him. Thus he concentrates on the particular look of Evans' evil picture, even though, as with Dud's bedpost, or Jason's Hindu deity, we never really get to see what these things are like. Only Powys would talk about being more interested in a person's skeleton rather than their visual appearance. when meeting them Powys is supremely literal, mechanistic, biological – childish. Unlike Lawrence with his blood-consciousness, Powys often looks no further than physicalities. Geard is someone who loves corporality– he loves sweat, dung, urine: for him all that lives is holy, and things have an aura around them (GR, p. 1117). Sylvanus, another wizard-figure, loves the sun and sea not in a poetic sense, but in actuality. Powys stresses the actual, empirical, actual experience. He stresses not the psychic or mystical aspect, but the very solid facts. Thus the Jobber is comforted by the feel of his stone, or Wolf his stick, or Dud his bedpost carving. This is the direct, immediate, sensory Powysian ecstasy, but it soon spills out into something wider. With a pungent enough catalyst, the self can move off in almost any direction. Often it is a form of escape, of moving into a dreamworld, which is yet also apprehensible from the bland sections of the planet, as Rook finds out in *Ducdame* (p. 265):

it came over him that this Cimmery Land of which she spoke was the thing that he had dreamed of lying on his bed listening to the sounds of the morning; dreamed of under the walls of old buildings in in the quiet places of historic cities, when the noons fell hotly and the shadows fell darkly, and from hidden fountains came the splash of water.

This vision – of a hot noon in some historic town square – recalls the paintings of Giorgio de Chirico. De Chirico fell dreamily into the soft melancholy of a sunlit afternoon:

> And now the sun has stopped, high in the centre of the sky. And in everlasting happiness the statue immerses its soul in the contemplation of its shadow.[43]

Powys's vision, which seems strange among novelists, is quite commonplace among painters and sculptors – and very common among poets. It is basically animism, the basis of all religions, with a tidal surge of imagination added.

Powys delights in multi-dimensionality, in opening up perception as much as possible (in the Blakean sense). His sensualisms always begin from modest experiences. Gleeful as a truant schoolboy contemplating a birds' nest, a patch of frogs' spawn or a gushing waterfall, Powys takes us into his version of the essence of things. This is the view of High Romanticism – the Blakean, Wordsworthian, Goethean stance, in which the soul alone actualizes the myriad things of Nature. Thus Goethe writes in his *Werther*:

> Ah, to view this vast landscape from there! Oh, distance is like the future: before our souls lies an entire and dusky vastness which overwhelms our feelings as it overwhelms our eyes, and ah! we long to surrender the whole of our being, and be filled with all the joy of one single, immense, magnificent emotion. (p. 44)

Nagel, in Knut Hamsun's *Mysteries*, has similar feelings of rapture:

> A tremor of ecstasy ran through him. He felt himself carried away and engulfed by the magic rays of the sun. The stillness filled him with an intoxicating sense of well-being...He felt exhilarated because life was good....There was not a soul in sight. He said yes to life once more... (*Mysteries*, p. 50)

Powys's ecstasies serve many functions. In the later works Powys begins to ætherealize his ecstasies. They become rarefied, more spun in the air, more intangible. This tendency is clear in *Maiden Castle* where the dominating element is the æther and the wind, after *Glastonbury*'s water,

---

[43] In *Giorgio de Chirico*, by James Thrall Soby, MOMA, New York 1955.

Weymouth's stone and *Wolf*'s fire. This occurs also in Powys's fear of physical love-making. He loves to get in close to the inanimate, and to animate it, but, when faced with something utterly kinetic and vital, such as a person, he retreats, unable to deal with it. This push-me-pull-you tension lies at the heart of Powys's art and his sensualism.

In the ordinary John Cowper Powys ecstasy, there is a focussing on some object; but then follows the spiralling outwards, towards the Past, myth and history. In the human-slanted ecstasies – the ones which begin with the contemplation of or love-act with another person – then Powys spins away immediately. So Sylvanus, Geard and Uryen lie with their people but do not penetrate them sexually. Powys's love-making on the magical plane is an ecstasy of sleep, a tidal but unconscious and unseen experience, such as in *Owen Glendower* (p. 715). Powys is excellent at self — nature conflicts, when people merge fervently with their surroundings. In love he fudges things. His whole life-philosophy, after all, is about ecstasy-in-solitude, not about trying to join in ecstatic union with someone else (one of the main themes of Western literature since the troubadours). Be like a cloud, he cries, or like some 'hard, round, impenetrable pebble-stones, at the bottom of a babbling river of propitiation.' (Sol, p. 217). Powys's love-making or drawing together of souls is fraught with problems. He cannot do it – his characters cannot do it. Only Nell and Sam manage it fully. More common for Powys to speak of 'the silence of lust drawn out taut and tense to its breaking-point' (*Morwyn*, p. 68). So, although 'the chief thing to do is to be forever losing yourself in the enjoyment of embracing life' (In Spite Of, p. 17f) it means a drifting apart from other people. Hardy's novels too feature this fear and desire of other people, this urge towards erotic conjunction and this disgust with romance. Powys moves towards the sky, the air, the æther, and, later, the Void. In *Rabelais* he speaks of 'inter-cosmic gulfs' (Rabelais, p. 399). The Void takes us into Oriental mysticism, the not-this-not-that Nothingness of Tibetan philosophy, Taoism and Buddhism. In the last works, the Void looms larger behind the narrative. The Void turns 'its very self inside out' in *Up and Out* (p. 47) leaving an Einsteinian black hole.

Powys's world is essentially an open universe – a multiverse. There is no heat death, but endless nothingness beyond everything. An egobound person like Powys could not countenance a closed spatiality and temporality to the cosmos. His is a multiverse, a mass of possibilities. How rigid is Hardy's world, bound by time, and by space, and by circumstance, and knocked by life's little ironies, time's laughing stocks, under the auspices of Fate, Destiny and the President of the Immortals. Powys, though, goes for a multi-levelled multiverse, because for him myth is too rich a source to be dried up by any mortal. Myth for him is endless.

The ætherealizing tendency in John Cowper Powys's fiction was present in the early books – in the swan-vision in *Ducdame*, for example. Adrian in *Rodmoor* says: 'I'm porous to things' (p. 288). The wind has a deadening power in *Wood and Stone* (p. 370f). The præternatural breeze in *Maiden Castle* is also as deadening and chilly as it is mythical. So the Powys-man ætherealizes, becomes like air and aether – pure spirit, the Hindu Breath of the Eternal of the Upanishads, the neo-Platonic *Nous*. Powys projects his characters' consciousness until it becomes 'pure and undiluted awareness' (In Spite Of, p. 110). In Oriental esotericism, breathing forms the sacred links that chain existence together. In Powys these breaths become exploded into a cosmic wind, which scatters the soul, just as the ashes of Powys own body were strewn over Chesil Beach – cast to the cosmic winds. Condensed as a person breathing, Powys's cosmic wind relates to the Hindu *aum*, used in yogic meditation. For Powys's wind is pure consciousness, in the Eastern manner. There, at the extremes of ecstatic practice, one realizes that *Thou Art That*. In Powys, as in Romantic pantheism, there is a stress on self — world identification, on the *participation mystique* with the world. Here the Gnostic *Logos*, the Hindu *Brahma* and the Tao itself merge into one, into *The One*. While these notions are historically and culturally discrete (and commentators such as R.C. Zahner loathe the idea of putting them together) they are, nevertheless, embroiled together – following the efforts of Jung, Huxley *et al*.

John Cowper Powys himself is fervently anti-doctrinal in his religious views, just as Thomas Hardy bitterly attacked Christianity (although liked to feel 'churchy' himself). Powys loves to blend together all kinds of mysticism. He is a magpie of religions (think of the religious substructure of *Porius* and *A Glastonbury Romance*). His vision is basically pantheistic (and 'pan-en-henic') – a view upheld in Christian mysticism by such great thinkers as Meister Eckhart, who wrote: 'all blades of grass, wood and stone, all things are One.' All is indeed One, if God is in the world, for God is the world. We all partake of the Body of Christ – it is all the same mystery. Powys's vision usually moves up to include the whole planet (as did Lawrence when he was in his apocalyptical mode). Powys often speaks of an oversoul, a worldmind, a great 'planetary consciousness'. This is the precursor of the 'global village' and the new age, scientific ecological concept of *Gaia*. The idea is (as Sartre pointed out) that we are all in this together, and that we are all responsible for the whole world. This vision is common in Powys – the buildings, streets, hills and furniture of his Glastonbury all add to the book as much as the characters. It is the same with Durrell and his Alexandria – the city-as-God, the Augustine City of God. In particle physics, all is one anyway – everything is made up of the same stuff. A view such as this is the ultimate in reductionism – Freud and Marx taken to psychotic extremes. All is merely a bunch of molecules. The outcome of this reductionist viewpoint is naturally cynical and deadening – life becomes worthless. People become bags of chemicals, easily controlled by drugs (Powys sees people often as skeletons). If all is just a matter of molecules, then feelings are destroyed, and dropping a few nuclear bombs means nothing – it's just a case of turning one type of matter into another. What does it *matter* in the long run? So Powys, never quite as cynical as this, holding as he does onto the individual ego-alone, moves nevertheless up into the Void. Such a philosophical outlook is not unusual in post-war atomic-age fiction – think of Beckett, Durrell, Cary *et al*, who move towards the Oriental vision of things. Powys was writing, after all, just before the onslaught of Leary, the Beat poets, hippiedom, drug-culture, magicke and New Agism became *de rigeur*.

So there is a strong argument for seeing John Cowper Powys's sensualism as escapism – the ultimate kind of escapism – into phantasy worlds, away from other people, in sensual solitude, shirking all societal responsibilities. In *Owen Glendower* he created a 'mythology of escape' (p. 889). In *The Inmates* Powys wrote: 'Every living soul has one right…to be free and alone in our thoughts' (p. 273). Well, fine. Off you go to your country retreat, your ivory tower, your backstreet tenement block, to be alone. But *you're never alone!* You are surrounded by people, by culture – embedded in yourself. Masses of education, of person-to-person influences, of history, of input, of parental pressure, of memories, of experiences, of scars, of socialization and enculturation. Telemachos yearns in *Atlantis* (p. 239) 'to escape from the whole business', but you can't. No one can. The desert island dream is a lie.

Six

Nature in Thomas Hardy's Fiction

It was the first day of June, and the sheep-shearing season culminated, the landscape, even to the leanest pasture, being all health and colour. Every green was young, every pore was open, and every stalk was swollen with racing currents of juice. God was palpably present in the country, and the devil had gone with the world to town. Flossy catkins of the later kinds, fern-sprouts like bishops' croziers, the square-headed moschatel, the odd cuckoo-pint, – like an apoplectic saint in a niche of malachite, – snow-white ladies'-smocks, the toothwort, approximating to human flesh, the enchanter's night-shade, and the black-petaled doleful-bells, were among the quainter objects of the vegetable world in and about Weatherbury at this teeming time...

Thomas Hardy, *Far From the Madding Crowd* (pp. 125-6)

The great novel of human/ nature integration is *Tess of the d'Urbervilles*. Despite being crude and cartoon-like at times, Thomas Hardy's use of setting and symbolism is very powerful. *Tess* would lose much if it lost its settings. The earth itself becomes a narrative force From the pastoral languor of the Vale of Marlott with its pagan customs (the Mayday dance, p. 49) Tess moves to the unknown lands of Trantridge. She knows it is a strange place, because strawberries are already in season there (p. 81). She is raped among 'the primæval yews and oaks of The Chase', in total darkness (p. 119). After her dazed time with Alec (p. 125) she returns to her homeland a changed person. She retreats into herself, nursing her bruised body and soul. But she is resilient – indomitable. She is still alive and open to experiences. From her bedroom window

> under her few square yards of thatch, she watched winds and snows, and rains, gorgeous sunsets, and successive moons at their full...She knew how to hit to a hair's-breadth that moment of evening when the light and darkness are so evenly balanced that the constraint of day and the suspense of night neutralize each other, leaving absolute mental liberty...On those lonely hills and dales her quiescent glide was of a piece with the element she moved in. Her flexuous and stealthy figure became an integral part of the scene. At times her whimsical fancy would intensify natural processes around her till they seemed part of her own story. (*Tess*, p. 34)

As Jude is the 'natural boy' so Tess is the natural girl, fully enmeshed with Nature, with her surroundings. She embodies Nature and Nature is the embodiment of her. Tess is a Goddess, for, as woman, she is identical with Nature and the earth. The seasons flow through her. Her story is the story of Nature, except that Tess's tragic end stems not from a failure of Nature but from the failure of her men to really see her for what she *really is*.

It is the women in *Tess*, not the men, who are fully in harmony with the landscape. Women become part of Nature, while men build machines that move across the surface, scratching away at Nature's skin. Men treat Nature like dirt – they build the trains, threshing-machines and so on, which divorce people from the soil. The field-women, however, assimilate themselves with their environment (p. 138).

Talbothays and its surroundings is not as beautiful as Marlott Vale, but is 'more cheering' (p. 157). Here there is a 'change in the quality of the air from heavy to light, or the sense of being amid new scenes where there were no invidious eyes upon her, sent up her spirits wonderfully.' (p. 157) Here Tess blossoms. The Midsummer dawn trysts are some of Hardy's best passages. Sexuality and Nature are fused. Blood and passion are heated up in the sun (p. 207). Tess is a rich liver of life – 'she lives what paper-poets only write' says Angel (p. 225), admitting covertly his own inadequacies. Angel distances himself, while Tess moves in closer. She really lives.

After the awful honeymoon night, Hardy is none too subtle in his symbolism and *mise-en-scène*. Angel is thus confronted by the ashes from the fire. The same crude symbolism occurs when Tess compassionately kills the maimed pheasants (p. 352). Pheasants, those soft, plump and beautiful birds, the targets of men of leisure, will later bring Connie and Mellors together in Lawrence's last novel.

Flintcomb-Ash, with its frozen fields, speaks for itself. Tess's long, gruelling walk to Emminster is heart-rending. It is fully described – for here Hardy can pull together many places in his beloved Dorset. The work on the threshing-machine is also exhausting. Tess is an immensely active protagonist – she is not a disaffected wanderer, like many of the characters in Powys, Huxley, Waugh and Forster. The degradation continues, as Tess and her family camp outside King's Bere church. Hardy's comparison of the family on the bed outside and their ancestors in their tombs inside the church is again crude, but it does the trick. It is a brutal set-up – the family so alive, fleshy, hungry and poor on one side of the wall, and the knightly forebears once spiritually and financially rich, but now materially just useless dust on the other side. Much of the novel uses spatial *mise-en-scène*: Tess placed in the coffin by Angel, Tess happening to pass the preaching Alec. Hardy loves orchestrating his series of accidents and coincidences.

Tess adrift in Sandbourne (Bournemouth) is Tess fully displaced. She is a real outsider, a stranger to this lazy life of finery and hanging about in hotels. There is nothing for her to do. She is in a town, displaced from Nature. The setting is a town with no history, a place dedicated to leisure, not to labour (Bournemouth is now the largest non-industrial connurbation in Europe). This is all Alec can offer her – sex and money. The modern world has already overcome all things natural and spontaneous, with this dead tourist centre.

The irony of Stonehenge, with all its links with the Past, with ancient weather and star-watching people, with the whole of paganism, is a bitter irony. It is obvious and clumsy, this Stonehenge setting, yet Hardy brings it off. There is the suggestions of a mythic Return to the paganism of the opening pages – the Maydance – a suggestion that life is cyclical. But Stonehenge is bleak – exposed to the elements, desolate. It is a site of death, a temple to the dead as much as to the sun. The solar power of Stonehenge is dead now – it cannot save Tess. There is no escape in the ancient Past, or, symbolized by Wintonchester, in the middle ages. With Winchester we return to the old capital of Wessex. Tess's many journeys have led her to this old Centre. Hardy cleverly introduces the city as a historic and beautiful place – 'in all the brightness and warmth of a July morning' (p. 488). He then goes on to describe the modern red-brick gaol, rising *in front* of the old city. In the same way the train is compared with the figure of Tess. The train invades the countryside, superimposing itself upon the ancient landscape. So the new, the harshly modern, is not integrated with the old and the traditional, but simply thrown down upon it. Other spatial *mise-en-scène* in *Tess* includes the threshing-machine, the empty house where Angel and Tess hide (contrasting with the Sandbourne hotel), the coffin, the Cross-in-Hand and so on.

Tess and *Jude the Obscure* are full of travels, of people drifting, of the fragmentation of communities, the loss of cohesion. *Under the Greenwood Tree*, *The Return of the Native*, *The Woodlanders*, *The Mayor of Casterbridge* – these take place in one location (mainly). There is always a certain cohesiveness in their communities. The triumph of *Tess of the d'Urbervilles* is that it transcends Hardy's often brutish use of Nature, place, season and symbolism. It is also amazingly interlocked. It is difficult to extract an element without destroying the unity. Setting is essential. It is hard to imagine Hardy's novels taking place outside of Wessex, despite his claims of universality. Similarly with Durrell's Alexandria – the place is so important to the whole effect. So much of art and religion is a product of place – think of the Renaissance, how different it was in Northern and Southern Europe, or of Taoism in China. There is nothing quite like Taoism in the West. Somehow Taoism could not have originated in the Occident.

Wolf Solent is a novel in which characters and settings are closely bound up together. Ramsgard is merged with Wolf's father and the Past, while Yeovil is associated with love and the Present. The Gerda — Wolf romance takes place on Poll's Camp, while the first time they make love is among the yellow bracken in the shed. These settings add to the meanings of the scene, they provide frameworks for the drama. But Powys's landscapes are often projections of his characters' inner states, as in much of modern fiction from Lawrence to Ballard. (In some ways, Wolf images up that lonely shed, so that he can make love with Gerda.) How restless is *Jude the Obscure*, moving from town to town – or Lawrence's *Kangaroo* and *Aaron's Rod*, part of that 'savage pilgrimage'.

The savage pilgrimage is the search for a place which will fulfil the yearning in the individual for richness and ripeness. For many writers spirit of place is an essential factor in their lives as well as their books. Durrell sees people as 'expressions of their landscape' (*Spirit of Place*, p. 157). Landscape for Durrell shapes culture, character, art – and the artist seeks a nourishing soil, a sacred ground upon which s/he can create. Durrell writes:

> The great thing is to try and travel with the eyes of the spirit open, and not too much factual information. To tune in, without reverence, idly – but with real inward attention. It is to be had for the feeling, that mysterious sense of *rapport*, of identity with the ground. You can extract the essence of a place once you know how. (Spirit, p. 162).

This talk of essence gives Durrell's sense of place a Gnostic/ Greek feel. Both Hardy and Powys spoke in terms of essence. With nature-loving writers it is really a case of *essence through presence*. Like Hardy, Durrell suggests you sit quietly and sniff out the essence of a place. In Hardy's *Tess*, though, Tess very much is the place, the landscape itself.

The terms vary but they all contain the same basic principles:

sacred ground, miracle ground, private country, personal landscape, deus loci, spirit of place, God-in-nature, heartland, dreamland, bliss-space, motherland, gnost–alghia ('homing–pain'), magic circle, ivory tower, sacred grove, homeland, ambience, atmosphere, mythic Centre.

Lorenzo wrote: 'The island of Great Britain had a wonderful terrestrial magnetism or polarity of its own', adding: 'Men are free when they are in a living homeland.'[44] This is so true of Hardy – he is so thoroughly at home in his Dorset, as Powys is in North Wales.

As for the landscape itself, Hardy was clearly deeply in love with Wessex. For him it had some of the best scenery in Britain (Preface to *The Woodlanders*, Per, p. 20). Wordsworth in the Lakes, or Thomas in Wales would dispute this. But Hardy is sure about it. In one of his best incantations to Wessex, the poem 'Wessex Heights' he wrote:

> There are some heights in Wessex, shaped as if by a kindly hand
> For thinking, dreaming, dying on, and at crises when I stand,
> Say, on Ingpen Beacon eastward, or on Wylls-Neck westwardly,
> I seem where I was before my birth, and after my death will be.
> (*Complete Poems*, p. 319)

A poetico-mystical experience had by standing on top of a hill is quite common. Caspar Friedrich painted it many times. In his book *The Power of Myth*, Joseph Campbell talks of the Indian shaman Black Elk who stood on the central mountain in South Dakota and had a vision, realizing that the sacred central mountain is everywhere.

> That is a real mythological realization. It distinguishes between the local cult image, Harney Peak, and its connotation as the center of the world. The center of the world is the *axis mundi*, the central point, the pole around which all revolves. The central point of the world is the point where stillness and movement are together. Movement is time, but stillness is eternity. Realizing now this moment of your life is actually a moment of eternity, and experiencing the eternal aspect of what you're doing in the temporal experience – this is the mythological experience. (Power, p. 89)

---

44 *The Spirit of Place,* in *Selected Literary Criticism,* p. 301.

The Centre is right where you are – the mythic and the personal Centre. So the mythic Centre can be a Dorsetshire hill, or John Cowper Powys's Glastonbury, or Lawrence's ugly Midlands, or Naipaul's Wiltshire, or Nin's Paris, or Joyce's Dublin. It can be anywhere you are. The important thing is the realization. Mircea Eliade says exactly the same thing (as do most religions):

> Wherever one is, there is a *center of the world*. As long as you are in that center, you are at home, you are truly in the real *self* and at the center of the cosmos. (Ordeal, p. 100)

So Wessex is a spiritual and mythical Centre. Powys deals more with the mythical aspects of the Centre – Hardy hides his mythic discourse under a huge amount of detailed local colour. But Wessex is essentially a mythical both for both writers.

Certainly you feel at the centre of things when you stand on The Knoll near Swyre, in West Dorset, with that tremendous view to the west towards Lyme Regis and Devon. Or in the nave of Sherborne Abbey, or even better, at Avebury stone-circle.

Here, at Avebury, you've got the centre of prehistoric Britain. Avebury is pure magic in stone – truly a Cathedral to the parish church of Stonehenge. Here at Avebury you've got a cluster of megalithic monuments of exceptional magnificence: Silbury Hill, West Kennet Long Barrow, the Sanctuary, the Avenue, Windmill Hill and the gigantic henge itself. Here is Britain's equivalent of the Egyptian pyramids or India's temples. To stand amongst the sarsens at Avebury is to be in a mythical Centre of immense proportions. Avebury doesn't need the epic, expansive treatment of Turner or Homer – it already has it. Maybe this is why so few writers use such magnetic places as centres for their stories. Hardy and Powys both used Stonehenge, but their characters only lingered there a short while. These sacred sites have such an formidable grandeur of their own – too much for the ordinary, humble novel. They are overwhelming. Avebury Circle is, literally, magic solidified – the Unknown made into stone.

For Thomas Hardy, Wessex was a whole world. In *The Mayor of*

Casterbridge he writes: 'To the liege subjects of Labour, the England of those days was a continent, and a mile a geographical degree.' (p. 27) Wessex was clearly a realm rich enough for Hardy. The region contains many kinds of landscape – hills such as Pilsdon Pen, woods such as The Chase, beaches as strange as Chesil, and marshes such as Sedgemoor. In the towns and villages too, Hardy could find a rich array of people and architecture: Salisbury, Powerstock, Lyme, Dorchester, Abbotsbury, Studland, etc.

Here Thomas Hardy's sense of drama could unfold. This was the domain of those 'sequestered spots' in which deep rivers of passion run. The characters are isolated, really out of the centres of culture, politics, decision and discussion. Yet they too *burn*.

In the claustrophic tree-enclosed parish of *The Woodlanders*, the enduring Marty South and the reserved Giles Winterbourne go out at dawn:

> Hardly anything could be more isolated, more self-contained, than the lives of these two walking here in the lonely hour before day, when grey shades, material; and mental, are so very grey. And yet their lonely courses formed no detached design at al, but were part of the pattern in the great web of human doings then weaving in both hemispheres from the White Sea to Cape Horn. (p. 59)

Usually thought of as a pragmatic, stolid kind of writer, there is in Hardy a wealth of superstition, folklore, Biblical learning, mythology, philosophy and the supernatural. In this passage above Hardy moves easily from the local to the universal, ending on a note of global awareness so typical of Powys.

Tess, for instance, though a country girl, a provincial character, is nevertheless explicitly described as a Great Mother Goddess. She is at various moments a Saint, a Mystic, a Philosopher, a Poet, a Whore and a Slave.

Hardy's novels also feature much tree-worship – in his Green wood Tree, Woodlanders, *Return* and *Tess*. J.G. Frazer notes that 'Nothing could be more natural' (*The Golden Bough*, p. 109)

Thomas Hardy's country people are open to these poetic experiences of

Nature. They enjoy unclassifiable, uninstitutionalized revelations of the world around them. Giles, Oak, Tess, Eustacia, Marty – they are all open to the wonder of things. Oak sucks up the mystery of the stars; Eustacia opens to the erotic dream of the moonlight; and Tess, in her idosynctratic fashion, says 'The trees have inquisitive eyes, haven't they?' (p. 180).

Hardy's country-dwellers have to keep open to Nature and the elements because their livelihood depends on it. Thus 'the multitude saw in the god of the weather a more important personage than they do now.' (*Mayor*, p. 210) Goddess-in-nature is more important who live off the land than God-in-Heaven. For as Angel thinks bitterly: 'God's *not* in his heaven, all's *wrong* with the world!' (*Tess*, p. 225) But a heavenly Father is no use to people who live on an earthly Mother.

Rural people are more naturally Goddess-worshippers. They work on the sacred Body of the Great Mother. Nature is a provider, like the mother-figure of myth. Woman, Nature, sexuality, fertility, cycles, vegetation and the seasons have all been bound up together since before palæolithic times. Hardy's Tess is a modern Earth-Goddess who is raped by the deathly machinery of patriarchy.

Elsewhere in *The Mayor of Casterbridge* Thomas Hardy writes: 'To learn to take the universe seriously there is no quicker way than to watch – be a 'waker'; as the country-people call it.' (p. 135) This is Oriental meditative poise here – look and let it unfold, in its own way, at its own pace. This is also the Powys-man's way. A nature-contemplation that is like Taoist repose.

Tess of the d'Urbervilles opens with a pastoral vision of Wessex. Yet it is worth remembering that Tess herself thinks she is living on a 'blighted planet'. Even in her youthful, innocent phase, she is cynical. She does not expect to be given anything by her world. But it does give her this vision of Wessex, one of Hardy's best evocations of his beloved country:

> The traveller...is surprised and delighted to behold, extended like a map before him, a country differing absolutely from that which he has passed through. Behind him the hills are open, the sun blazes down upon fields so large as to give an unenclosed character to the landscape, the lanes are white, the hedges low and plashed, the atmosphere

colourless...The atmosphere is languorous, and is so tinged with azure that what artists call the middle distance partakes also of that hue, while the horizon behind is of the deepest ultramarine. (p. 48)

This is a painterly vision. Hardy invites us to see the country as a landscape painter might. The colours – azure, ultramarine – are the most precious hues of the Renaissance (blue being more expensive than gold). This is a rich vision, rich in precious azure, a vista drenched in the glow of *lapis lazuli*. It recalls the Arcadian views of Claude Lorrain (who is also referred to in *Wolf Solent*). The last time we see Tess is at Stonehenge. The trajectory of her tragedy is embodied in these two landscapes – the beginning so soft, languid, pastoral – Tess so fully at home within it. The ending at Stonehenge so dark, hesitant, reserved. She is sleeping on the sacrifical stone, a stained victim. The two landscapes tell us as much about her experience as the plot or the characters.

In writers such as Durrell, Hardy, Powys, Lawrence, Cavafy, George Eliot and Naipaul we have this exploration of people interacting with their landscape. The novels of Lawrence, Powys, Naipaul and Durrell are particularly intense and poignant because they were written in exile. Exile often gives an edge to fiction which relies so heavily upon the spirit of place. In exile, working through time and space, one communes with a multitude of former selves. The vanquished writer has to bend time and space, to twist memories about, to re-activate the Past. As Mircea Eliade writes:

One rediscovers the whole past in space: a street, a church, a tree. Suddenly time past has been regained...I rediscover precious things through such nostalgia. And in that way I feel that I never lose anything, that nothing is ever lost. (Ordeal, p. 101)

Everything is here. It always has been. Like the mystical experience, art is the ultimate in travelling-without-moving. Thus the past – of oneself, other people, history, events – is regained, reborn. In artistic creation one is continually making oneself anew. The restlessness, the eternal searching, the aching and questing for fulfilment, is typical of the modern artist. We see the same unease and yearning in artists such as Rothko, Schiele, Part, Svevo, Joyce, Beckmann, Hemingway and Picasso. Lawrence summed it up in *Sons and Lovers*:

Paul was dissatisfied with himself and with everything. (p. 271)

The restlessness of the modern artist produced many savage pilgrimages in the 20th century. Americans such as Pollock, Rothko and Newman explored their native American myths; others went to North Africa (Gide, Camus); while the English writers who lived in exile included Douglas, Stark, Lawrence, Graves, Durrell, Aldington and Huxley. Italy was a favourite destination on this bourgeois, existential inter-war Grand Tour. It was from Italy that Lawrence created his astonishing vision of England in the three versions of *Lady Chatterley*:

And she went in the thrilling wonder of the first twilight of spring, while the birds still called wildly, and the yellow light of evening mingled among the tree-buds that were just for opening. What lovely ghostly presences of life the wood was full of! (*John Thomas and Lady Jane*, p. 115)

For Lawrence, as for other expatriots, there was a visceral love-hate relationship with Britain. It was a fascination and a revulsion, such as Aaron feels in *Aaron's Rod* (p. 148). In Italy Aaron finds a 'bigness', a boldness, an exposed world: 'the walls of English life will have to fall' he thinks (ib, p. 239). A similar rebellion against England is found in *Kangaroo*, and in *The Insurrection of Miss Houghton*: England seen from a channel ship is described thus: 'England looked like a grey, dreary-grey coffin sinking in the sea behind' (*Kangaroo*, p. 286)

This *ennui*, this lassitude and disgust is an acute ingredient of Durrell's view of the world, but is curiously lacking in the devotional Thomas Hardy and John Cowper Powys. At times Durrell hated the English: 'Fuck the English' he wrote to Henry Miller, hating the people's mean-spirited ways, their puritanism, lack of culture and non-respect for the artist, their hypocrisy and so on (Letters, p. 79). But later (in 1958) Durrell wrote:

> In England the landscape is good, nourishing; one can work there. There isn't any hostility to the artist. What is killing is the spineless and revolting life they have built up around themselves, the habits, the boredom, the lack of *la bonne chere*. No belly worship! (ib., p. 334)

For poets such as Graves, Durrell and Lawrence, life in England was deadening. They needed the Mediterranean sunlight. Life in England was not rich enough for them. They wanted to be around people who were fully alive. When Powys came back to Britain he soon moved to North Wales, which is quite another country from cosy little England with its hedgerows, lanes and toy houses. Powys, too, needed a certain wildness.

Thomas Hardy has not quite reached that state of weariness, although it permeates some of *Jude the Obscure*. On the whole, Hardy loves his Wessex people. His Wessexscape is a labour of love, his theme is 'Wessexuality', Wes-sex-mania, Western sexual politics. *Tess* is his farewell to Wessex – he rounds off the kingdom there. *Jude*, with its fragmented lives and train journeys, shows Wessex falling apart. In *Jude the Obscure*, too, Hardy's hatred of the mob shows through. He describes so incisively the way society cannot tolerate anything out of the ordinary. The animosity that the ever-so-slightly different love-affair provokes from their neighbours is brilliantly portrayed in the scene where Sue and Jude are painting in the church (it has to be in a church, site of the 'true religion! Ha-ha-ha!' as Jude puts it, p. 463). Various visitors watch the lovers and gloat. Sue cries out:

> I can't *bear* that they, and everybody, should think people wicked because they may have chosen to live their own way! (p. 272)

The contempt of the social mass for the individual features in much of Hardy – so graphically in *Mayor*, for example (Lucetta and Henchard are targetted as scapegoats). But in *Jude the Obscure* Hardy does not hide his contempt for his society's contempt for the individual.

Jude the Obscure, with all its many urban settings, describes the demise of the old world. What is left of true landscape and true folkways in Britain will only now be found in pockets, in hidden corners, here and there. Hardy and Lawrence in their fiction moved from a rather uncritical love of England in the early works, to a disenchantment in the later books. You have to hunt harder and harder to find the authentic England now. Thus Lawrence in the short story *England, My England*:

> The sunlight blazed down upon the earth, there was a vividness of flamey vegetation, of fierce seclusion amid the savage peace of the commons. Strange how the savage England lingers in patches; as here, amid these shaggy gorse commons, and marshy, snake-infested places near the foot of the South Downs: the spirit of place lingering on primeval, as when the Saxons came, so long ago. (*Collected Short Stories*, p. 286)

What Lawrence wanted was wildness. Not for him cosy tea-and-biscuits England. He wanted Something Else, as do his characters – Kate, Ursula, Somers, Connie. They *yearn* for a landscape to make their expansive souls expand. Lawrence put it best in his story *St Mawr*, when Lou speaks for him:

> There's Something else even that loves me, wants me, I can't tell what it is. It's a spirit…It's here in this landscape. It's something more real to me than men are, and it soothes me, and it holds me up…It's something wild, that will hurt me sometimes and will wear me down sometimes. I know it. But it's something big, bigger than men, bigger than people, bigger than religion. It is something to do with wild America. (in *Complete Short Novels*, p. 428)

This is a classic piece of Lawrencean yearning. He ached for something bigger, wilder and stranger than England. And so did Hardy and Powys. Their Englands are mythical countries, suffused with folklore and legend. The Wessex of Hardy and Powys is the topography of fields and hedgerows and houses, but underneath it there is the mythopoeic world. Their Wessex had a substructure of myth, dream and the supernatural. They show how the workaday world can be so easily overturned, to reveal the extra-ordinary things going on under it. At the crises-points, the occulta emerge.

Soul, soul, soul – Powys loves the soul in things too, like Lawrence. Wolf's attitude to life was 'a worship of all the separate, mysterious, living souls he approached' and he includes trees, fish, planets, people, houses and landscapes among his objects of devotion.

No institutionalized religion such as Christianity is big enough for the yearning souls of Hardy, Powys and Lawrence. Their philosophies are naturally pagan – delimited. Over T.F. Powys's Wessex God presides. But it is a God-in-creation, apprehensible to the sensuously-open self: 'He wakes in spring to see the rich meadows covered with yellow buttercups, while the most delicious scents fill the lanes.'[45] (Llewelyn Powys is essentially pagan, delighting in the stone circles and the wilder places in Dorset. Of the cliffs at Bat's Head, west of Lulworth, he wrote in his *Dorset Essays*: 'I think there are few places more fitted for such moods of religion receptivity than this undisturbed sea-cliff.'(p. 156)

---

45 *Mr Weston's Good Wine*, New Phoenix Library 1950, p. 182.

Seven

The Visions of Thomas Hardy and John Cowper Powys

I feel that Nature is played out as a Beauty, but not as a Mystery. I don't want to see landscapes, i.e., scenic paintings of them...I want to see the deeper reality underlying the scenic, the expression of what are sometimes called abstract imaginings. The 'simply natural' is interesting no longer. The much decried, mad, late-Turner rendering is now necessary to create my interest.

Thomas Hardy, January 1887[46]

---

46 In *The Life*, p. 185.

Thomas Hardy is an immensely *visual* writer. He has been called a 'cinematic novelist'. There are many scenes which impress themselves on the mind's eye: Tess on the white road, Henchard on Grey's Bridge, Gabriel and Bathsheba in the thunderstorm, Giles disappearing up a tree in the mist. While in the earlier novels Hardy describes things very much as they seem, as in a still-life, from the outside, in the later books he moves towards psychoanalysis, towards revealing the inner feelings of people and places. Thus Sherborne, Dorchester and Shaftesbury are described historically and psychologically before the visual aspect is rendered. Hardy moves towards modernism, summed up in his piece on Turner, above. Turner is the painter for Hardy (as championed by Ruskin), not the Impressionists (although he enjoyed them too). The big, sweeping visions of skies and coasts in Turner's *Picturesque Views of England and Wales* are the visual equivalents of Hardy's landscape descriptions. Only Turner really captures those soaring clouds driven over Wessex by the south-west wind. In his watercolours, for example, of *Weymouth* (c. 1811, 5 x 9in, Yale Center, New Haven) or in his even more expansive *Poole and Distant View of Corfe Castle* (c. 1811, 6 x 8in, Private Collection, UK).

Turner is the painter to portray those vast skies over the Dorset coastline. In tiny watercolour drawings, often just six by eight inches, Turner filled out scenes of vast skyscapes, sunlight and space, and managed to include a welter of local detail and incident. *Tess* is filled with an Apollonian lightness and lucidity – in Talbothays, which is described as aquæous and water-filled, like Turner's Venetian watercolours. The sun and its pagan solar power and magic flood the lush fields east of Dorchester in *Tess*. As in Turner, Hardy's use of sunshine here is 'cheerful', as Ruskin put it (Works, xx, 489f). Turner is the artist to visualize Powys's Wessex as described in *Wolf Solent*: 'In one warm inrushing wave the fragrance of the whole West-country seemed to flow through him.'(WS, p. 226)

While early Hardy is a Hobbema or Vermeer, later Hardy moves towards Turner, Monet, even Van Gogh at times. Corot too seems to crystallize some of Hardy's mix of the pastoral and the psychological in his canvases. The brooding Heath in *Return* needs a Turner to paint it properly, to give it that sense of Cimmerian twilight and Sophoclean grandeur which Thomas Hardy fought so hard to render in words. The Brontëan heathland – 'the powerful, eternal origin seething with production' as Lawrence called it in his *Study* (p. 27) – requires a treatment in oil of Turner mixed with Dürer, or Corot melded with Velasquez. Hardy wrote: 'Turner's water-colours: each is a landscape plus a man's soul' (Life, p. 216). Hardy wanted the late Turner of intense subjectivity and Apocalyptic visions, the mad Turner of the vortex works which culminate in the extraordinary vision of *The Angel Standing in the Sun*. Not for Hardy the phanstastical detail of John Martin. Turner's vision is apocalyptic *emotionally*. Turner creates an intense bond with the natural world. His skies are full of feeling, his world full of ferment and fervour. Turner is not only England's greatest painter, he is also the greatest painter *of* England. No one else has depicted the British landscape as Turner has. Turner is astonishing, but his paintings are always based on a direct study of the world, under the open sky, with a sketchbook and a leather pouch of colours. Turner's art is, like Hardy's, 'done from the real'.

In his novels we find many references to Turner, Correggio, Crivelli, El Greco, Rembrandt, Raphael and the Dutch school, among others. Hardy used painters to help him visualize people and landscapes. Thus Ethelberta is Reynolds-like, Angel is as haggard as a Crivelli, and Jude's great-aunt looks like Sebastiano del Piombo's Lazarus. In landscapes Hardy uses Turner, Hobbema, Terburg, Poussin, Danby and Douw (all these in *Far From the Madding Crowd*). In *Wolf Solent* there are direct references to Claude Lorrain, Poussin, Alma-Tadema, Gainsborough and Holbein.

Thomas Hardy wrote (Life, p. 177): 'My art is to intensify the expression of things, as is done by Crivelli, Bellini, etc., so that the heart and inner meaning is made visible.' This is the true Hardy, the poet who desires an *intensification of expression*. Hence his movement in the fiction from the static luminescence of Dutch art to the ardour of the late Turner. And beyond we can extend Hardy's urge towards intense expression to Van Gogh, Beckmann, Kirchner and the Expressionist. Hardy would surely admire the painful and humanist vision of Beckmann. And, as Hardy too moved towards abstraction, he would appreciate Mark

Rothko. Egdon Heath as it appears in *Return* if abstracted might approximate to some of Rothko's large, dark, sombre and religious canvases. In his novels Hardy becomes more subjective in his visions – hence his liking for the Impressionists, which he used in *Tess* and *Jude the Obscure*.

This love of the urge towards intensification in Bellini and Crivelli (he had seen these painters in the National Gallery, London, in the early 1860s) is entirely undertandable, given Hardy's other concerns. Hardy wants to paint a sympathetic, humanitarian portrait of life, and this is certainly depicted in Bellini's images. Bellini's noble figures exude deeply-felt emotions – the darkness and sadness under the skin, in the soul, pouring forth (as in his *Pietà*, late 1460s, Pinacoteca di Brera, Milan). This 'sorriness underlying the grandeur of things' which Hardy was so interested in (Life, p. 171) is also to be found in Leonardo, Martini, Mantegna, Dürer and Titian. The intense *Crucifixions* of Roger van der Weyden and Matthias Grünewald are equivalents of the later Hardy. Jude's crucifixion and martyrdom is intended to be as tragic and as as full of pain and rage as Roger's *Descent from the Cross* (1443, Prado, Madrid) with its geometric orchestration of anguish, or Grünewald's *Isenheim Altarpiece* (1515, Musée d'Unterlinden, Colmar) which is the most extraordinary depiction of despair in the Renaissance.

Hardy was attracted to those painters who expressed the darkness underlying things. He liked the Northern light and humanist outlook – that strain of existential beingness visualized in the works of Friedrich, Munch, Nolde and Beckmann. *Tess* moves inexorably towards darkness – from Corot and the Impressionists, let's say, to Turner and Munch. Much of Netherlandish and Northern art seems to have been painted not on a white but on a black ground. Netherlandish paintings rise up out of black – this gives them that luminosity that Hardy so loved. But it makes them full of a dark presence – like the deep blacks you find in Zurbaran, Velasquez and de la Tour. *Jude the Obscure* (the title indicates this darkness) begins with the underlying darkness that ends *Tess*. And only intermittently does Jude rise to normal full-colour tones. The blackness is not a late addition to Hardy, either. *Under the Greenwood Tree*, with its subtitle 'A Rural Painting of the Dutch School' (referring to Hobbema and

Ruisdael) is painted out of black. Always Hardy spoke of 'seeing into the heart of a thing' (*Early Life*, 1928, p. 190).

The love of darkness underlying things (which finds its apotheosis in painting in Rembrandt) can be found in many scenes in Thomas Hardy's art. In the opening of *The Woodlanders*, for example, there is a Rembrandtian vision conjured up out of Marty's house. Her living door is ajar 'so that a riband of light fell through the opening into the dark atmosphere without.' (p. 46) Hardy continues to describe the interior of her house with an eye for visual detail that is Netherlandish: there is the black oak, the blazing fire, the brass candlestick, the hazel rods, Marty's red palm and brown hair – all these images are picked out by Hardy with a fastidious exactness.

Like Turner and the early Flemish painters, Hardy likes to open out from these intimately detailed and finely sculpted scenes to something wider and more expansive. These vaster visions of landscape stem in part from the High Romanticism of Wordsworth, Keats and Shelley, Hardy's perennial favourites. Keats' 'To Autumn '– 'Season of mists and mellow fruitfulness' – appears in the description of the apple-fragranced Giles, while the relationship between the knightly lover and the enthroned Beloved of Keats' extraordinary 'La Belle Dame Sans Merci' influences Sue and Jude (and most of Hardy's young couples). The aching in Keats' 'Ode to a Nightingale' lies at the heart of Hardy's poetry, while Shelley's mythic West Wind blows through the fiction of both Hardy and Powys.

Shelley's skylark and Thomas Hardy's darkling thrush lie behind the erotic force in Gerda's bird-whistling during the courtship scenes in *Wolf Solent*, while Shelley's 'The cold earth slept below' lyric, with its wintry imagery, could have been written by Hardy:

> The cold earth slept below
> Above the cold sky shone...
> The wintry hedge was black...
> The moon made thy lips pale, beloved.

How well this vision of nature fits in with Hardy's – the cold, wintry night and the strange, wraithlike beloved, perhaps culled from memory, perhaps from wishful yearning, or perhaps from an encounter with a dream-lover. Strange things are bound to happen if you linger around graveyards as much as Hardy.

A typical Hardyan midnight tryst occurs in his poem 'The Well-Beloved', when the poet goes 'by star and planet shine / Towards the dear one's home / At Kingsbere' (CP p. 133). Past the ancient hills, the pagan temple, the trees and the green he goes, eventually meeting a spirit who resembles his beloved closely. In a ballad-form, ancient in folk poetry, Hardy meets his beloved's spirit-familiar, who says: 'I am thy very dream!' The poet, always yearning, gets what he has so fervently desired and imagined. The sprite turns out to be a Shelleyan seraph, a slyph, a neo-Platonic essence, an *anima*, a fairy queen truly in the spirit of Keats' 'lady in the meads'. The night-wraith appears years later in the poetry of Robert Graves as the White Goddess. Graves' poem 'A Love Story' successfully summarizes this romantic trend in English poetry. It brings to an apotheosis the wintry fervour of Keats, the idealism of Shelley and Donne, the passion of Spenser and Traherne, Hardy's supernatural trysts, the Baudelairean Fatal Woman and the Dark Lady and bitter realism of Shakespeare:

> But fell in love, and make a lodgement
> Of love on those chill ramparts.
> Her image was my ensign: snows melted,
> Hedges sprouted, the moon tenderly shone,
> The owls trilled with tongues of nightingales.
>
> These were all lies, though they matched the time,
> And brought me less than luck: her image
> Warped in the weather, turned beldamish.
> Then back came winter on me at a bound,
> The pallid sky heaved with a moon-quake.[47]

The yearning, the ecstasy, the love reflected in the blossoming of the surrounding landscape, the self-delusion and the deluding ikons, the realization and the ensuing disgust, the detachment and the re-making of the experience in poetry – all this is fundamental in Western love-poetry from the troubadours to Robert Graves.

---

47 R. Graves, *Collected Poems 1975*, p. 121.

From the Romantics Thomas Hardy and John Cowper Powys gathered a fire to energize their descriptions of landscape. Thus Hardy writes: 'I view the evening bonfires of the sun', an image straight out of Shelley illustrated by Turner ('A Sign-Seeker', CP, p. 49). Perhaps the most spectacular piece of Hardy's visionary prose comes in *The Woodlanders*, when Fitzpiers, a plodding Tannhauser-figure, rides away from Grace quoting Shelley to himself. He moves through a 'gorgeous autumn landscape' (Woodlanders, p. 259) and fades from Grace's view, while Giles, the would-be lover, rides into her life, described in sensuous Keatsian terms as an Autumn god (p. 261). Giles is the fruit of Little Hintock and its forests, just as Eustacia grows out of Egdon Heath and forms is apotheosis. Giles is ripe, a harvest, a blossom waiting to be picked. Giles' fate, though, like Tess's, is that no one comes to pick him. Nor can he pluck Grace and carry her off. Fitzpiers on his horse does that, as does Alec with Tess on the night in The Chase. Giles falls to the ground, over-ripe. The good apples (the good characters) die, or live on in an everyday stasis of non-life. The outsiders – Alec, Fitzpiers, Troy – are clockwork oranges, machine-like fruits – fake people. They bring with them patriarchal disaster. Tess is raped before she is ripe, but even when she blossoms despite her blight, at Talbothays, Angel is not whole or brave enough to claim her fully. Angel can't save Tess because he can't save himself. Education has killed his true soul, as with Clym. Hardy's fiction is full of lovers meeting each other at the wrong time – either when one of them is not ready, or when it's too late. A rearrangement of the time-structure of Hardy's novels would create many more successful love-matches. Giles and Grace are granted a moment's glory and unity, however, when the sky opens up before them and heaven shines forth radiant:

> With their minds on these things they passed so far round the hill that the whole west sky was revealed. Between the broken clouds they could see far into the recesses of heaven as they mused and walked, the eye journeying on under a species of golden arcades, and past fiery stalactites and stalagmites of topaz. Deeper than this their gaze passed thin flakes of incandescence, till it plunged into a bottomless medium of soft grey fire (Woodlanders, p. 262).

A resplendent green and gold – rarely does Hardy allow himself such opulence. Turner of course painted this sunset thousands of times (literally). How Turner stared into the sun, and stared into the sun, and stared into the sun, blinded by its brilliance. Many writers, such as Durrell, Pater, Ruskin, Nin and Rimbaud work in this elaborate, indulgent, often euphuistic mode constantly. Powys more often let himself go, as here:

> The memories!...That smell of pigs' wine, urine, mingled just as it was a year ago, with the smell of the flowering hedge, gave him a thrill of delicious sadness, and all Dorset seemed gathered up into it! Little wayside cottages, fallen trees, stubblefields, well-heads, duck-ponds, herds of cattle visioned through frames of shed-doors – all these things flooded his mind now with a strange sense of occult possession. (Wolf, p. 626)

Like Paul Klee, Powys takes us for a walk. The Powys's novel-structure is centred around a walk, in which time and space expand, from a single moment, to fill out a whole chapter, a whole book. Powys is atomic – his books explode, and keep expanding, from a single, primary vision or ecstasy. The sculptor Brancusi wrote:

> I am within the essence of things themselves.[48]

In Thomas Hardy's fiction we begin also with a walk, but soon events begin to accelerate, and the elysian walkabout turns into a tragic exploration of the relationships between the sexes, and between the individual and her/ his society.

Powys, like Klee, lives in a world of personal symbols. Klee talks of an explosion of tiny details like a 'fish swimming in all directions'.[49] This corresponds to Powys's multiplicity. 'Art makes visible' says Klee (ib.), and it is the same with Powys. Powys is like the Greek Atomists, portraying an abundant world always in motion. To the vision of Democritus Powys adds the pluralism of Empodecles. He also believes in

---

48 In David Lewis: *Constantin Brancusi*, Wittenborn, New York 1957, p. 43.
49 P. Klee: *The Inward Vision*, Abrams, New York 1959, p. 5f.

the Platonic unity of things – all are One. But the ancient philosopher he is most like is Heraclitus. Powys, like Miller, fully endorses the Heraclitean doctrine that 'everything flows'. Powys's post-Einsteinian views also chime in part with thinkers such as Bergson, Whitehead and Heisenberg. Powys is not a New Physics man – his multiverse, though, blends well with Oriental thought, as does quantum mechanics. Powys is regarded as a mix of Hercalitus and Chuang-tzu. Hardy, too, has a Schopenhaurian sense of non-attachment and despair. Hardy's thought, especially in the later works, moves towards Buddhism. Hardy's characters are caught in the samsara, the wheel of life. They are struggling to attain maximum *karma*, to get themselves flung off the wheel into timelessness. The urge towards self-transcendence lies at the heart of Powys, Hardy and Lawrence. Their characters' struggles are religious, ontological, existential, epistemological, hermeneutic. The search for meaning is a difficult one. But it can only be strived for if society has also been placated. Many of Hardy's people do not even get that far.

Powys's vision has much in common with world mysticism – the many deities of Hinduism, for example, of the pacific doctrines of Buddhism, or the embracing acceptance of Taoism, or the irony and innocence of Greek philosophy. Hardy too studied Classic philosophy. He was more heavily influenced by Christianity than Powys. Christianity for Powys, as for Dostoievsky and Lawrence, is mystical. They concentrate on the Sacred Body of Christ. Hardy, in philosophy, absorbs Schopenhauer and Nietzsche, Darwin, Mill and Huxley, as well as many 19th century theologians. In Hardy the rational/ scientific world of Darwin and the empiricists is in conflict with the Romantic extravagances of Blake and Nietzsche.

John Cowper Powys does not weigh much on the realist side of things. He is wholly internalized. There is no really strong political or ideological subtext in Powys as there is in Thomas Hardy (and Lawrence, Conrad and James). Hardy fuels his fiction with political and societal polemical fire. His concerns are as much social as romantic. In Powys the political ciphers, such as Red (the Communist) who is set against Philip Crow (the Capitalist) are crude. They slip into self-parody. They have no weight. There is no heavyweight ideological debate in Powys as there is, for instance, in Hardy's *Mayor* or *Jude*. Powys shows up his weaknesses here, when he tries to include political themes in his novels. He has rage, true, but he does not know how to direct it as Hardy and Lawrence so ruthlessly do. Powys's political awareness is like those of Robert Graves anti-mechanistic, anti-patriarchal, humanist, intuitive, poetic. Like Graves, Powys just wants to be left alone (Merlin calls for 'more gentleness...'). In this respect, in the call for self-dignity and solitude, Powys is not unlike Sartre, Camus and other existentialists. Powys is essentially a personal writer, someone who concentrates on the individual. It is when he is writing about the individual that he is at his best. He is a geographer of the psychic interior, like Nin and Ballard.

Paul Klee speaks of the inner workings of trees: 'An apple tree in bloom, its roots and rising saps, its trunk, the cross section with the annual rings' (ib.). Like Klee, Powys looks beyond the surfaces of things. This passage from Klee could easily appear in one of Powys's books. In Hardy there is a search for the essence as well as the surface. This getting-behind-of-things, this search for an inner essence, is also expounded by artists such as Beckmann, Newman, Nolde, Van Gogh, Mondrian and Redon. Powys is like Van Gogh, not Cézanne. Essence and expression, not presentation for him. He is a Klee, not a Matisse – symbols not patterns. A Blake and a Delacroix of the pen, not a David or a Manet.

Hardy is like Turner balanced by the social documentary portraits of Hogarth. His landscapes are like those of Corot and Courbet – particularly Courbet's seascapes, and Corot's paintings of softly wind-blown trees and lanes. John Cowper Powys often moves into Munchian introspection. Munch is the artist to paint the erotic tension in *Wolf Solent* in Christie's bedroom (in Munch's famous picture of the virgin cowering under her own shadow, for instance). Hardy interiorizes more in the manner of Cézanne (going for a detached probing of the subject) or Velasquez and Ribera (going for a rounded rendering full of *chiaroscuro*). Lawrence is like Sickert in his early novels – Sickert moving into Kokoschka. Hardy and Lawrence dwell on sexuality at times like Egon Schiele – all contorted bodies expressing angst-ridden psyches. Powys is the Romantic rebel who dives in fully-clothed, regardless of the consequences. Powys wants to drown himself – he wants the raw experiences of a Van Gogh, who, like Powys, amplifies whatever is in front of him. Only Van Gogh could paint Wolf's ecstatic vision of the golden buttercup field. Only Van Gogh (and perhaps Turner) is suitably soaked in the elements, in the out-of-doors world, under open skies. Van Gogh aches for *radiance* – a Joycean epiphany taken to extremes. Van Gogh, like Powys, is all about *intensification*.

> I want to paint men and women with that something of the eternal which the halo used to symbolize...[50]

In this visionary painter we can see the visualizer of the Powysian ecstasy. Van Gogh's flowerpieces, cornfields and interiors have that dizzying exaggeration of hallucination and heightened perception so much a part of Powys's intoxications. When Powys is feeling vast and elemental the equivalents are Turner, Claude, Poussin and the Romantic Sublime artists. Hardy and Powys love odd-looking characters – the sort of people Bosch, Memling and Goya loved to paint. There is a dark side to Powys, too – like the nightmarish scenes of Fuseli, Goya and Rops. At his most extreme, when his trance-like states veer off into the truly bizarre, Powys is like the romantic Abstract Expressionists, who say: 'We are reasserting man's natural desire for the exalted'.[51] Then, apart from the Surreal and Expressionist and Early Renaissance aspects of both Hardy and Powys, there are the more eidetic Impressionist elements –particularly Monet, with his visceral colouration. Again, as with the Flemish painters and Van Gogh, there is an exaltation of the commonplace. Monet turned ordinary haystacks into fervent objects of desire reverently worshipped these days by the middle classes in their millions. Sisley wrote: 'Every picture shows a spot with which the artist himself has fallen in love.' (in Goldwater, 309)

A painter such as Poussin fell in love not only with a particular kind of post-Hellenic landscape, but also with a late afternoon light, coming from a westering sun (not seen) usually placed on the left. Poussin's skies are (unlike Turner's) the creations of his imagination. Poussin does not paint from life (look at his human figures). Claude, however, paints every leaf

---
50 *The Complete Letters of Vincent Van Gogh*, Greenwich, Conn., 1958, iii, p. 25.
51 Barnett Newman in *Tiger's Eye*, New York 1948, 6, p. 53.

lovingly and in shadowy greens. Powys is like this way of seeing, populating his landscapes with Claudean mythological scenes. It is the secular paintings of artists such as Sickert, Courbet, Corot, Sisley, Turner and Girtin which really capture the flavour of Hardy's and Powys's landscapes. They painted odd little streetscenes, or going-nowhere lanes, or misshapen houses – all those odd, out-of-the-way spaces in which the characters of Hardy and Powys rejoiced. Powys (and Hardy) will speak with joy about a particular line of trees, or a wayside stone, or a particular clearing in a wood. They celebrate the insignificant spots on earth as well as the more grandiose. Much of Hardy's landscape is small-scale – the walks between Stinsford and Dorchester, for example, or the lanes leading down into Beaminster.

Thomas Hardy and John Cowper Powys survey Nature like landscape painters. Picture Hardy wandering in the countryside with a notebook or pencil, like an Impressionist painter, scrawling on dead leaves with bits of stone when he becomes inspired. Powys was excited by old landscape paintings which spoke to him of old walls and old roads in his search for 'an Inanimate rendered holy and fetish-like by its contact with humanity' (A, p. 302). In old landscape paintings Powys found a nostalgic but elemental vision of Nature solidified. 'Landscape pictures have certainly played a part in my life that I sometimes think goes down to the very bottom of my soul.' (ib.)

Both Thomas Hardy and John Cowper Powys loved secluded lakes. The fierce ocean works well for expansive poets such as Rimbaud or Keats (and Powys in his louder poetic voice) but the small lake surrounded by trees suffices for Hardy and the quieter Powys. Wolf has to confront his desire to suicide at Lenty Pond. What stops him is the look of the Pond itself. Wolf reacts to the Pond with physical revulsion. His body shrinks from 'immersion in that localized, particular, cubic expansive of starlit oxygen-hydrogen!' (WS, p. 560) Typical of Powys to use such an odd way of describing water. The forerunner of Powys's Lenty Pond is Hardy's Rushy Pond. This and other ponds (Heedless William's Pond, Greenhill Pond, Oker's Pond) feature in the fiction and the poetry (so powerfully in 'Neutral Tones', for example). These are intimate, quiet spaces. At night they are magical – lakes are often the sites of serpents, færies or other strange goings-on. Lonely, yearning poets such as Hardy and Powys and Keats and Edward Thomas are bound to be drawn to them, with no nearby hills or oceans to use as launchpads for journeys into infinity, memory, desire and history. Hardy's poem 'At Rushy Pond' is archetypal: the poet visits the place on a moonlit night. The poet contemplates the reflection of the moon in the water (like Birkin in *Women in Love*). He recalls how, once, 'in a secret year', a long time ago, he had a meeting with a woman there. She is gone – and the poem ends on a familiar ghostly note:

> And the troubled orb in the pond's sad shine
>   Was her very wraith, as scanned
> When she withdrew thence, mirrored, and
>   Her days dropped out of mine.
> (CP, p. 714)

Hardy poeticized these places intensely. He made the ordinary poetic, making mytho-cosmological statements out of simple, everyday events. Hardy's gestures, like those in Poussin or Titian, are mythical. In Hardy the ancient pagan and the mediæval Christian combine to create a dramatic unity of poetry equivalent in painting to Angelico mixed with Delacroix. Or, summed up in one painter – Botticelli, an artist who depicted hauntingly melancholy goddesses while being wracked by the hypocrisies of Christianity. Tess is a Botticelli *Madonna*, but Angel is no Pan.

Hardy, and Powys, love to intensify things, as Leonardo spoke of intensifying the light and shadow in faces.[52] Art is (partly) for revelation. Hardy is exactly like the modern painter here – like Van Gogh, Klee, Miro, Beckmann, Rothko, Malevich and Kandinsky. With his painterly handling of colour and light Hardy hopes to render the invisible visibly. Hardy is true to life, his descriptions are 'done from the real'. Van Gogh also stressed the realistic core of his paintings. But objective vision does not exist. Put a group of artists in front of the same landscape – Monet, Schiele, Marden, Claude, Leonardo, Hardy, Powys, Lawrence, Naipaul, Petrarch and Sappho – and their depictions will all be different. Monet will paint a

---

[52] In Goldwater, ed., p. 53.

myopic mass of reflected colour. Schiele would sketch an edgy, angular drawing which would tell us more about his state of mind than the landscape itself. Brice Marden might produce a sequence of meticulously constructed softly-coloured panels. Claude would turn the landscape into a post-Renaissance Arcadia, populated by mythic personages that were not in the original landscape. Leonardo might render the prospect in the fashion of his astonishing, fervent *Adoration of the Magi*. Hardy might imagine the scene from the viewpoint of a solitary walker going towards the beloved's home, or he might describe the human structures – hedges, lanes, fields, houses, in the landscape and what they mean to him. Powys might crouch down to observe a particular stone or plant, letting his soul sink into it. Lawrence might try to describe the 'spirit of the place', or comment on how civilized or savage it is, or he might talk about the shyness of some flowers. Naipaul would quietly discuss in detail the topography of the landscape, and how humanity has altered it. Petrarch would give us a love-soaked countryside – and say *how dreary and faded the flowers are now, since she has been gone (these twenty years)*, while musing bitterly upon time and mortality. Sappho might also infuse the landscape with love, but in an emotional, not an idealized way.

Which is the real, authentic version? The landscape with angels, with figures, with classical architecture, with exaggerated lights and darks? Every approach has its function – the elemental, the poetic, the nostalgic, the mythic, the idealized, the materialist, the incoherent, the confused.

Hardy is one of those rare writers who can be highly symbolic and deeply realist at the same time. He shows us a person on a white road, on his Great Western Way, and, yes, people *do* walk along roads, which are often white – it is utterly ordinary. At the same time, Hardy says a lot about the human predicament. He manages, through his impressionist approach, to make people 'enlarged and dignified', as Virginia Woolf put it. Hardy's ability to dignify and elevate people is partly what makes him 'the greatest tragic writer among English novelists'.[53] Hardy has the Dostoievskian gift of making the trivial universal. Like Lawrence, Hardy works on many levels. His dramatic scenes are superbly realized symbolically. The symbolic discourse rarely usurps the dramatic one. It's

---

[53] V. Woolf, *The Second Common Reader*, Hogarth Press 1932, p. 253f.

easy to see how such symbols as a tree or a snake can play two roles – dramatic and symbolic – in a text, whether painting, poem or novel. An utterly ordinary phenomena such as light, though, also has a plethora of symbolisms attached to it. There are light-mysticisms in Zoroastrianism, Islam, Greek religion, Hinduism, Tibetan Buddhism (with its *clear light of the void,* that wonderful phrase) and Christianity among others. Painters have to work with the mysticism of light, although they might not be conscious of it. In many ways, the world is reflected light. Much of philosophy is based on visual information, on what we know of the world through the reflections of light. The Western world is founded upon light, in many ways. Certainly sight is the main sense, and vision is the dominant discourse – television, with its vast audiences, testifies to that fact. The visual is put above the other senses – in art as in everyday life. So when Hardy describes light – and he usually pays attention to lighting – he is using one of the major fields of Western symbolism.

Light takes us to the sun. We are – physically – born from the sun (our planet and our bodies). From the sun we can move into solar religion, paganism, astrology, phallicism, Nature, colour, climate – all kinds of correspondences suggest themselves. You can start anywhere, take any symbol, and hook up with the whole vast interconnecting network of hermetic correspondences. Thus Tess on the white road could be an alchemical symbol (referring to the black-white-red process of 'alchymie'), or it could be connected with Mithraic/ Gnostic/ Zoroastrian thought (white and black in conflict, the eternal fight of good and evil), or Christian (the retribution them)e, or Buddhist (Tess alone in the Void) and so on.

Hardy tries to retain a certain objectivity, although, like Powys, he moves towards abstraction as the fiction progresses. Frank Stella has written that modern abstract painting has its roots in the 'Northern, realist, landscape tradition'.[54] There are parallels here with Hardy and Powys and regional fiction. Both writers move towards spiritual realism and abstraction. In the psycho-cultural movement from Hardy/ Turner to Powys/ Klee, there is a new sense of perception, of volume and space, a movement from illusionism to abstraction. Powys is interested in the

---

54 F. Stella, *Working Space*, Harvard University Press 1986, p. 134.

thing-in-itself, in elementalism, in the abstract physicality of a thing, as in some modern sculpture (such as Brancusi or Gaudier-Breska). In modern painting, the art-object has its own kind of beingness. It is an object in its own right – it has its own kind of isness or thereness. Symbolism and abstraction merge, and presence speaks for itself. Similarly, in Powys – his elemental ecstasies are there for themselves, not as representations, but as essences-in-themselves. Hardy clings on to illusionism – he is of that tradition. But in *Jude the Obscure* the ontological space of Wessex is breaking apart, much as pictorial space did a few years later with Cubism.

John Cowper Powys's sensualism is tremendously visual. He begins like Thomas Hardy, with the seen source. Where Lawrence is immediately diving for the emotional and psychological, Powys uses the vision to begin his ecstasies. Like Leonardo, he quietly contemplates the mysteries of Nature. Powys extemporizes. He writes on the wing. He is open to impressions, to experiences, like the Hardyan 'natural soul'. Hardy has a plan, however, a structure – some idea of what he's looking for. The Hardy base-structure is a sequence of events and how they relate to character and place and motive and ambition. Lawrence, meanwhile, looks for the *relationship* between things, especially between people. In Powys, history and background are touched in later. Lawrence starts with background (he gets scenic groundwork quickly out of the way). Lawrence asks, always: *who is this character? why is she here? where is she going?* Lawrence throws himself and his characters into the fire, into the future. He starts grappling with big issues immediately. Powys lets his people float about a bit Powys's people live in the Now. They yearn, but not like Hardy's and Lawrence's characters. The latters' characters yearn for action, for change, for progression. Powys's people are static, preferring to sink into quiet thinking. Powys's characters enjoy the 'in-seeing' of Rilke, the inwardness of poets such as Graves, Valéry, Mallarmé and Eliot. Here is an example of Powys's spatial mysticism, from *Wolf Solent*:

Wolf tried to visualize the whole course of the [river] Lunt, so as to win for it some sort of coherent personality. By thinking of all its waters together, from start to finish, this unity could be achieved; for between the actual water before him now, into which he could thrust his hand, and the water of that tiny streamlet among the mid-Dorset hills from which it sprang, there was no spatial gap. The one flowed continuously into the other. They were as completely united as the head and tail of a snake! (WS, p. 109)

If we imagine Hardy's colours, we would picture much light and dark, with a reddish-brown tone between the two. He paints his scenes out of a Dutch darkness. Many scenes occur in twilight – either at dawn or dusk. Twilight is Hardy's favourite time of day. It is the time of the 19th century world – after the bright afternoon of the Renaissance, the noontide of Christianity and Classic cultures, and the morningtime of prehistory. The twilight of the Victorian/ Romantic era precedes the nuclear midnight of the (post) modern age.

Like Turner, Hardy creates scenes full of contrasts – light and dark, truth and lies, love and hate, passion and indifference. Colour and light are both natural and symbolic in Hardy. Tess is a dark spot in the distance on Hardy's Great Western Road. This is an everyday occurrence – the lone traveller. But Hardy transforms it with his painterly eye into an image of existential vacuity. The image is stark, like a Munch painting, and its blackness is Beckettian. Tess is now not integrated with Nature – she stains the landscape. Her rebellious act has upset the natural order. She is now a hunted victim. Nature, once lush and green and full of promise is now desolate and white, drained of colour. Tess, once blooming, full of life and blood, is now an outsider, an intruding dark blemish on the scheme of things.

Thomas Hardy is full of this visual, symbolic shorthand. He touches in his dramas with simple but powerful visual devices. His visual descriptions function to render the scenes for the reader in the conventional manner. Thus he uses a naturalistic palette to depict clothes and lighting – yellow, rusty, snowy, etc. But in the later works the use of colour and light becomes more extreme. The focussing becomes both sharper and more diffuse. Hardy moves from Impressionism in *The Woodlanders* to Turnerian *chiaroscuro* in *Tess* and *Jude the Obscure*. White, black and red feature prominently in *Tess*. Scarlet and black are the colours of Hell. Alec combines the white-black-red configuration when he appears in Tess's Paradisal garden dressed as the Devil – in his white smock, before the red fire, complete with pitchfork. White, black and red are the colours of the drama of life. They are the colours of birth, love and death, and also of the Goddess. Tess herself is a Goddess, and it is truly fitting that she should be associated with these primeval, magical colours. Hardy's use of these very bold colours is a manifestation of his desire to describe life as honestly as possible, in all its raw power.

By the time of *Jude the Obscure*, Thomas Hardy's use of colour and light darkens dramatically. He moves into a zone of dialogue and abstractions. His vision is intensified. Turner went the other way, piling on the white until there was hardly anything left of humanity. His *Norham Castle* is pure incandescent whiteness. Hardy loved this intense chaos, this over-spiritualization of the world.

What an amusing image it is: Turner standing on a box in top hat and tails in the Royal Academy, smudging in loads of white paint into his skies. Turner wanted to 'outwork and kill' other painters – particularly Constable. Hardy too wanted to go further than literature had gone before. Hence his *Jude the Obscure*, with its polemical rage. Turner shivers into boiling brilliance, and Hardy trembles into ethical anger. Both artists in their late works move into abstraction. Turner breaking open the way into modern painting, and Hardy opening up the path towards modern fiction. There is no way beyond Turner, except the all-white canvases of Malevich and Robert Ryman. There was still some way to go after Hardy – Lawrence, Beckett and Burroughs.

Hardy noted that Turner aimed to create a 'pictorial drug' with which to intoxicate the viewer with the full effect of the real (Life, p. 226). The aim is Symbolist synæsthesia. Hardy tries for similar effects in his prose – the visual is for him the way into a six-sense experience so that the reader/viewer will be awakened to 'the tragical mysteries of life' (Life, p. 192). Hardy wants an experience of the revelation of life as profound as that rendered in oil by Turner in his *The Angel Standing in the Sun*. Like Turner's Blakeian Angel, Hardy's later characters are haloed by the intensity of their feelings. Hardy's aim is to pierce the halo of emotional light surrounding a person, to lay bare their feelings. Hardy's characters are struggling to be released from the Stendhalian crystallization that surrounds them. For Hardy, as for Ruskin, light is spiritual as well as physical.[55] Turner, with his transcendent lambency, is the painter for Hardy. Turner, not Constable. Not Constable's weary, too tame rendition of Salisbury Cathedral, but Turner's vast *Salisbury from Old Sarum* (c. 1828, part of the *Picturesque Views*, Private Collection). This watercolour, with its soaring rain-clouds split apart by shafts of sunlight, was a favourite of Ruskin's.[56] It is the same with Stonehenge. Not, for Hardy or Ruskin, Constable's flaccid version, but Turner's Apocalyptic Vision of stormlightning and electrical death (*Stonehenge*, c. 1825-8, private collection). Ruskin compared the cathedral and the stone circle in Turner's watercolours, those monuments of 'the two great religions of England – Druidical and Christian' (*Works*, vii,p. 190).

Throughout his fiction Hardy compares the pagan and the Christian. In *Tess* he contrasts these two spiritual structures on Wiltshire Plain. Tess and Angel pass through Salisbury (Melchester) by night – no glorious Biblical entry into the City of God for them. 'The graceful pile of cathedral architecture rose dimly on their left hand, but it was lost upon them now' (*Tess*, p. 483). This is another example of Hardy's shorthand – it is none too subtle here. Christianity is experienced in darkness, the two protagonists blind to it now, its effect dimmed. Hardy's visual/architectural notation does the trick, though. Tess is beyond the reach of Christianity and God. Something older and more powerful controls her destiny. Call it paganism, Nature, Fate, the old dark gods, the President of the Immortals, whatever. Stonehenge is as good an embodiment of 'It' as anything else. Stonehenge is for Tess the last in a long line of pagan structures – from the opening Maydance, to the ancient Chase and the Cross-in-Hand. Tess goes through most of the experiences in life: childbirth, motherhood, death of her child, rape, marriage, prostitution, murder, self-sacrifice, homelessness, labour, ecstasy and death. The novel is a catalogue of her disasters, and Hardy needed landscapes rich enough to enmesh with Tess's deeply-felt experiences. Hence his tendency, like

---

55 See Ruskin, *Works*, xxviii, p. 614.
56 *Modern Painters*, v, *Works*, vii, p. 190.

Powys', to over-rich Nature descriptions. Hence also the use of a passionate, visionary painter such as Turner. Hardy's province, though, like Turner's, is the realm of experience beyond the senses. *Tess* and *Jude the Obscure* are records of emotional and spiritual tragedies. Nature in them begins by being fused with the protagonists, but ends up as a total not-self Other. The Quest through the forest of symbols for Hardy's people is a tragic journey. How sad that Hardy's people could not ask the right questions at the right time, like Arthurian heroes in the Grail legends. Hardy's people are too silent for too long. If only Eustacia, Giles, Marty, Henchard, Tess, Sue and Jude had said what they really wanted to say earlier. They knew in their hearts that the Grail – life – served *them*, as well as the other way around. They – we – are not slaves. They – we – are also kings and queens and gods of all we survey in the landscape of the heart.

Eight

Paganism and Folklore

The instincts of merry England lingered on here with exceptional vitality, and the symbolic customs which tradition has attached to each season of the year were yet a reality on Egdon. Indeed, the impulses of all such outlandish hamlets are pagan still: in these spots homage to nature, self-adoration, frantic gaeities, fragments of Teutonic rites to divinities whose names are forgotten, seem in some way or other to have survived mediæval doctrine.

Thomas Hardy, *The Return of the Native* (p. 452)

Thomas Hardy is full of pagan imagery, pagan scenes and pagan themes. In *Tess of the d'Urbervilles* there is the club-walking, the sleepwalking, the mistletoe, Tess and her star and sun-worship. In *The Mayor of Casterbridge* Elizabeth and Henchard meet at Maumbury Rings, there is the skimmity-ride, and Henchard visits the shamanic Conjuror Fall. In *Far From the Madding Crowd* Bathsheba divines using the *Bible* and a key. There is also the Gothic coffin scene. In *The Return of the Native* there is the wonderful Maydance, the bonfires, the mummers' play, Susan pricking Eustacia in church and later making a wax-image of her. In *The Woodlanders* there is the Midsummer revel and the tree-planting. Hardy punctuates his fiction with the grotesque, the macabre, the Gothic and the supernatural. There is a poetic, pagan 'Thomas Hardy' who erupts from under the cool surface of the rational, scientific one.

There are pagan characters too: the local shaman, Conjuror Fall, a weather-prophet; the Mephistophelean reddleman, Diggory, covered in blood-coloured dust; Oak, a latter-day Pan with his flute and nocturnal reveries; Susan Nunsuch who curses witchlike the waxen image of Eustacia – she is more of a sorceress than Eustacia; there is the ghost of Mrs Jethways' son, who haunts Elfride and her lovers; a ghost visits Cytherea; and Rhoda Brook has an incubus.

There are many Gothic and ghostly goings-on in Thomas Hardy, which counter the pessimist and realist that people see in him. He very much wanted to see a ghost. He wrote, after all, in the great epoch of Spiritualism, ectoplasm, graveyard-vigils, charaltan-magicians and all kinds of psychic phenomena. Hardy was partly a country-believer and a city-doubter. In *The Life* he wrote:

> Half my time – particularly when writing verse – I 'believe' (in the modern sense of the word) not only in the things Bergson believes in, but in spectres, mysterious voices, intuitions, omens, dreams, haunted places, etc., etc. But I do not believe in them in the old sense anymore for that. (pp. 369-70)

Return is the most folky and pagan of Hardy's books, while in Tess paganism is set against Christianity, and the pagan nature-way wins. In *Jude*, Christianity wins out over paganism. These conflicts are summed up so ironically in the figure of Sue Bridehead.

The elements of folktale, balladry, pagan and traditional customs always supersede in Thomas Hardy over the scientific, modern Christian elements – until *Jude the Obscure*. It is no good being *obscure* in the modern age: you get killed. Hardy's novels are book-length versions of ballads – the folktale fleshed out to form a novel. Even his sense of Christianity was folkish. He spoke of feeling 'churchy'. He liked the trappings and æsthetics of Christianity but not the dogma. How clear this is in Greenwood Tree, when the Mellstock Quire meet around the centrepiece of the church not really for religious but for social purposes. They are a band of friends, not priests. How tender is Hardy's humorous battle in this novel between the older William and the younger guests at the Tranters' party who want to dance:

> 'If you do have a party on Christmas-night 'tis only fair and honourable to the sky-folk to have a sit-still party. Jigging parties be all very well on the Devil's holidays...' (*Under the Greenwood Tree*, p. 49).

Dancing is the Devil's doing for the more God-fearing persons in the populace. So they have to wait until after midnight. Here the older members of the community dictate the pace of things (and it is old William who lays down the law – patriarchy at work again). Things have not changed greatly in Hardy's world, for by the time of *Jude* Sue has to lie about the statues of Venus and Apollo, telling her pious landlady they are St Peter and Mary Magdalene (*Jude*, p. 142). Hardy is supremely economical again here. He turns the Goddess of Love, Venus, into the pentitent whore of Christianity (the Magdalene is also a Black Goddess, associated with heresy, Gnosticism and occultism). Apollo becomes St Peter, one of the founding fathers of Christianity, and one of the people responsible for the hypocrisies of sin—sex—death buried at the core of the millennial religion.

The pagan versus the Christian is often surpassed by a conflict between the religious (whether pagan or Christian) and the scientific – a battle between the old and the new, in essence. Hardy wrestles with these issues as his characters wrestle with their destinies in love and tragedy.

Like John Cowper Powys, Thomas Hardy has his action occur on special days of the year. The stories are woven into the fabric of time, nature and the seasons. Thus Angel and Tess marry on New Year's Day, *Return* opens on Bonfire Night (a remnant of the Celtic fire-feast of Samhain), Greenwood Tree opens on Christmas Eve, while Powys uses Maundy Thursday, All Soul's Day, Midsummer Day and Candlemas Eve. What Hardy does (and so do Lawrence, Graves and Powys) is to set off what *should* happen on these festival days, with what actually *does* happen. Thus the Maytime dances, which should end in the blossoming of romance and eroticism, end for Tess in a trip to the pub to fetch her drunken father. It is a shabby, sober end to her Mayday rituals. She has no illusions at this point about what life can offer her.

Occasionally, the seasons and people harmonize: as in the Midsummer picnic in *Maiden Castle*, or the Midsummer night in *The Woodlanders*, when Fitzpiers, the rake, seduces not Grace but Suke Damson. The folk is of the mass, it is anonymous, unlike the individual. Fairy tales speak of nameless protagonists, archetypes in archetypal stories. The folk is of the community and of the past, but Hardy and his characters are individuals, of the present. His characters are the artists and individuals in their communities. Powys's people are even more shamanic – they stand out a mile from their neighbourhoods. Hardy aims to tie together the particular and the archetypal, while Powys flies between tiny details and huge universes. The mass/folk/Past is not enough for Hardy's characters – they must have more than their environments can provide. Hardy's limitation is to see this journey towards wholeness and self-achievement as always tragical.

Powys's biggest mystical statement is in *A Glastonbury Romance*. There is religious fervour in the novel. In Sam's story is the most dramatic of all Powys's mystical initiates. There are other moments of spirituality in the book: Geard at Mark's Court, John Crow's visions of Arthur's Sword on Pomparles Bridge, Geard's 'miracle', Evans' masochistic ecstasy during the Pageant, Cordelia in the rain, and the Flood.

Sam's vision of the Grail is Apocalyptical: he has a vision of power and wholeness, of a cosmic force embodied in the 'World Fish'. John Cowper Powys here binds up ideas of the New Millennium, of cosmic Time (with its intimations of the new age of Aquarius succeeding the Christian Age of

Pisces). The themes of fish, of the world as a fish-tank, of water, glass, Glastonbury (the city of glass), of blood, nature, sensualism, Christ, Arthur, Merlin and the Revelations – all these are tied up together in the Grail vision.

Sam is split apart in his experience of the Grail. The world cracks open, and pain crashes in (GR, pp. 938-9). Powys's Grail is described thus:

> But when the vision appeared it came sailing into the midst of this bleeding darkness that was Sam's consciousness, healing everything, changing everything, each detail of what he saw he saw with a clearness that branded it forever upon his brain. He saw a globular chalice that had two circular handles. The substance it was made of was clearer than crystal; and within it was dark water streaked with blood, and within the water was a shining fish. (p. 939)

This is a menstrual Goddess-soaked vision of the Grail as a world-womb in which Ichthus, the World-Fish, swims. Ithyphallic consciousness, clad in sensuous feminine guises is embodied in the Fish, but the blood is not of Christ – it is menstrual blood, matriarchal, hot with life, intensely fecund, pouring from the Welsh Goddess Cerridwen. It is the water of life, the blood of rebirth. Powys's whole creation of the scene is sexual. It is an anal, sadomasochistic and intensely painful experience. Sam's battle with Nell and his domineering father is also sexual. The upshot is that Sam is reborn – he is torn apart, but the Grail reconstitutes him. Again, as in Lawrence's later philosophy, Sam becomes a neophyte of a mystical Christ, not a theological Jesus (p. 943).

John Cowper Powys's occultism is a curious mixture of Spiritualism, telepathy, Gnosticism, anthroposophy, alchemy, Qabalism, neo-Platonism and Taoism. He believed in certain paranormal occurrences. G.Wilson Knight relates how the ghost of Powys appeared to him one night, in a psychic æther. Powys appeared to Theodore Dreiser, and, after his death, to Knight again.[57] Powys believed he had thaumaturgic powers. His view of magic was sexual. In Powys magic and sex, mysticism and masturbation combine to make that 'cosmic eroticism' (A, p. 531). With his ecstatic, masturbatory view of the cosmos, Powys is quite different from most other novelists. Perhaps it is these strange, elemental ideas that

---

[57] See Colin Wilson, *The Occult*, pp. 63-9, 639-643.

keep Powys on the fringes of literature, not his bad prose, loose form or weak characterization or dubious politics.

John Cowper Powys's occultism veers from the benign magicianship of Shakespeare's Prospero (in Geard, Sylvanus, Merlin) to a peculiar kind of esoteric elementalism (in Larry Zed, Wolf, Sir Mort). With his delineations of visions, animisms, psychic imprints, æther, magicke, ghostlore, Grail legend, alchemy, Tarot and Spiritualism, Powys creates a world in flux, an everchanging spirit-world in which souls drift about dreamily. Underneath the ordinariness of Powys fictive world lies an abundance of sprites, mages, ghosts, gods and planetary powers. The links with *The Tempest*, with fairy tales and mediæval romance are strong in Powys. He tries to keep alive an archaic spiritual world, in which strangeness is the norm (much as contemporary horror films try to do). Powys's concerns are more mystical than religious, more mythic and mystical, but more elemental than mythical. His mania is irrational (A, p. 331). He wants the magical not the doctrinal Jesus (ib.). He is a dualist, a self-confessed Gnostic (p. 353). A strong sense of ethics, of good and evil, pervades his writing, as it does in Gide, Brontë, Thomas Hardy, Dostoievsky, Greene. At times Powys believed himself to be possessed of a 'demonic formidableness' (p. 408, 457, 462) He identified with Taleissin, with the Druids, with ancient cults of all kinds (p. 454). In his cult of sensualism, mind becomes matter. What the brain thinks becomes real, externally. 'Thought is a real thing...It creates; it destroys; it begets' says Geard in *Glastonbury* (p. 457). Of course thought does. This happens all the time in artistic creation. The painter thinks of a picture, and then, after a struggle, the painting is made flesh. People image up pyramids, skyscrapers, whole cities. They think of them, and then they become real. 'All's vision' says Uryen (MC, p. 237).

Powys's hermeticism is often Shakespearean, theatrical – Wolf converses with his father's skull. Groddeck is not far away here. Powys's characters have an 'It' coursing through them, for all to see. The source of Powys's occultism lies in his childhood, in the ecstasies he felt looking at the ocean at Weymouth (Wey, p. 29). These childhood ecstasies are bound up for John Cowper Powys (and his characters) with parents, with the whole œdipal drama (A, p. 5).

Thomas Hardy thought himself a serious (though not professional) chronicler of Dorsetshire customs and life (in Anne Smith, ed, pp. 108-9). His use of folklore and tradition is essentially poetic – not inaccurate but poetically true. In the same way Lawrence in *Sons and Lovers* gives us a valuable record of the daily lives of Nottinghamshire coal-miners. These poetic accounts beat any by journalists or historians. The artists tell us what it was really like. They offer up an intuitive penetration into people and their habits.

Thomas Hardy uses the ancient rhythm of the seasons to counterpoint his stories: from Old and New Lady Day, through Mayday and Midsummer Day, to the harvest, through to Autumn, Christmas and the New Year. This love of seasons, customs, folktales and ballads gives Hardy's fiction a vivid sense of life – of full-bloodied and full-bodied life. Amazingly, Hardy can he joyous in his use of festival days and customs. This folkloric strain has its apotheosis in *Return* and *Tess of the d'Urbervilles*, but is there throughout the fiction, poetry and miscellaneous articles and essays. See the poems 'At the Entering of the New Year' and 'If It's Ever Spring Again', for example.

Hardy was trying for an poetic account of his subject. He wrote that 'the road to true philosophy of life seems to lie in humbly recording diverse readings of its phenomena' (Per, p. 39). Here Hardy plays down his clever manipulations of his material. He is no simple provincial documentor, but a complex and great novelist. He knew what he was doing (which cannot always be said of Powys, unfortunately).

Two pagan days feature strongly in both John Cowper Powys and Thomas Hardy: Mayday and Midsummer Day. These are bound to be favourites with nature-lovers – particularly fresh May, when everything is bursting into bud, when the world is made anew and the plants as yet have not been frazzled by the hot summer sun.

Mayday is certainly crammed full of folklore and poetic associations. It opens *Tess of the d'Urbervilles*, Hardy's most complete and satisfying novel. Mayday is associated with fertility, sexuality, trees, flowers, bonfires and all things pagan. Mayday Goddess include Flora, Maia, Luna, Asherah, Danu and Tanit. Mayeve is the German *Walpurgisnacht*, the night of witches, orgies, drinking, dancing and the Celtic bonfire feast of Beltane. There is a May Queen and King, dancing among the sacred oak trees. In England, the Morris-men, flouncing about with their scarves and bells, seem ridiculous – what a national dance! Yet their dances and games are all about fertility and sexuality, and, at times, with their use of scapegoats, Morris-dancing uses ritual violence.

Mayday is certainly a rich time for all manner of happenings. These customs have not completely died out. In Rochester, Kent, there is the cheeky, Puckish Jack-in-the-Green who leads the dancers at dawn into a day of ceremonies still vivacious and hypnotic.

No wonder, then, that Hardy uses these festival-days, with their fusion of sex, love, fertility, magic, nature and the Goddess, involving the whole community. It is significant that he focuses on women in these rituals (in *Tess of the d'Urbervilles*, *The Woodlanders* and *The Return of the Native*. especially). Chapter Two in *Tess* moves from the long-shot descriptions of the 'fertile and sheltered tract of country' (p. 48 – the adjectives could apply also to Tess herself) to the history of the place. The Mayday dance is introduced by reference to the ancient forests of the region (Hardy is accurate here as ever, for Maytime rituals are bound up with tree-worship, symbolized by the Maypole). Hardy then describes the Cerealian sisterhood of the girls' club-walking. In invoking Ceres, Hardy makes his village maidens latterday upholders of a Goddess-cult. There are strong undertones of matriarchy here, of feminine ritual and vitality. Indeed, the images of female solidarity are one of the most uplifting parts of the novel: Tess and her friends are set against the barren spirituality of Angel and his brothers; Tess and the milkmaids; Tess later on, downtrodden, finding sanctuary with Mirian.

As Ovid says, at the Ceres festival white is the main colour. White is Tess's colour – purity stained with red blood.[58] Thomas Hardy evokes the scene vividly and with thinly veiled eroticism. The wisdom of the grandmothers and crones adds to the dimension of witchcraft. But the narrator's interest is in those 'under whose bodices the life throbbed quick and warm.' (*Tess*, p. 50). These girls dance alone. They do not need men. When the men arrive, they only offer dissatisfaction. It is a crisis time for Tess, so pure and virginal yet so cynicial too, and so aggressively

---

58 Ovid, *Fasti*, Loeb 1967 iv, p. 393.

described by her creator – she has a red ribbon, hot blushes and a 'pouted-up deep red mouth' (p. 52). If only Angel could have made the connection with Tess at the beginning. But it was 'too late'. Tess, with life and its red-blooded passions overtaking her, is harvested not by her true soul-mate, but by one who is only interested in her blossoming body. The pagan—Christian conflict is so rigorously brought out in this scene, as are the other themes of sexual maturity versus virginity, and youth versus old age, and ignorance versus experience – unknowing (in *Tess of the d'Urbervilles*) and wisdom (in the old women).

Two people meant for each other who miss each other occurs in the Midsummer Night in *The Woodlanders*. Midsummer, the Summer Solstice, the high point of the year for the sun and its energies, is a time for fire and lovers, as Frazer notes in *The Golden Bough* (p. 153):

> In modern Europe...the great Midsummer festival has been above all a festival of lovers and of fire; one of its principal features is the pairing of sweethearts, who leap over the bonfires hand in hand or throw flowers across the flames to each other. And many omens of love and marriage are drawn from the flowers which bloom at this mystic season.

The love–marriage, and its defeat at the hands of circumstance, was Hardy's great theme. He liked to use these fire-festivals to focus his narratives, to provides frames for the action and themes. Midsummer is the mid-point, the turning-point, the time when the zodiacal constellations change – the planets which control human destiny. The spirit of the year turns from waxing to waning. Hence the use of the wheel in the ground-plan of Avebury, Stonehenge and the prehistoric stone-circles.

The mid-point of the Hardy novel is a crucial time. Beginnings in Hardy's texts are critical too: events are set in motion. The mid-point in *Tess* (the wedding) is a crisis-time, as is the mid-point in *Mayor* when Henchard's fortunes topple over at the exact minute that the furmity-woman testifies in court. Henchard's ghost-crime haunts him as does Tess's. In *The Woodlanders*, the Midsummer revel is a turning-point. The wheel of fire and life turns at this point, and the group of village girls hope for a glimpse of their future partners. As with Mayday festivals, Midsummer masquerades take place in the sacred groves. Hardy carefully sets the scene: the trees have faces, the moon rides above the green shades below. It is a night when færies and spirits run abroad, as in Shakespeare's play. Hardy's emphasis on the moon suggests the whole weight of Goddesses, witchcraft, sexuality, nature, the unknown and a whole mass of moon-magic. J.C. Cooper writes: 'Midsummer is the most magically powerful of all times'.[59]

Thomas Hardy's cinematic sensibilities come into play as Grace and Marty pass Giles' house and they hear him hammering and packing up his furniture ready to leave the next morning. Hardy has to underline things thus, to make things just a little obvious. He likes to give us an insight into what each character is doing at this crisis time. Crises implicate everybody, Hardy says, meaning the whole community. These days, in a global village world, one nation's crisis is everyone's crisis. Hardy is filmic: he uses sound here to communicate the guilt that Marty feels but Grace cannot feel. Hardy uses tracking, panning, montage and *mise-en-scène* (as in the opening chapter of *Return*).

As in the Maydance in *Tess of the d'Urbervilles*, Thomas Hardy creates a solid matriarchal configuration: Grace, her mother and Grammer Oliver (Marty has a tribal Mother-figure, Grammer Oliver, while Grace has a middle-class parent). The Celtic Feminine is very much present here – the trinity of matriarchal figures, the moon, the woods, Midsummer, and so on. Hardy's use of tree-lore is displayed too: 'Grace and her stepmother paused by a holly tree; and at a little distance stood Fitzpiers under the shade of a young oak' (p. 195) The oak, always associated with Midsummer (at which the Oak-King is burned as a sacrifice) also has the necessary phallic connotation for Fitzpiers).

Like witches, the girls begin the incantations which will spirit up their future lovers. Like Ursula, Grace stands 'in the full face of the moonlight' (p. 196). Grammer Oliver tries to engineer the proceedings so that Grace will run into Giles. But of course all aspirations are thwarted in Hardy. Grace's mother does the same with Fitzpiers. The two suitors are bound up together and contrasted in this way, guided by The Mothers (of *Faust* and Briffault). Hardy moves his characters around like a director on the stage, sometimes with Shakespearean accuracy. Marty South, 'always

---
[59] *The Aquarian Dictionary of Festivals*, Aquarian Press 1990, p. 148.

doomed to sacrifice desire to obligation', helps to guide Grace towards Giles. How clearly Hardy forces his characters to confront one another, and to confront their own, deep selves. Fitzpiers captures Grace – neither Giles nor Marty have the strength nor the inclination to stop her. Giles' non-action, like Angel's, is part of his downfall. His passivity is useless when faced with the dashing force of Fitzpiers. The moon, the night, the Midsummer ritual have helped to join Grace and Fitzpiers together: 'new relations between them had begun'. Hardy's vivid cinematic treatment continues with a love-chase between Fitzpiers and Suke Damson. An ironic pastoral love-scene among the hay-cocks ensues, complete with a sarcastic night-hawk taking the place of the usual nightingale. Fitzpiers, associated like Alec with the Devil, gets to satisfy his lust. The other characters are in disarray. The plot changes here – the wheel has turned, new relationships are set in motion. With a dramatic economy rare in literature, using a fusion of pagan ritual, natural imagery and mistaken identity, as in *A Midsummer Night's Dream*, Hardy points out the new directions this narrative will take.

John Cowper Powys's use of occultism and paganism is rather different from Thomas Hardy's. There is still the loving recreation of particular festivals, as in *Maiden Castle*, but Powys is more interested in resurrecting an ancient feeling for mysticism, in rebirthing a mystical cult (as in *Glastonbury*). Powys has a feeling for authentic mysticism, like Arvo Pärt, the Russian composer, who is trying to use mediæval plainsong in his new music, or, in sculpture, Eric Gill, with his re-working of ecclesiastical direct carving.

On the last page of his *Autobiography* Powys wrote that the two main strands in his life had been his self-realization (his sensualism) and his

> magic trick of losing myself in the continuity of the human generations. By this continuity I mean the way in which from father to son our life-sensations are handed down from the past, creating a sort of 'eternal recurrence' of the poetic mystery of the *little-great* ritual, the daily acts by which we all must live. ...The astronomical world is *not* all there is. We are in touch with other dimensions, other levels of life. (A, p. 652)

Here Powys's philosophy is similar to the 'eternal return' of Nietzsche, Joyce and Mircea Eliade, in which nothing is lost, and everything returns. Keeping the spirit of this 'poetic mystery' alive is the aim of the Powysian and the Hardyan self. Hardy wrote of the villages in *Return*: 'Paganism was revived in their hearts' (p. 321). The cult of the strange, the unreal and the supernatural is very important for both Hardy and Powys. Hardy at times is unreal, ghastly, theatrical – overburdened with occult references. Powys wallowed in this field of thought.

Feminine magic is subverted by a dark masculine force in John Cowper Powys's picnic scene in the chapter 'Midsummer's Eve' in *Maiden Castle*. Powys uses the ritual of running through a fire – here Uryen drags Wizzie and Thuella through it. It is his ætherealized way of making love to them both. The ambiguity of Uryen's new religion is symbolized by these two Powysian sylphlike girls. While Hardy brings his concerns into close-up, Powys's treatment is more diffuse. It has to do with Wizzie's love being transferred from Dud to his father. But the whole feeling of the scene is ambivalent, and difficult to isolate. The scene is not mentioned again in the novel.

The other major fire-festival in Thomas Hardy is in the opening of *The Return of the Native*, on November the fifth. Bonfire Night takes over from the Celtic feast of Hallowe'en. The connotations – a Northern European series of bonfires lit at the onslaught of winter, with its emphasis on witchcraft, Autumn and Celtic/Cimmerian twilight – have all the right ingredients for the setting of Hardy's full-blown tragedy. Hardy uses the string of bonfires to lead us into history and legend – to Hallowe'en, a Dantean Inferno, Norse legend, the Saxons and Druids and the Gunpowder Plot. With these autumnal fires Hardy hopes to give his tale the feel of Scandanavian myth. He means to say that the world we are entering is dark, Northern, passionate and legendary. He hopes to elevate this scrubland in Dorset up to the stature of a battleground of the gods. There are implications in a Hallowe'en fire of the burning of witches, and Eustacia is called a witch later on (p. 101). Significantly, she drowns herself, showing that she cannot pass the witches' test. She grows out of the Heath, she completes it (p. 63), and she goes back into it. Her first act (we see) is to stand atop Rainbarrow – to pierce the sky, to be elevated above the earth. Her first act is rebellious, Promethean, romantic. She strains upward and outward. When she dies she sinks downward and inward, the force of the water is above her. Her spirit, however, flows down to the ocean, just as rivers do – and this is where she wanted to be along.

As scene-setters, the bonfire and Heath chapters are superb. Hardy does not need to go on to describe Eustacia as a Goddess, as a suitably solemn and stately Queen of the Night. We know she is. All he needed to say is:

> Moreover to light a fire is the instinctive and resistant act of man, at the winter ingress, the curfew is sounded throughout Nature. It indicates a spontaneous, Promethean rebelliousness against the fiat that this recurrent season shall bring foul times, cold darkness, misery and death. Black chaos comes, and the fettered gods of the earth say, let there be light. (p. 67)

Fire is indeed one of *the* marks of humanity, and is one of the earliest objects of mystery and worship. Fire is linked with sexuality, life, love, purification and so on. It is the *fiat lux*, the creative male Word, the Heraclitean energy. Fire is associated with seeds, sperm, soma, light, life and divinity. As La Barre says (*Muelos*, pp. 80-3), 'fire is the earthly form of heavenly light'. The origin of the word deus is **diew* – 'the shining one'. Anyone who has seen Venus rising on a clear Spring evening will understand the mystery and splendour of this ancient experience of divinity. The sky is the first manifestation of the Sacred – it is transcendence actualized. Fire works so well here, in these opening chapters of *Return*, showing how humanity rages upon the face of he earth – how passion will burn, how Eustacia will rebel against the earth that birthed her. Eustacia's revolt after all, is partly against herself, against the constraints that have been enculturated inside her by other people. It is the same with Tess, and Jude – and Ursula, and Connie in Lawrence. How they *yearn*, and how their stories touch us, deeply – really deeply.

Nine

Love

Poets understand love as the union of complementary souls, an ecstatic event which sets the world on fire and allows them to transcend the loveless limits of time, space and circumstance.

Robert Graves [60]

---

[60] Foreword to *Poems About Love*, Cassell 1969, p. 5.

Thomas Hardy's characters yearn so painfully – Eustacia cries out for a great love to help her escape. 'To be loved to madness – such was her great desire.' (*Return*, p. 121) Love – the great yearning – proves to be her downfall. She dies for love, like Cathy in *Wuthering Heights*. Hardy's women yearn, but rarely do they get an earthlover like Heathcliffe. Intense love means intense death. Love now but die later – this is the Romantic credo. The love between Clym and his mother (a precursor of that depicted in Lawrence's *Sons and Lovers*) is equally intense, and destructive. It reaches a profundity of painfulness (*Return*, p. 247).

Tess lives, for a season, in 'spiritual altitudes' which are ecstatic (Tess, p. 257). Her tragedy is also Eustacia's and Marty's, and Ursula's – her yearning for love is not reciprocated. Love is not returned, passion burns itself away and is thrust out from the soul into the darkness of the universe. The self is ultimately alone – the modernist post-Romantic stance. This aloneness is confirmed by the fiction of White, Golding, Ballard, Beckett, Auster and Carver, among others.

The narrator (and Phillotson) see Sue and Jude as two halves of one whole – a Gnostic love-union of selves (the *syzygy* [*Jude*, pp. 293-5, 361]). In fact, their togetherness is very shaky. The dialectic of their love is continually shifting – from desire to disgust, and all the shades in between. There is no easy, simple dualism for Hardy. Sue and Jude drift apart and come back together in waves. They fuse then fragment, like particles in some subatomic experiment. It is a bout of Empodeclean Love and Strife for them, a state of Heraclitean flux, a Hegelian neurotic tension, shot through with the world-weary detachment of Schopenhauer. In Sue and Jude the big themes – the pagan and the Christian, the traditional and the modern, the spiritual and the sexual – are at war. And they embody them so well, and this is Hardy's great success.

Sue and Jude are the last in a long line of dissatisfied Hardyan yearners. But Ursula, in *The Rainbow*, is the biggest yearner for love of them all. Ursula out-yearns everybody. 'I want to go!' she yells, but no one and no thing is big and deep and wide and rich enough for her. For Ursula, ecstasy is very bitter. But the rainbow is slowly forming inside her soul. She yearns for a deep connection, for a pure and authentic *relation* with Something. It is *inside her*, she realizes, as do Powys's characters.

Hardy and Lawrence depict love-in-flux, always being modulated, changed, destroyed, rebuilt, transfigured. Sue and Jude fly together involuntarily – in their kiss on the silent road, when they 'kissed close and long' (*Jude*, p. 278). But soon they fall apart again. It is the same story with Ursula and Anton, Ursula and Birkin, Paul and Miriam, Wolf and Christie, Perdita and Skald. The pattern was laid down long ago in figures of myth such as Isis and Osiris, Ishtar and Tammuz, Anna and Baal, and in the later figures such as Anthony and Cleopatra, Heloise and Abelard and Petrarch and Laura. Both Hardy and Powys are heretical about love. They do not believe in marriage. Their ideas on love have much in common with the mediæval cults and heresies of courtly love, the Cathars, Templars, Sufism, Albigensian heresy, alchemy and the cults of the Grail and the Black Virgin. Though it is not as strident as in Durrell and Lawrence, there is in Hardy and Powys the urge towards spiritual sublimation, the transcendence of the flesh and the mysticization of the erotic.

John Cowper Powys's concept of love and sexuality is unusual. In some ways it is the typically masculine, misogynist, self-centred and unemotional love of Western literature. But he also has some odd ideas on love. In Powys it is more common for two lovers' psychic *aura* or *eidola* or astral essences to touch, rather than their genitals. Spiritual ravishment is the order of the day – Wolf and Christie, Dud and Thuella, Larry and Perdita. In his book *In Defence of Sensuality* Powys talks of super-human love:

> For the love of two really lonely human creatures is like an encounter between life and death, between Being and Not-Being, between day and night. (Def, p. 141)

Love is the meeting of day and night – a typical poetic image, but Powys really means it. He means the lovers *are* day and night. The elemental, not the metaphorical, for John Cowper Powys. Two loves create a third love, the power of love which then affects the lovers. A third party is created, as in Hegelian dialectics. Usually this is the love-child, though it is not necessarily made of flesh and blood. The third agent can be made of spirit, like the fairy changeling. Spirit is enough for the ætherealizing lover. Graves too has a theory concerning the third element in a love-affair. But Powys brings in Sir Thomas Browne and his concept of the *quincunx*. The two selfs and the two not-selfs add together, with the mystic third element, to create a five-fold vision of love, the *quincunx* (Def, p. 141). Thomas Browne's *quincunx* was later taken up by Durrell in his *Avignon Quintet*, who used its as the ground-plan for his complex architectural–literary edifice. Lawrence spoke of love as the meeting two five-pointed stars – a marvellous image of balance and occultism.

Love for Powys is a miracle (Def, p. 143). Love can occur between people in different places – for love compresses space and time (Def, p. 144). These ideas are very ancient. Graves was a great believer in this kind of miraculous love. Here love becomes mystical, spiritual, occult, supernatural, more-than-natural.

Love in Hardy and Powys is about two people trying to 'follow their bliss' (Campbell's term). When you follow your bliss 'you come to bliss.' (*The Power of Myth*, p. 118). You have to follow the 'pollen path' of the Navaho Indians, as Campbell here defines it:

> The Navaho have that wonderful image of what they call the pollen path. Pollen is the life source. The pollen path is the path to the centre. The Navaho say, 'Oh, beauty before me, beauty behind me, beauty to the right of me, beauty to the left of me, beauty above me, beauty below me, I'm on the pollen path' (Power, p. 230)

This is the journey – towards the centre, the life source. Paradise, the Golden Age, Eden, was not back there then, but it is *now*. 'Eden is…this is it, this is Eden.' (Campbell, ib.) Powys is as mystical as this. In *A Philosophy of Solitude* he wrote: 'Simplify your desire till you enjoy with sacramental ecstasy every single physical sensation you have.' (Sol, p. 185) In *A Glastonbury Romance*, life flows out of the Grail. And this ecstasy of being alive must intermingle in a Rabelaisian fashion 'the excremental with the sacramental' (GR, Preface, p. xvi) In Hardy the urge of the lovers is to escape, to find, like Sue and Jude, Angel and Tess, their own niche in the world, away from other, interfering people. Hardy put it utterly plainly and so passionately in his poem 'The Recalcitrants':

> Let us off and search, and find a place,
> Where yours and mine can be natural lives,
> Where no one comes, who dissects and dives
> And proclaims that ours is a curious case,
> Which its touch of romance can scarcely grace.
> (*Complete Poems*, p. 389)

This is the great dream of lovers – to re-create the world and to find a place in which to really live and breathe. Nin described this yearning for a sacred space away from the crowds in her book *Cities of the Interior*:

> And at times this absolute which Rango demanded, this peeling away of all externals to carve a single figure of man and woman joined together, appeared to her as a desirable thing, perhaps as a final, irrevocable end to all the fevers and restlessness of love, as a finite union. Perhaps a perfect union existed for lovers willing to destroy the world around them.[61]

The problem is that society and all kinds of other factors subvert this lust for loneliness. 'Love is the burning-point of life' says Joseph Campbell (Power, p. 205) and the tragedy of Hardy, as Lawrence notes, is that the pioneers in love die in the wilderness (Study, p. 21). Escape, but die. Remain, and live. The Kierkegaardian risk-taking is everything. Without risk there is no life. Life is lived on the edge. Powys's characters, like those of Hardy and Lawrence and Gide and Miller and Dostoievsky and Brontë, live on the edge. They are artists of desperation.

This risk-taking for the glory of love is the main theme in Thomas Hardy. The way he deals with it makes him great – as with Dostoievsky or Shakespeare or Sappho. 'His feeling, his instinct, his sensuous understanding is, however, apart from his metaphysic, very great and deep, deeper than that perhaps of any other English novelist,' as Lawrence wrote of Hardy (Study, p. 93)

Sex in John Cowper Powys's fiction is a strange, nervy, obsessive, ambivalent, voyeuristic phenomena. Many of his characters are voyeurs, like Hardy's, but Powys concentrates on sadism, homosexuality, sex-magic and other kinds of eroticisms. A deep and nervous yearning is the source of his characters' sexuality. Powys delineates a network of

---

[61] *Cities of the Interior*, Peter Owen, 1978, p. 273.

disconnection, of dissatisfaction, disillusion and dissolution. Love in Powys combines desire with visceral loathing. But above all he exalts solitude.

Women-hating does occur in his novels – in the depictions of Christie, Mary, Cordelia, Curly and Wizzie, for example. Powys thinks of sexuality in a similar way to Joyce, Lawrence and Mailer. The bedroom scene at the Malakites' in *Wolf Solent* is particularly painful. 'She will let me undress her' thinks Wolf, leering, sinking deeper into autism (WS, p. 458). The sex act itself is a rare occurrence in Powys – it is even rarer in Hardy. Powys instead ætherealizes sexuality. It becomes a power-source for other discourses, often of a neurotic, magical or psychic kind. Sex in Powys is potentially a source of mythic revitalization.

His most memorable love-scenes are those in which no physical contact takes place with Larry and Peridta (Wey, p. 168ff), or with Thuella and Dud by the 'scummy pond':

> the absence of actual contact between them evoked, in place of any twinge of tantilization, an intensity of imaginative lust that was transporting. Thuella seemed to know to a point of exquisite clairvoyance how to play on the psychic nerve of his [Dud's] cerebral desire... (MC, p. 200)

John Cowper Powys is vague. He eschews detailed descriptions of love-making. He does not know quite what he is trying to do. John Crow makes love in a vicious way (GR, pp. 387-8) but Powys is vague about it. Dud's love-making is sterile. For Wizzie it must be un emotional, male-centred, non-orgasmic and very unsatisfactory. The orgasm in Powys is given over to psychic lust, or to sublime evil, not to the sexuality of the body.

John Cowper Powys tries to reach that realm of transcendent sexuality of D.H. Lawrence. Lawrence was so much better at describing intense sexual acts: 'And he touched her with the poignancy of wonder, and the marvellous, piercing transcendence of desire.'[62] Like Lawrence, Powys intensifies the erotic until it becomes magical, until it moves into other dimensions. Both writers allude to anal sex (as do Joyce and Mailer and contemporaries such as Amis and Diski). In Powys the anal is an essential

---

62 *The Escaped Cock*, in *Complete Short Novels*, 596.

part of the mystical. The Grail-ecstasy pierces Sam anally. In Powys, the anal realm must be activated in the drive towards elemental and sensual wholeness. In Lawrence anal sexuality is bound up with taboo, guilt, purgation and release. In Powys the anal is religious.

The Powys-character has to face something deeper than love – solitude. Porius has to come to terms with his 'crazy loneliness' (P, 681) while Morfydd realizes her identification with the world and with Nature (P, p. 619). She is like Tess, Bathsheba and Sue in this. When Wizzie hears Dud speaking of the 'ecstasy of life' she laughs and thinks: 'I wouldn't be a man for anything...*They* talk; but *I* feel' (MC, p. 327). Powys's insights into women have been far surpassed by Lawrence, Zola, Flaubert, Shakespeare and Hardy, while these 'greats' have themselves been surpassed by Woolf, Nin, Griffin, Rich, West, Stein.

Women writers know that 'There is no way to love without being changed.'[63] Wolf, Dud, Magnus and John – the four Powys-men in the Wessex novels – have not deeply changed after their experiences. Dud is still sterile, Magnus still ineffectual, John still impervious to others, and Wolf still egocentric.,

Women-hating is there in Powys, but it is diffuse, or odd. His misogynism is not as strident as Miller's or Mailer's. Powys feared menstruation (A, p. 191), and admitted to being a voyeur and a sadist.[64] Like Graves, Powys exalted women as Goddesses (ib, p. 103). He could be courtly – as when Wolf walks out with Gerda. This courtship is straight out of Hardy. Gerda is compared, as women were in Hardy, with various Goddesses (Daphne, Artemis, Helen and Leda).

Thomas Hardy, too, is full of supernatural sensibilities. He conversed many times with his dead wife, Emma: 'Would that I lay there/ And she were housed here!/ Or better, together/ Were folded away there/ Exposed to one weather/ We both...' ('Rain on a Grave', CP, p. 341). Hardy yearns to be united with his decayed lovers, in the Brontëan manner: 'The eternal tie which binds us twain in one/ No eye will see/ Stretching across the miles that sever you from me.' (CP, p. 321)

This is wholly Romantic, this yearning for absolute togetherness-in-

---

[63] Susan Griffin, *Viyella*, in Laura Chester, ed. *Deep Down: New Sensual Writing by Women*, Faber 1988, p. 138.
[64] *Letters to G. Wilson Knight*, pp. 61-68.

death. Robert Graves wrote:

> Having at last perfected
> Utter togetherness
> We meet nightly in dream[65]

The romantic idea of lovers meeting over distances, or at night, in dreams, or after death, extends the Western notion of the soul to its logical extreme. In Powys we find similar kinds of rarefied sex-magic. Powys's sexual rites have something in common with Tantrism – in which the body is 'made cosmic' and the initiates gradually feminize themselves – awake the Eternal Feminine (the Goddess) in themselves.

John Cowper Powys speaks of awakening the Feminine in himself. In his *Autobiography* he wrote of being thrilled by a 'fleeting, floating, fluttering fantasy of femininity, a kind of Platonic essence of sylph-hood' (A, p. 205). These objects of 'sensual lust' are the Powysian sylph-like boy-girls. Love in Powys is Platonic – a merging of essences. He does not advocate that people actually touch each other, not skin-on-skin, God forbid! Powys's idea of love-making is detached, Platonic, impersonal and there is also some disgust for the body, for deep, sensual love-making. There is a disgust for full-blown sexuality in Hardy too. Think of his characters Sue, Angel, Grace or Bathsheba, or Powys's Christie, Wolf, Dekker, Persephone, Marrett, Dud or Thuella.

Like Wordsworth, John Cowper Powys merges his elemental sensualism and his impersonal lust for sylphid boy-girls. This passage from the *Autobiography* (p. 275) illustrates this position clearly:

> When I write my essay about my great master Wordsworth, I shall show how his cerebral mystical passion for young women is intimately bound up with his abnormally sensual sensitiveness to the elements. He wanted his girl to be an Elemental. And in his poetry – where people betray their deepest souls – he loved, above all, to imagine himself a girl. I myself idolize the particular type of girl I call a slyph to such a tune that I want to destroy everything that is not sylphood. But I still want to make love to what attracts me!

So in Powys love-making heightens nature-perception, and vice-versa.

---

[65] *Collected Poems*, Cassell 1975, p. 465.

Sex and nature are bound up together in Powys's conception, for when he talks about Wordsworth he also talks about himself. There is a similar ambivalence about sexuality in Lawrence, Gide, Proust and Joyce. The homoerotic undercurrents are dealt with in a hesitant, equivocal manner. Powys works through the five senses – he is synthæsthetic, like Rimbaud and Keats and Rilke. Rilke speaks of the five senses melding with 'that supernatural plane which is precisely the plane of poetry.'[66] This occult apperception is a merging of sensation and memory – it is not a question of technique, as Proust says, but 'of vision' (ib., p. 79). Powys agrees with Schopenhauer that 'the task of the novelist is not to narrate great events but to make small ones interesting.' (ib, p. 92)

Ambivalence, androgyny, sylphood, elemental rapture – the key notes of John Cowper Powys's concept of love-making. How strange is the sudden, fierce love-making between Porius and the giantess (P, p. 518) after which her skull is smashed in by her enraged father. Certainly that sex-scene is one of the most bizarre in all of Powys.

The best love-scene in Powys is in *A Glastonbury Romance* – the chapter 'Consummation'. Knight calls it the finest insight into a woman's sexual experience in literature.[67] Other writers, such as Andrea Dworkin, Mary Daly, Susan Griffin, Anais Nin, Virginia Woolf and Adrienne Rich would not agree with this judgement at all.

It is, though, a great piece of prose. Nell dutifully does the housework and prepares the love-room while Sam wanders up the river in an erotic trance. Powys describes in detail Nell's thoughts and acts. Sam, meanwhile, is 'roused to the magic of sex' (GR, p. 305). He has reveries – dreams of being a wave, a crystal, a plant and a fish (p. 307). He comes back and they make love. The gates of ecstasy are opened wide (p. 310). Powys is none too subtle with his similies and metaphors here. The ecstasy comes like this:

> They took such spacious draughts of it [ecstasy]; they plunged into it so desperately, so utterly, that in the mingling of their identities there seemed no portion of either of them – body, soul or spirit – left over, that was not merged and not in the other. (p. 311).

---

[66] *The Creative Vision*, ed Block, p. 50.
[67] G. Knight, Sat, p. 37.

So John Cowper Powys allows one great orgasm to overwhelm his lovers – a rare thing indeed. This may be the best Powys can do, but D.H. Lawrence does so much better:

> Darkness cleaving to darkness, she hung close to him, pressed herself into the soft flow of his kiss, pressed herself down, down to the source and core of his kiss, herself covered and enveloped in the warm, fecund flow of his kiss, that travelled over her, flowed over her, covered her, flowed over the last fibre of her, so they were one stream, one dark fecundity, and she clung at the core of him, with her lips holding open the very bottomless source of him. (*The Rainbow*, p. 497)

But Anais Nin, in her journals, does it even better than Lawrence:

> I want to dance. I want drugs. I want to know perverse people, to be intimate with them. I never look at naive faces. I want to bite into life, and to be torn by it. Henry does not give me all this. I have aroused his love. Curse his love. He can fuck me as no one else can, but I want more than that. I'm going to hell, to hell, to hell. Wild, wild, wild.[68]

Another fleshly union in Powys's fiction is when Zoyland and Persephone make love in the boat near Whitelake cottage. Here sex and nature merge – the sounds of the river, the smell of mud, a falling star, the movement of the boat, and the 'sudden rising of a great, broad-winged heron' during Zoyland's orgasm – 'all these things gave to the bastard's sensuality that sort of romantic elemental margin, which was the thing of all things that he relished most in the world.' (GR, p. 833) Here the sex-act becomes an elemental ecstasy, in which the orgasm is extended beyond the body to include all of nature. Powys here is searching for new forms of expression, for new ways of describing the raptures of sexuality. Like Lawrence, Powys is always looking to extend sexuality beyond the personal level, to make it mythical, elemental, hypersensual or religious. Paul Eluard wrote:

> La vie sans cesse a recherche d'un nouvel amour, par effacer l'amour ancien, l'amour dangereux, la vie voulait chainger d'amour. [Life unceasingly searching for a new love, to obliterate the old love, the

---

68 *Henry and June*, W.H.Allen 1987, p. 179.

dangerous love, life wanted to change love.']⁶⁹

This is the search of Lawrence in *The Rainbow*, of Hardy in *Jude the Obscure* and of Anais Nin in her *Cities of the Interior*. The aim is to make writing like love -- to write and love, to make the act of writing love itself, to make desire concrete in art, the two fusing, love and art, into one life, so that, as Eluard says: 'speaking/ May be as generous as kissing' (ib, p. 39). The aim is to fuse life and love and art. As Hardy wrote in his poetry: 'Love lures life on.' ('Lines', in CP, p. 458).

Love in Thomas Hardy is Keatsian. In Powys it is Shelleyan. Hardy is fleshly, sensuous but also doomed. His love-affairs take much of their flavour from 'La Belle Dame Sans Merci'. Elfride, in her vanity, asks Stephen from her pony: "Do I seem like La belle dame sans merci?" (*A Pair of Blue Eyes*, p. 57). The reference probably suggested itself to Hardy as he constructed this scene. The fairy queen/ knightly lover motifs feature also in the romances of Bathsheba and Oak, Sue and Jude, Eustacia and Clym.

The dark sensualism of Keats is well suited to Hardy, as it is to Graves. Hardy is a slave to love, as a poet, as he is a slave to women, to Woman, as is Skelton, Donne and Herrick. Hardy's women are Muses who throw down enchantments over the initiate's soul and senses. Hardy's beloveds are the Symbolist and Decadent Fatal Women, the pale wraiths eulogized by poets such as Baudelaire, Swinburne and Coleridge, and by Moreau and Rops in painting. Graves has his Laura Riding, as Hardy has his Emma Gifford. The poetry records a haunting of the poet-alone by the Elf-Queen. The antecedents of this scenario are many – the classic one in English literature being of course Shakespeare and his formidable Dark Lady, she 'Who art as black as hell, as dark as night.' (last line of sonnet no. 147)

Another ancestor is Merlin's enthrallment at the hands of Ninue – a set-up that intrigued John Cowper Powys greatly. In Keats and Shelley and the Elizabethan poets we find the powerful spirit of Arthuriana, embodied in those figures such as the Lady of Shalott or Morgana Le Fey, before they became trivialized in Tennyson, late Victorian poetry and Pre-

---

69 From *Uninterrupted Poetry*, New Directions, New York 1975, pp. 22-23.

Raphaelitism. These romantic ideas surged throughout Europe in the late 12th century and afterwards with the troubadours. But England was late in accepting Arthurian legend. The new concepts and *mœurs* of love and individualism took hold in the Elizabethans. In Campion's exaltation of the 'fairy queen Prosperina' (in Hiller, ed, p. 117) for instance. Nothing new about these sorcerous Madonnas, however. Giraut de Borneil, Arnaut Daniel, Bernard de Ventadour and the other troubadours, *jongleurs* and minstrels had all done it before, and so well, too. Shakespeare is the apotheosis in English literature of this kind of love-poetry. Romanticism is the end of it all – though a wild, chaotic and intense kind of end. Hardy arrives at the very tail-end of this extended demise. What raises up his love-poetry is the authenticity of his experience and poetic voice, as with Graves, who was perhaps the last great love-poet in the Western romantic tradition.

Hardy is not as violent, nor as high-flown, as the Elizabethans. Nicholas Breton wrote: 'to kill love's maladies,/ Meet her with your melodies'.[70] This is the answer – when stabbed to death by love, re-birth yourself in art, in love-poetry. Or as Keats would have it:

...if thy mistress some rich anger shows
Emprison her soft hand, and let her rave,
And feed deep, deep upon her peerless eyes[71]

Thomas Hardy is not as assertive as Keats or Shakespeare, though there is still the same masochistic misogyny in some of his poetry. Hardy though, like Shakespeare, wants to be slain by his beloved. 'Kill me outright with looks', implores the Shakespearean poet, while Jude, at the terrible climax of his romance with Sue, also implores his black Mistress:

'Don't go – don't go!...This is my last time! I...shall never come again. Don't then be unmerciful, Sue, Sue ! we are acting by the letter, and the letter killeth!' (*Jude*, p. 468)

The letter, the vicious law of a dying religion, Christianity, certainly does kill. So the poet begs for *merci*, that key blessing in Renaissance and

---
[70] From *The Passionate Shepherd*, in G. Hiller, ed, p. 244.
[71] J. Keats, 'Ode to Melancholy', *Poems*, Oxford 1909, p. 141.

chivalric love-poetry. But the poet knows it is useless – it is all over, just as Tess cries, but hopelessly 'Have Mercy!' (p. 298) A similar pleading for *merci* from the Goddess occurs in the Wolf – Christie affair. The romances of Wolf – Christie and Jude – Sue have a Shelleyan subtext to them. They are built upon an ætherealizing orientation of spirit-over-sex. Shelley's poem 'When Passion's Trance is Overpast' forms the philosophical basis of Hardy's and Powys's romances:

> If it were enough to feel, to see
> Thy soft eyes gazing tenderly,
> And dream the rest – and burn and be
> The secret food of fires unseen,
> Could thou but be what thou hast been.[72]

Love without touching, sex through spirituality, a deeply sensuous love-act transcending skin and ordinary sense – this is a common ambition in both Hardy and Powys. Think of all those poems of Hardy's, in which the poet meets some beloved by night, but they do not touch or kiss, just talk. Hardy aims to spiritualize love, but in a heterodox, not doctrinal, manner. *Jude the Obscure* records the failure of this sacralization of love, its near-impossible fusion with everyday domestic and economic life. Hardy's holy love, like Shelley's, needs a sacred, secret place away from other people, in which to flourish. But there's none left. No places left, so you have to create your own – and how difficult that is! Hardy's lovers aim to do this: 'Let us off and search, and find a place' Hardy wrote in 'The Recalcitrants'. But they fail. Robert Herrick wrote the same pæan: 'Come, let us go while we are in our prime' (in 'Corrinna's Going-a-Maying'). It is an anti-social ambition, an escapism in love almost wholly unrealizable.

Hardy is very bitter about this secular failure to recapture an earlier hermetic love-time. In his poem 'She to Him i' he wrote: 'That Sportsman Time but rears his brood to kill' (CP, p. 15). This is the bleak view of Tess, who wishes she'd never been born into this cynical game of the gods. Hardy tries to look honestly and clearly at life – to go after the 'offensive truth' (Per, p. 26). His pessimism is really 'evolutionary meliorism' (ib, p.

---

[72] P. Shelley, *Selected Poems*, Dent 1983, p. 163.

52). As he says in the poem 'In Tenebris': 'if a Better way there, it exacts a full look at the Worst' (CP, p. 168). Hardy depicts people full of 'fret and fever' (Per, p. 32), the idea being 'given the man and woman, how to find a basis for their sexual relation' (ib, p. 19). Hardy quotes his beloved Shakespeare in support of his claims: 'life [is] time's fool'.[73] The flipside being 'Love's not Time's fool' (Sonnet no. 116). The work of Shakespeare and Hardy is the result of the attempt to fuse these two viewpoints – the hopeless and the idealistic. Love's not time's fool, but life is – how typically of two harshly realist and determinist artists to be so ambivalent. They know love and life and art and time and death cannot be simply reconciled. In both Hardy and Shakespeare Time marches on, unstoppable, even though, sometimes, it 'must have a stop'. No. It eats everything away, demolishing all as it sweeps by. Love in Hardy ends up as a drowned body in a heathland river, or a hanged woman in Winchester, or a derelict dying in Oxford, or a corpse in a Dorset wood.

How desolate is Thomas Hardy's view of the outcome of love! He is an optimist blasted by life's shocks into bitter realism. His works record satires of circumstance, life's little ironies and time's laughingstocks, those human shows with their few moments of vision, offensive truths hidden amongst post-pastoral Wessex tales.

How forlorn Hardy actually is can be adjudged from the endings to his tragic novels, and throughout his poetry. Tragedies must end in death, it seems, but how *awful* and ludicrous is Viviette's collapse at the end of *Two on a Tower*. There is much doom and gloom in the poetry. It is there in the early poems – in 'Neutral Tones', for example. Hardy's imagery in this short lyric is bleak, while the poem's sparseness looks forward to Beckett: the white sun, dead pond, barren earth (these are stage-settings for *Waiting For Godot* or *Happy Days*). Hardy rages here, too, though in a quiet way – the poet learns that 'love deceives' and thus the sun, the innocent, utterly non-human sun, becomes 'God-curst' (CP, p. 12). This is typical of the love-poem in the West: the jilted lover must have the outside world reflect his/ her desolation.

The futile scene in 'Neutral Tones' is picked up in Hardy's last novel – it forms the opening of *Jude*. Jude, the 'natural boy', works in the 'wide and

---

[73] Per, p. 47, quoting *King Henry IV* (i), V, iv, 81.

lonely depression of the empty field' (p. 52). The depth of Hardy's rage is clear from the way he develops this scene – Jude soon gets beaten up by Farmer Troughton, and whirled around like a toy. The target of Hardy's anger is made explicit – it is not God, nor the birds nor nature, but the *human* world in which Jude lives (p. 55).

How bitterly ironic Thomas Hardy was to use Shelley as one of the major discourses in *Jude the Obscure*. For Powys, Shelley was a 'most exquisite poet', full of poignant sweetness and an 'ethereal transparency of passion', someone who goes over the edge, taking us into another dimension.[74] Hardy counters his grim realism with a Shelleyan aching for sweetness and release. It is this quivering yearning that powers Eustacia, Tess, Sue and Jude, and also Pierston in his Platonic search for a Shelleyan 'Beloved'. Eustacia, Tess and Sue are Shelleyan heroines, yearning for a delicacy of touch and spirit that the workaday world simply cannot provide. The gulfs between the two form the tension at the heart of the Hardy novel (Life, p. 272). These conflicts force the Hardyan anti-hero to cry, with Shelley: 'O World, o Life, of Time'.

Hardy is ultimately an optimist. He does weave in an escape-clause at the end of his novels, most prophetically in the figures of Angel and Tess's sister, as a New Adam and Eve. And in 'The Darkling Thrush', with its heartfelt synthesis of Keats, Shelley and Wordsworth, Hardy rejoices that out of the waste land a bird can still sing, and that 'there trembled through/ His happy good-night air/ Some blessed Hope' (CP, p. 150).

---

[74] *Visions and Revisions*, pp.xvii, 129, 132, 135.

Ten

The Oedipal Rebellion

But nowhere is absolute power over other human beings more unquestioned than in parents. And parents, oddly, are no better than the ordinary run of people.

Weston La Barre, *The Ghost Dance* (126)

The fiction of Hardy and Powys is full of an ambiguity regarding parents. œdipal ambiguity plays a large part in the relationships between, for instance, Tess and her drunken father and pushy mother (who are compared ironically with Angel's pious parents); Sam's puritanical father has a strained relationship with his son; Tess is a mother to her brothers and sisters (and to her dead child); Eustacia has an old seadog for a father; Grace has a domineering father and step-mother; Marty, however, has Grammer Oliver; then there is Clym and his possessive mother, a forerunner of Lawrence in *Sons and Lovers* and also of Wolf and his dominating mother; Jude is an outcast, an orphan, trying to make peace with the curse of his ancestors and with the patriarchal ghosts in his society, symbolized by Oxford; Dud has a dead father and dead wife; Wolf too has a dead father with whom he communes; Geard is surrounded by Goddess-like feminine figures; there are the similarly matriarchal 'Aunties' in *Porius*; Wizzie's 'father' and lover is Funky, while they have a child; Thuella is very ambivalent about her father; Gypsy May is a strange surrogate mother to the urchin-orphan Larry Zed; then there is the incestuous set-up of Malakite, Christie and Olwen; and the confused hereditary of Henchard, Susan and Elizabeth-Jane in *The Mayor of Casterbridge*.

Certainly Hardy's and John Cowper Powys's attitude to œdipal issues is intensely ambivalent. The examples above illustrate how strange are the configurations of familial relations in both these Wessex writers. It is rare to find in either Powys or Hardy an ordinary familiar scenario. Psychologically, the parents are inside the individual – in art they are extensions of the self, the parents are expressed outwards, into the artwork. Much of Hardy's and Powys's fiction deals with the parents, with their influence and legacy. Powys's people are usually older than Hardy's (Wolf, Dud, Magnus). Hardy's characters are young(ish), just out of teenage and in their early twenties (Tess, Jude, Eustacia, Grace). Bathsheba, after all she has been through with her three lovers and one murder, is only twenty three at the end of the tale. Hardy's figures have to make the leap from youth to adulthood, from innocence to total self-responsibility (this is how Lawrence describes Ursula's task in *The Rainbow*). Hardy records his characters' failure or success in achieving this self-responsibility and socialization. He describes their journey, their struggle in overcoming various obstacles, their torturous passage across many thresholds. It is a journey of rebellion and crises – in the stories of Eustacia, Jude, Swithin – and also pain, anguish, despair of all kinds. The characters in Hardy and Powys embark on a quest for the father, just as the hero does in classic mythologies, and in fairy tales (such as *Jack and the Beanstalk* for example).

Hardy's people are on a vision quest for adulthood. Hardy records rites of passage, a process of maturing and letting go of now-useless values and habits. Weston La Barre writes in *Muelos* that

> the critical individual, commonly in adolescence [must be] able to tear away the mildewed holy veil of œdipal symbols – and to substitute his own, if he needs to flee the anguish of remembered childhood realities. (p. 132)

Jude, Sue, Eustacia, Angel, Clym, Giles – they all fail to do this. They fail to clear away the old values and symbols of their parents and the constraints that society puts upon them. Here Hardy is a great novelist, teasing out so well the materialistic, social, political, religious and personal pressures that act upon the individual. His characters are young because they are bursting into life, into the world. They are at an age when everything in their life is changing. Choices have to made, values destroyed, habits broken and new challenges faced. Ursula bursts into the world and envisions a rainbow. For Hardy's characters the way forward is unclear. Hardy is unsure, hesitant. He clouds his emotions with many doubts. His people are still bound to values which are not truly their own. *Jude the Obscure* and *The Rainbow* are the great novels of this anguished rebellion. It costs the protagonists a lot: both Jude and Ursula pay a high price. Wolf is willing to renounce his past, partner and old world, but loses his 'mythology' too. In *A Glastonbury Romance* there is the powerful sequence of Sam's renunciation of Nell and earthy love. He goes instead for Christ and the Holy Grail, the religion of his father. The patriarchal ghosts win here. Powys's gift in the Nell—Sam—Dekker—Grail battle is to show Sam's Pauline renunciation as a success, not, as it would be in Hardy, a failure to face up to immediate duties. Powys has a deep sympathy with an unorthodox, individualized and mystical kind of Christianity, like Lawrence. Powys (and Lawrence) are more optimistic than Hardy. For Powys posits a real 'Afterwards', while for Hardy's characters 'Afterwards' is full of problems. Hardy's 'Afterwards' is an uneasy mix – even in the relatively 'happy ending' of *Under the Greenwood Tree*. When Hardy allows for an afterlife, as at the end of *Tess of the d'Urbervilles* or *The Mayor of Casterbridge*, he makes sure it will be a tough time for all concerned. Even in the tacked-on ending of *Return* things will not be easy. Hardy is equivocal, ambiguous. There is no easy answer, he says, to complex problems.

John Cowper Powys presents the œdipal problem in a very idiosyncratic and elemental fashion. Wolf relates to his father's *actual skull*, his actual dry bones, not his spirit (WS, p. 30). Their relationship is strange indeed, and largely one-sided. Wolf controls his father's influence, but he cannot control his overbearing mother. In *Wolf Solent* there is a strong undercurrent of incest – not only in the Malakite story, but also in that bizarre heated-up embrace of Wolf and Mrs Solent on the sofa. Much of *Wolf Solent* consists of the Powys-man's relation with his mother. It forms one of the major relations in the book, as also in *Sons and Lovers*. Wolf, like Paul, grapples with the Mother-figure, the All-Powerful Great Earth-Mother-Goddess. Wolf tries to escape. Magnus and Dud No-Man both grapple with their parents. Dud's relation with his wife is very Hardyan. The feeling of all those poems Hardy wrote about Emma (how obsessed he was with her after her death) re-surface in Powys's Dorchester Romance. How many times must Hardy have returned in spirit more than in the flesh to Cornwall and to her graveside. 'Woman much missed, how you call to me' ('The Voice', CP, p. 346). The *Poems of 1912–13* are fuelled by an intense, agonized melancholy. But it continues to Hardy's death. Hardy haunts gravesides as other people haunt pubs and town squares. Dud and Wolf go on Hardyan pilgrimages to graves at the beginning of their books. They want to visit the final resting-place of the lost loved ones. The pilgrimage depicted in Powys's Wessex quartet is spiritually a downward spiral towards the Past, the parents, the homeland and the deeper self.

Thomas Hardy uses space and season to suggest his mnemonic agonies

– such as in the brutally simple 'Where the Picnic Was'. The summery spot by the sea has now become cold and lonely. The place where the hot fire was is now chilly and charred. One wonders how Hardy can get away with such simplistic poetry. This is antiquated imagery – the Petrarchan conceit beaten to death by bad lyricism. It is the poetry a ten-year-old might write on a dud day – derivative, imitative, regurgitative. There is no subtlety here. This is also Hardy's strength, of course, this brutal honesty and simplicity. Here was love, he says, and now it's dead. You can overdo this, though, You get tired of this emotion and format. How long can one go on dredging up the same buried corpses from the lake? Hardy is morbid, not because his subject is death and the death of love, but because he goes over the same ground again and again with mind-numbing regularity. He is like a child who keeps prodding the fire to see if it is hot, who keeps getting burnt, but keeps going back for more. Or like a dog scrabbling away at the same piece of ground. Or, more sinisterly, like a psychotic murderer who haunts the grave of his victim. This comparison is vicious, but there's a lot of truth in it. Hardy's poetic subject is the Death of Love, so he simply keeps returning to Where Love Died, to the scene of the life-crime.

Hardy is like Petrarch in his incessant obsession with the Death of His Beloved. For Petrarch too had counted off the days since he had met Laura (April 6th, a magical date for him). Her death (on the same day, twenty-one years later) is also exalted in his poetry. Petrarch's *Rime Sparse*, like Shakespeare's *Sonnets*, is one of the great sequences of love-poetry in history. As with Shakespeare, Petrarch produced a highly stylized version of his love and agony, but, like Hardy, Graves, Donne, Eluard, Sappho and all true love-poets, he writes from his guts, from the direct experience of his heart-rending emotion. Petrarch is full of love-fever, hot desire, glory and self-chastizement. The metamorphosis is of love through memory. Thus he writes in sonnet no. 267:

> per voi conven ch'io arde a'n voi respiro,
> ch'i' pur fui vostro; et sedi voi son privo
> via men d'ogni sventura altra mi dole
> (For you I must burn, in you breathe, for I have been only yours, and if I

am deprived of you, it pains me more than any other misfortune.)[75]

Petrarch, like Hardy, writes: 'My lady is dead and has my heart with her' (ib., p. 436). Hardy's heart is buried with Emma's in Stinsford churchyard, both physically and spiritually. He lies in 'her haunting ground' now.

Many deaths in Hardy: he is tragic, and Victorian – melodramatic. Powys and Lawrence are not like this. People rarely die in their books. The father dies at the opening of *A Glastonbury Romance*, freeing up the plot in the classic fashion.

Death haunts the characters in Hardy. Death lies behind so many of his characters: Tess, Jude, Eustacia, Henchard, Giles, Viviette, Mrs Yeobright, Wildeve, Fanny, Troy – they all die – it's terrible! How melodramatic Hardy is, needing these dramatic conclusions so desperately. Here we see the problems of intertextuality – for Hardy was clearly pressurized into producing melodrama for the monthly magazines. The social and financial pressures on his art changed the nature of it. Here Hardy differs from Powys and Lawrence. The latter two novelists wrote full-length books pretty much as they wished. In *A Glastonbury Romance* Powys could spend a couple of hundred pages here or there writing about patches of moss upon sunlit walls, while Lawrence could burn up pages and pages with visionary polemic. Hardy, constrained by the demands of a magazine and a hungry Victorian audience, was compelled to write swift narratives, which could not dwell on one idea for too long. He moved in the upper-class and literary world of London, not Dorset. Bourgeoise notions and values infuse the works. He had to re-structure his original ideas, sometimes even changing the endings. This helped his writing, in some ways. He does not overwrite, for instance, as Powys does so often. Hardy is tighter than both Powys and Lawrence – tighter, indeed, than many novelists.

For John Cowper Powys and Lawrence, melodramatic death was not necessary. Lawrence was more concerned with re-birth (in *The Rainbow*, *The Escaped Cock* and *Lady Chatterley's Lover*). The short story 'The Horse-dealer's Daughter' takes place in a Hardyan world. It involves the

---

75 *Petrarch's Lyric Poems*, tr R. Durling, Harvard University Press, Mass., 1976, pp. 436-7.

rescue of a girl from a lake, and though it abounds in Lawrencean imagery of Nature and re-birthing, it comes straight out of middle-period Hardy.

What Thomas Hardy and a billion other artists are trying to grapple with is the extinction of the body, ego, soul, self, individual – whatever you want to call your self. La Barre writes: 'Death. No one can really contrive to believe in his own total extinction' (*The Ghost Dance*, p. 16). Bertrand Russell is similarly blunt. In his *Mysticism and Logic* he wrote that 'no fire, no heroism, no intensity of thought and feeling can preserve an individual life beyond the grave'.[76] Hardy confronts this issue. Darwin, Hume, Mill and Huxley lie behind his logical-scientific stance. Base matter, base realism. Emotions? Spirituality? Forget it. God will not save us either, Hardy claims. He searched for God for fifty years, but never found Him (Life, p. 234).

These rational, empirical concerns culminate historically in Einsteinian physics – most especially in the Second Law of Thermodynamics here tragi-comically summarized by J.L. Greenstein:

> (1) You can't win, (2) You can't even break even, (3) Things are going to get worse before they get any better, and (4) who says things are going to get better?[77]

Countering this deadening ratiocination is religion, poetry, art, architecture, ethics and other belief-systems. Hardy and Lawrence countered the patriarchal, scientific stance with their call for 'tenderness'. Powys called for sensual solitude, for more 'leaving people alone'. In *Tess of the d'Urbervilles* Hardy wrote: 'Tenderness was absolutely dominant in Clare at last' (p. 475)

Thomas Hardy's preoccupation with class and materialism plays a large part in his fiction. The families he depicts are falling apart. There are 'family curses', or hidden secrets – in *Tess*, *Jude* and *Mayor*. The Past modifies the present. The deeds of long-dead relatives conditions the acts of the living family. There are banes, murders, spells, incests and

---

[76] *Mysticism and Logic,* Norton, New York 1929, p. 47.
[77] *Scientific American*, 200 #1, January 1959, p. 46.

adulteries. Once-great families are now destitute ('how are the mighty fallen' is a key-line in *Tess*). Parents cannot control their children (how Jude disappoints his aunt, Tess her mother, Clym his mother, Grace her father, etc). Every generation makes its own mistakes. Children do not listen to their parents. Hardy's view of the family is severely jaundiced. Rarely does he show a family in action, as Lawrence does so extraordinarily well in *Sons and Lovers* and *The Rainbow*. There is no security for Hardy in the family, although he was much concerned, in a petty bourgeois way, with his family's decline in Dorset. There is nothing unusual about Hardy's ambivalence towards his origins and class – this kind of socio-economic unease is common among artists.

Children. Hardy was childless, as was Lawrence, while Powys thought his having a child was miraculous – he could not believe it had actually happened. Hardy's childlessness gives his fiction that strange, unsettled attitude towards offspring. The children are very hazily painted – there are Jude's children, some of them are not even named. Little Father Time is Hardy's most bizarre character, and the crucifixion/ hanging scene is Hardy's most extraordinary. Tess's child is vaguely treated. It is more common in Hardy for his young couples to break up before they can bear children. Marriage is not a fruitful time in Hardy: weddings are funerals. Children are out of the question. When they do come, they are soon slaughtered. Few of Hardy's lovers reach a child-rearing maturity. They are all young and immature. Even Sue and Jude who have a few children are still young, still immature in many ways. Lawrence too reveals his lack of knowledge of children as a part of a family. *The Rainbow* deals with pregnancy and child-rearing, but from a detached, strained point of view. Lawrence is brilliant at describing a family at home – in *Sons and Lovers* especially. But not as a parent. Powys's children are more colourful, but, like Lawrence's, they stem from an experience of brothers and sisters. In Hardy domesticity is death: it kills. Hardy has a impoverished view of children and the family. This is one of his weaknesses. His fiction lacks fullness in this area.

It is not easy being a child anywhere, but in Dorset children under six were working in the fields, according to a Royal Commission report.[78]

---

[78] In Wilhelm Hasbach: *History of the Agricultural Labourer*, 1908, p. 410.

Certainly Thomas Hardy was sympathetic to the plight of children, even if he writes as a kindly but distanced uncle-type. Some of his poems take the difficulties of being a child as their subject: 'To an Unborn Pauper Child', 'The Market-Girl', 'The Sheep-Boy', 'The Bird-Catcher's Boy' and in the angelic depiction of the lonely 'journeying boy' in 'Midnight on the Great Western' (CP, p. 516).

Eleven

The Transcendence of Work

I do not want to work. –You must,– comes the answer. But nobody wants to work, originally. –Yet everybody works, because he must, –it is repeated. And when he is not working? –Let him rest and amuse himself, and get ready for tomorrow morning…Work is, simply, the activity necessary for the production and sufficient supply of food and shelter: nothing more holy than that. It is the producing of the means of self-preservation. Therefore it is obvious that it is not the be-all and end-all of existence…We must eat to live. And living is not simply not-dying. It is the only real thing, it is the aim and end of all life. Work is only a means of subsistence. The work done, the living earned, how then to go on to enjoy it, to fulfil it, that is the question. How shall a man live? What do we mean by living? Let every man answer for himself: we only know we want the freedom to live, the freedom of leisure and means.

D.H. Lawrence, *Study of Thomas Hardy* (pp. 32-3, 38)

Thomas Hardy's characters work, unlike the characters of Powys's and other disaffected 20th century writers' novels. Hardy makes a distinction between a working class – Giles, Marty, Tess, Oak, Venn, Dick, Jude, Henchard – and a leisure-class, which does not usually work, which is bourgeois and often comes from outside the community – Alec, Fitzpiers, Troy, Boldwood, Mrs Charmond, Viviette, Sue. The typical Hardyan romance is between a working-class type and a bourgeois-type: Giles and Grace, Swithin and Viviette, Jude and Sue, Oak and Bathsheba. The love-matches of proletariat and bourgeoisie are often doomed in Hardy, while those between fellow working-class people are on the whole safe (Venn and Thomasin). The bourgeois couples are ill-fated – Eustacia and Wildeve, Eustacia and Clym, Bathsheba and Boldwood. Like must mix with like in Hardy.

Thomas Hardy's romances have an insistent materialistic undercurrent. This is most powerfully displayed in *Tess of the d'Urbervilles*. The Tess – Angel relationship embodies so well the clashes between the rural and the middle classes, between the values and *mœurs* of the country people and the bourgeoisie. Tess literally is the agricultural world – physically, culturally and spiritually. She is an Earth-Goddess, heavy with life, life-in-ascension. She is sensuous, pure, close to nature, accepting the rigours of existence, dealing with the present. Angel has a dry, distanced and impure kind of spirituality and religion. He is blind, and plays at farming. He does not see Tess fully, nor does he fully experience agriculture. His Christian religion sets up barriers – it is not as life-affirming as Tess's paganism. Hardy uses these two lovers to point out so many hypocrisies in society. In Tess and Angel he sets up the struggle between agriculture and industry, between paganism and Christianity, between a feminized culture of the land (of magic, Nature, growth, labour, season and community) and a patriarchal culture of the machine (Christianity, science, control, a city-life).

The life of the working-class people in Hardy is not 'better', or even preferred. Hardy is ambivalent about both classes (though he is bitter and resentful of upper class characters). He loves the traditional values and the way of life of the country folk, but also enjoys 'high culture'. He likes the debates in literature, philosophy and theology. He is critical of the working class. They are set in their ways, they are not 'progressive', they are often too easily manipulated. Angel and Alec exploit Tess, while Grace controls Giles. The working classes in Hardy are limited functionally – but they limit themselves, Hardy says: they blinker their world-view. The working class characters get on with things well enough, but so often they do not rise up to a challenge during a crisis. At the crisis, brought on by love, personality and circumstance, the lack of assertion in the peasant class encourages their downfall (in Tess and Giles particularly). They allow themselves to be used. They are victims partly because they see themselves as victims. *Once victim, always victim, that's the law* – this is Hardy at his most bitter. It is a profoundly depressing statement.

But Thomas Hardy is ambivalent about all this. Stay in the homeland, he says, and you'll suffer a life you don't value. Break out into the world beyond, and you'll die. There is no salvation in either course of action. There are no easy answers. Hardy told Graves that the only thing that poets could do was to keep on writing poems on the old themes. Hardy's people go on living in the old ways. Unlike Lawrence, Hardy could not really imagine a different sort of life for his characters. He cannot imagine a real future. Angel's sojourn in the wilderness of Brazil is hazily defined. In Lawrence this self-exile would be the main subject of a book (*Kangaroo, The Plumed Serpent*).

In the Angel–Tess romance Hardy is critical of all the things they represent. As with Sue and Jude, their affair is as much ideological and symbolic as it is emotional and sexual. In the clash of ideologies no one wins. Hardy wanted everything, all at once: the rural, pagan, ancient ways, where the weather rules and the inhabitants know each other well, where the rest of the world is kept at a reasonably safe distance. But Hardy also desired the big Outside, the Unknown, the cosmopolitan and the highbrow. He is fascinated, as only an amateur provincial bourgeois but resentful artist can be, by the ideas and environment of the city-based modern world. The modern world – as embodied in Fitzpiers, Farfrae, Knight, Sue, Angel and Alec – fascinates Hardy. He wants to know it, to be a part of it.

There are characters in his rural class who transcend their origins, who are what Lawrence called 'aristocratic' – Marty, Henchard, Tess. Marty in particular achieves a kind of transcendence through her stoically realist position. There is a certain kind of sacrality, Hardy says, in fighting onwards, in accepting, Buddhist fashion, all of life's little ironies and big shocks. Marty, at the end of *The Woodlanders*, reaches an apotheosis that is beyond love or spirituality or materialism. She gives up part of herself, in a supra-Christianity thrust of altruism, like Tess, Giles and Susan Henchard. These people transcend their origins, and themselves. The ontological apotheosis of Tess, Marty, Henchard and Oak is greater than that of Sue, Jude, Eustacia and Viviette. All of Hardy's protagonists are trying to find a way to live, as described by D.H. Lawrence in the above quote. Hardy's characters, though, are only just beginning to wake up to this aspiration. It is there in Eustacia (an early model for Ursula) but not fully realized. Eustacia yearns to live. The answer, she thinks, will come from outside – from Clym, from Weymouth or Paris. She is struggling to realize herself. In Jude and Sue the same struggle for wholeness, for being truly alive, continues, is more developed, but has still not reached up to the religious intensity of Ursula.

The Mayor of Casterbridge is Hardy's big social novel, charting in detail the ideological, personal and material battle between the rural insider and the bourgeois outsider. Henchard is a special case in Hardy – the local skilled worker who makes good, who becomes mayor. Hardy keeps the upper-classes and gentry out of his Dorchester, even when Henchard is the mayor, when he would be moving among such social types. Hardy keeps to the themes of shifting fortunes by surrounding Henchard with burghers and businessmen. Money and materialism dog Henchard. Hardy cleverly folds in the ideological equations of woman and property, of success in love with success in wealth. Hardy binds together sex, love, money, property, power, family and ambition. Everything affects everything else. This ideological milieu is very familiar to us in the 21st century Western world. The personal is political. The individual is integrated at every level into her/ his society, whether s/he likes it or not. A kiss becomes a political act!

The force that activates the socio-economic tensions in Thomas Hardy's fiction is love. Love upsets the comfortable equilibrium of the known world. Love rushes in to Hardy's world, as the sensual ecstasy floods Powys's world. The irony is that love does not invade the characters from some foreign Outside, but wells up inside them, from some unconscious reservoir. Love is the plague that overcomes certain susceptible members of the community. Romeo in Kathy Acker's *Blood and Guts in High School* puts it like this: 'Fuck this social political economic sickness. I am sick. I am diseased. I am in love.'[79]

There now emerges a hierarchy of Hardyan characters: the bourgeois outsider, the middle class controllers, the working class, the noble labourers, the odd Lord or Lady and land-owning gentry, the folk who dwell on the margins (Venn, Conjuror Fall, Captain Vye, the urchins and stragglers), and finally the restless souls who do not fit into any single category: Eustacia, Tess, Jude, Troy, Henchard. The rustic types stay fixed in their social status – content, but resigned to their way of life. Some of them act as a chorus, others, such as Susan Nunsuch or Suke Damson, affect the main narrative directly. Clearly Hardy had a lot of fun creating these rural types. Their names alone hit the right notes of comedy and irony: Matthew Moon, Joseph Poorgrass, Old Andrew Satchel, Timothy Tangs, Grandfer Cantle, William Worm, Solomon Longways, Izz Huett and Dairyman Jinks.

John Cowper Powys's rustic characters are conceived with colourful names: Mother Legge, Abel Twig, Bert Cole, Elphin Cantle.

Thomas Hardy himself had a 'triple existence unusual for a man' – for him the 'professional life, the scholar's life, and the rustic life [were] combined in...one day' (Life, p. 32). The people on the edges of classes – Eustacia, Tess, Jude, Henchard – these are the dispossessed. The homeland is jettisoned. They become wanderers. Eustacia stalks around the Heath, but Tess and Jude migrate across most of Wessex. Hardy could show this displacement psychologically, but he has his protagonists physically move. This is because he is very concerned with labour, mobility, sociology and materialism, as well as passion and despair. He binds his love-affairs up with notions of class, wealth, inheritance, family and labour. Basically, a cross-class relationship will be full of problems, Hardy says. He sites each of his characters into a particular class-space.

---

[79] *Blood and Guts in High School,* Picador 1984, p. 273.

The two novels which chart the tragic trajectory of men in decline, *The Mayor of Casterbridge* and *Jude the Obscure*, use the working class character as a vehicle for meditations on the dangers of crossing the boundaries of class and status. Hardy is cynical at times. His view of the potential of people to live is tarnished. His theme of 'the poor man and the lady' is too narrow. He tries to show that the romance of Swithin and Viviette (or Giles and Grace) fails because of their different social standing. This pessimistic, and inauthentic. It is too reductionist, too over-simplified.

Tess of the d'Urbervilles is the best example of Hardy's concerns of class, labour, materialism, sexual politics and social status. *Tess of the d'Urbervilles* brilliantly exposes the hypocrisies found in the notions of inherited and earned rank, in labour and economy, in property and ownership. Hardy ruthlessly highlights the brutality inherent in these problematical areas of the human condition. Alec's gift to Tess is sex and materialist wealth. He buys her disinherited family a horse; he gives Tess a kind of home in the Sandbourne hotel. Angel gives her spirituality, but nothing materially. Alec, though a false aristocrat, is practical. Angel, more noble, is impractical. His Brazilian escapade goes terribly wrong. John Durbeyfield finds out he is a descendant of a titled and prestigious county family, but he is not able to do anything with this knowledge. Joan Durbeyfield is more practical. She sends Tess away, but also withholds important information from her daughter concerning men. Tess is not only a great novel of the tensions between nature, sexuality, character and spirituality, it also engages face-on the vicissitudes of class, labour, wealth, knowledge and economic politics.

Hardy's Wessex is not only a world of nature, emotion, personality and the spirit of place, it is also a world of great social change, in which the market forces at work are changing rapidly. The working class figures – Marty, Oak, Tess, Jude – try to cling on to the old ways of earning a living. Tess and Marty carry on working in the way they have always done. But they are overtaken by a new group of controllers, who have new methods. The way that Tess and Jude try to earn a living is far below what they are capable of doing. They are fully-alive human beings. But Jude, pathetically, becomes a stone-mason, so he can be near the colleges in

Oxford, so he can work with the very building-blocks of the colleges. œdipal forces are at work here – Hardy's father and grandfather (the patriarchal ancestral ghosts) were both in the building trade. How harsh Hardy is in *Jude the Obscure*, describing Jude's nighttime entry into his long-beloved Christminster, listening to the ghosts of the intellectual city, and brushing his work-hardened hands over the walls and carvings of the colleges (It is interesting to compare the young Jude's entry into his New Jerusalem with that of the seventeen-year-old Turner's:

> Sunday July 22.92. Left London in Evening reached Oxford at 3 in the morning – which was delightfully clear and the stillness of the scene gave additional solemnity to the venerable assemblage of Gothic buildings in this City.'[80]

Both young men fell in love with the city – Turner, typically, languishing in the visual atmosphere, while the Hardyan anti-hero feels the philosophical ghosts of the Past blowing coldly through him.) How *deluded* Jude is! He calls the city beautiful (p. 128) even though it has so far given him nothing (materially). Jude lives in a dreamworld. He buys books to learn, but then can't afford to have a fire in his damp room (p. 134). He thinks the answer to his problems is simply to get money and book-knowledge. These are no answers, however. Jude does not realize that yet. The book is the record of his journey towards the existential realization that nothing can provide an 'answer' to the human condition – not love, nor money, learning, God, religion, children, art, work nor even death. Jude the man begins his life in the world of late 19th century rural values, but ends up firmly embedded in 20th century anguish and self-disgust.

In *Jude the Obscure* Hardy takes on all of society. Hardy grapples, as Jude does, with the problems of paying your dues, of placating the ancestral and patriarchal ghosts, dealing with notions of genealogy and œdipal tensions. Hardy tackles Western philosophy, Christianity, hypocrisy, theology, paganism, materialism, ethics, morality and divinity. He tackles these subjects head-on. What a magnificent effort *Jude the Obscure* is – great scream of rage compressed into the conventions of

---

[80] J.M.W. Turner: *Collected Correspondence*, p. 11.

the late 19th century novel. Such passion, and so rigorously controlled. Many of the problems are unsolvable – especially that prime Hardyan theme of the reconciliation of the sexes, the attempt to find a meaningful and authentic love-relation. Hardy's *Jude* is immensely cathartic. In it Hardy grapples with the whole process of enculturation – he tries to shatter it and examine it as honestly as possible. He falls into many epistemological and hermeneutic traps, but the struggle is glorious. Like Lawrence's *The Rainbow*, *Jude the Obscure* is the novel Hardy should have writing all along, from the beginning. It is his 'black book', a book of revelations, a manifesto and creative credo that lies at the heart of his whole work.

Life is not easy for Thomas Hardy's Wessex characters. Many of them work hard – Jude, Tess, Marty, Giles, Henchard, Clym, Oak. Generally, Hardy regards labour reverentially: it is noble, it adds value to life. For Hardy, love and work are bound up together. The nature and quality and conditions of one's working life directly affect the nature and quality and conditions of one's love-relations. Thus a noble and hard-working figure like Marty is also seen as a noble and passionate and diligent lover.

Hardy exalts those who work – those who don't (Viviette, Mrs Charmond, Lucetta, Troy, Fitzpiers [these two are dilettantes]) are seen as destructive people. Work is creative in Hardy, as is love. But the conditions of labour are often very poor. Dignity through work is achieved at a great cost. Tess has her independence and nobility, yes, but she pays dearly for it. Tess goes down to the bedrock of socio-economics. She is alone, she must eat to live, so she works. Her London education does not help her at all. Her solution is entirely practical. 'Social life is essentially practical' wrote Marx.[81] Hardy's novels operate in the Victorian worlds of cruel socio-politics, of Marx's philosophical materialism and revisionism, or extreme poverty and rapid change. 'The socio-political systems of the era did help to strengthen the domination of the bourgeoisie over the proletariat' wrote Lenin (in ib., p. 57).

Education was one way out and Hardy dealt with the issues of increased mobility, choice, status and material wealth achievable through education in the characters of Fancy, Tess, Clym, Sue, Angel and Jude.

---

81 *Selected Works*, I, Lawrence & Wishart 1942, p. 473.

Education helps Hardy's characters to transcend their intermediate social class. But Hardy is ambivalent about the whole issue. His tragedies often pivot on the destructive nature of education. He resents the foreign influence that educated people bring into a community. His educated characters are often also outsiders (Angel, Troy, Fitzpiers). Education raises their social expectations, and they cannot fit in to the community. The insiders who hope to elevate themselves through education (Tess, Clym, Swithin, Fancy, Jude) are viewed more sympathetically, but their journey is still problematical. Marx's right when she says that 'the educator must himself be educated' (ib., p. 472). Although social life may be essentially practical, the solutions must involve the issues of psychology, spirituality, art and culture, as well as materialism.

Part of the Hardy's success with the ideological issues of class, labour, education and social ambition is that they are so rich and complex in his novels. His is a dense and ambiguous fiction. Questions of work and class are woven deeply into Hardy's narratives. They are not tacked on afterwards, as a beautiful piece of nature-writing might be. While *Tess* is brutally straight-forward, and *Jude the Obscure* is bitingly sarcastic, *The Woodlanders* is complex in its fusion of class and character, labour and narrative. Hardy creates a hierarchy of characters: Marty-Giles-Grace-Fitzpiers-Mrs Charmond. The hierarchy moves from the hard-working proletariat to the land-owning layabout gentry. Below and behind Marty are Jack South and Grammer Oliver they are links with the ancient, tribal, pagan Past.

Cleverly Thomas Hardy binds all these characters together through their actions. Marty and Felice are joined through the sale of Marty's hair; Giles and Mrs Charmond are connected through her ownership of his cottage, and so on. Grace stands in the middle of this claustrophic web of relationships and potential clashes. She is unable to reconcile Marty and Mrs Charmond, or Giles and Fitzpiers. Hardy is critical of everyone here, though Giles, the archetypal Hardyan villager who aims to improve himself, to step up the societal ladder from his intermediate status, dies a pathetic death of self-sacrifice and martyrdom. Giles' death, like Little Father Time's and Viviette's, strains the conventions of the realist novel. We don't believe in these deaths, these quasi-suicides. Hardy is as unreal here as he is in Jack South's demise following the disappearance of his haunting tree. Hardy moves into what would later be called 'magic realism'. Marty, such a passionate, dignified and enduring figure, gets nothing at the end of the book except the opportunity to tend undisturbed the last resting-place of someone who never loved her. "You are mine, and only mine" she says to Giles' grave. But, in fact, by the standards of materialism and practicality, by which Marty herself lives, she has *nothing*. Hardy's criticism of Fitzpiers is typical – he views Alec and Troy in the same way. But at least Fitzpiers followed his passions through – at least he had assertive qualities – all those which Giles lacked. The capitalist middle-class characters are unethical, selfish and destructive, but they get what they want more often than the would-be socialist labourers. Nothing is simple in Hardy's Wessex, however. There is a blurring of all kinds of social, economic and political boundaries. Hardy sees any kind of aspiration as problematical, but he equally criticizes a lack of ambition in the proletariat.

Gender and received gender roles play an important part in Hardy's socio-political Wessexscape. It is true that the women in his novels are too often stereotypes – the possessive mother, the betrayed maid, the neurotic Lady, etc. The role of working women in a patriarchal society is a central concern of Hardy's. He knew that women could be cruelly underpaid (Per, p. 186). In *Tess of the d'Urbervilles* he shows how a woman wanting to work on her own, outside of a domestic situation, will be the victim of all kinds of masculine manipulation. Tess is a prey to rape, hard labour, bad pay, patronizing male attitudes, patriarchal double-standards and an inadequate male-made justice system. Though we think of Hardy's age as archaic, poverty-stricken and quite different from our own, some things have not changed. Women still earn on average 74% of what men earn. Poverty, disease, famine, slavery, prostitution and dictatorship are still at work in our early 21st century world. These problems are far worse now than they were in Hardy's era, because the number of people suffering is millions and millions more.

Twelve

Philosophy

So that a true philosophy cannot be spun out of mere abstract concepts, but has to be founded on observation and experience, inner and outer... Philosophy, just as much as art and poetry, must have its source in perceptual comprehension of the world.

Arthur Schopenhauer, *Essays and Aphorisms* (pp. 118-9)

Avert thy face from world deceptions; mistrust they senses, they are false. But within the body, the shrine of thy sensations, seek in the impersonal for the 'Eternal Man', and having sought him out, look inward,; thou art Buddha.

Tibetan Book of the Golden Precepts[82]

Philosophy aims at the logical clarification of thoughts. Philosophy is not a body of doctrine but an activity... The world is my world: this is manifest in the fact that the limits of language (of that language which alone I understand) mean the limits of my world. The world and life are one. I am my world.

Ludwig Wittgenstein, *Tractatus Logico-Philosophicus* (pp. 25, 77)

---

82 In F.C. Happold, ed., p. 171.

There are many 'Thomas Hardys' – the poet, the dramatist, the topographer, the historian, the social commentator, the philosopher. In the fiction there is a fundamental tension between the poetic pagan and the scientific rationalist. We cannot extract one 'Hardy' without upsetting the others, they are nestled in so tightly together. Poetry and science have been merging into one another for decades now, since Einstein. The New Physics and Oriental mysticism meet at many points in our post-war post-atomic era. Hardy too tried to bring together different life-views. The philosophical discourse in his fiction swings from the empiricism of Darwin and Hume to the subjectivism of Nietzsche and Schopenhauer.

In Hardy we can find aspects of Camus' and Beckett's absurdism; the existentlaism of Sartre and Heidegger; he naturalism of Darwin, Spencer and Huxley; the Buddhist resignation of Schopenhauer; the exaltation of the individual in Nietzsche and Jung; the æsthetics of Ruskin, Pater, Emerson, Turner, Scott and Shelley. There are similarities too between Hardy's thought and that of Otto, Tillich, Berdyaev, James, Freud, Frazer, Jung and Rank.

Thomas Hardy did not, however, formulate a philosophic system, unlike, say, Graves or Blake. Hardy's philosophy is constructed out of a series of seemings, of impressions, of questionings, of intuitive explorations, not out of a rigorous exploration of concrete reality (Per, pp. 19-20, 27, 32, 39, 41, 45, 51-52, 56-57, 61, 81, 112-3). In the Preface of *Winter Words* Hardy wrote: 'I also repeat what I have often stated on such occasions, that no harmonious philosophy is attempted in these pages – or in any bygone pages of mine, for that matter.' (Per, p. 61)

Hardy is a tragi-poetic humanist, open to new data. He believes, poetically, in phenomena that science disproves. He knows as all artists do, that art and religion 'modulate into each other' (Per, p. 56). Hardy is a humanist in the Renaissance manner: the human individual is the ultimate measure of the universe and of life. Hardy is psychological: he knows that everything must ultimately refer to humanity, if it is to be at all meaningful. Hardy's targets are not Nature, God or other non-human phenomena, but people and their constructs. Tess and Jude fight against social systems, human-made institutions – the family, domestic life, education, religion, marriage, love. They set love against the Law. Love is not enough, however, and Hardy's novels record the defeat of the psychosexually immature at the hands of a ruthless, world-weary social machine. His concern is societal injustice, the tension between the individual and her/ his society. From this central theme – absolutely fundamental to Hardy – spring his discourses on religion, paganism, art, politics, class, labour, marriage and love.

He write in his Preface to *A Laocidean*: 'Some of these novels of Wessex life address themselves more especially to readers into whose souls the iron has entered.' (Per, p. 15) We can see how deeply the iron has pierced the souls of Jude, Sue, Phillotson, Clym, Tess, Eustacia, Wildeve, Angel, Henchard and Elizabeth-Jane by the end of their stories.

Life is painful much of the way, Hardy says. In a letter, he wrote: 'Pain has been, and pain is' (Life, p. 315). Thomas Hardy is compassionate, though. He sympathizes with all kinds of pain – not just human pain, but also the suffering of animals (Tess and the pheasants, for example) and of the vegetable world (Marty and the trees). Hardy resigns himself, Buddhist-fashion, to much of the world's suffering. He acknowledges that it is a part of existence, but also that much of it could be avoided. He claims that some institutions, such as hunting, marriage, Christianity and labour, do not need to inflict so much pain. His plea is simple, but the answer to it is very complex, and involves (as does the 21st century notion of the 'global village') everybody on the planet. As Sartre says of the 'one world' idea: 'it means that everyone is responsible for everything that goes on in the world.'[83] Hardy is never as direct or as polemical as Sartre – in fact it is clear he did not have many answers (unlike Lawrence, who thought he had an answer for every problem facing humankind). Hardy does condone the 'one world' view. He moves closer and closer towards it in each novel and poem. In *Tess* and *Jude* the whole of Wessex is bound up with the suffering of the protagonists. 'Life is a battle' says Ethelberta (*The Hand of Ethelberta*, p. 131).

Hardy, then, is close to Buddhism, to existentialism, to Western thinkers such as Schopenhauer, Camus and Gide. The sentiments in *Jude the Obscure* are close to those in *L'Etranger*. Like Buddhists, Thomas Hardy sees suffering everywhere. Pain must be taken inside, it must be

---

[83] *Reflections of Our Age*, Columbia University Press, New York, 1948, p. 67.

integrated in some way. Hardy's protagonists have to grow up, to learn to live with pain and frustration. No one said life was going to be easy, and there is no deep consolation to be found in the cultural defences promised by religion or art. One must learn to live with pain (among other things) if one is to achieve Jungian individuation, Lawrencean wholeness, Schopenhauerian existence, Heidegger's being, Buber's I—Thou relation, Freudian maturity, Lonergan's authenticity, Berdyaev's transcendence, Campbellian bliss, Wilson's Faculty X, Tillich's ontology or Chong Trungpa's self-luminosity.

Pain must be made conscious, like death. Hardy is a Gnostic. How often his characters voice Gnostic epithets – *I wish I'd never been born!* they cry. Schopenhauer takes up the same Gnosticism. Both Hardy and Schopenhauer aim to tease out the many 'vanities of existence'. Hardy is no systemic thinker, however, and it is difficult to pin him down to anything but the loosest of life-views. He veers from total disillusionment to dogged meliorism. It is difficult, also, to separate the author from his characters and his text. This is clear in Sue and Jude, the embodiments of the many dichotomies in Hardy's philosophy. Hardy wavers – he is hesitant, open, loose, suspicious, self-doubting. He never created a complex ideological system like Lawrence did in his *Study of Thomas Hardy* or his *Apocalypse*, for example. Lawrence has a vast Biblical vision – he takes on the whole *Bible*, the whole of Christianity in his works. Powys is also ambitious, and his sensualism is a deep source of inspiration. Hardy, though, has no sure-fire way to bliss. He wants people to work it out for themselves. In *The Life* (p. 310) he wrote:

> After reading various philosophic systems, and being struck with their contradictions and futilities, I have come to this: let every man make a philosophy for himself out of his own experience...Let him remember the fate of Coleridge, and save years of labour by working out his own views as given him by his surroundings.

A subjective, individualized philosophy for Thomas Hardy then, based on personal experience and one's surroundings. This is the modern stance: *rely on nothing that has gone before, reject all previous systems, because nothing can save you, you're on your own, so rely on nobody else, there are no certainties, and no solid comforts*. This means looking at life face-on, with no œdipal veils or religious aids or rose-tinted poetic glasses. Hardy, like many artists before him, tried to record and interpret life as honestly as he could. He aimed for a purity of vision.

As with Lawrence, Lacan and Bataille, Hardy saw most of life's pain and ecstasy and ontological problems focussed in love and sexual politics. Sexual love is Hardy's chief terrain. The only transcendence he acknowledges is through authentic loving. He agrees with Schopenhauer in *The Metaphysics of the Love of the Sexes* when the latter said that even 'satisfied passion also leads oftener to unhappiness than to happiness'.[84] Hardy, like Schopenhauer, has a bleak view of passion -- it hardly ever turns out right. Sometimes, like Schopenhauer (and a host of other 'philosophers of love') Hardy is misogynistic. He cannot hide his linking of women and nature and sexuality and how these things contaminate the sanctity of male life. This idea goes back to Plato – this contamination of maleness by femaleness.

When things reach a painful low-point Thomas Hardy does resort to a belief in the powers of loving-kindness. Loving-kindness, the old English term for compassion, is exalted in Hardy, as it is in Shakespeare, above love. In Hardy's atheistic, tragic humanism, loving-kindness is the highest emotion one can have. To attain compassion is to reach the heights in Hardy's moral ontology. Marty in *The Woodlanders* achieves this ethical apotheosis. She surrenders herself, in an act of maximum altruism. Other altruistic characters include Tess, Jude, Oak, Clym and Elizabeth-Jane. Characters such as Henchard, Eustacia, Bathsheba, Angel and Grace do not give up much of themselves. They cling on too much. Here the Hardyan self is like the humanist, Christian mystics – Ruysbroeck, Hildegard, Suso and Tauler. Rarely does the Hardyan self burn like St Teresa, Rolle, Catherine of Siena or St Bernard. The Powys self among mystics is like Swedenborg, Blake, Paracelsus, Agrippa, Dee, Eckhart – those deeply individual mystics whose philosophies lie on the edges of the Western mystery tradition.

In Thomas Hardy, as in Camus, life is absurd, but nihilism and violence is no answer, even though rage and intolerance drives much of their

---

[84] In *The Philosophy of Schopenhauer*, ed. Irwin Edman, Carlton House, New York, p. 369.

philosophies. Hardy's revolt, like Jude's, is religious as well as social. But Hardy knows the solutions must come from and operate within the societal sphere. Hardy is more of an ethical rather than a metaphysical thinker. His thought, like Powys', is often confused and badly expressed. His view of 'the good life' is essentially the same as that of Bertrand Russell: *'The good life is one inspired by love and guided by knowledge.'*[85] With God dead (killed by Darwin and Nietzsche among others in Hardy's time) there are no solutions to be found in a Divine Being, or in a religion founded more on fear than love.

Hardy and Powys are part of the British mystical tradition (Rolle, Julian, Law, *The Cloud of Unknowing,* etc). They move towards the poetic mysticism and mystical poetry of Donne, Herbert, Vaughan, Traherne, Blake, Wordsworth and Shelley. There was a great catastrophe in the middle of the 19th century – the Death of God. Hardy and Powys are separated from the Romantics by this theological and cultural calamity. They are post-Romantic, post-Renaissance, post-mediæval writers. They do not commune with God, but with Nature. God is not Nature – the two are not confused in Hardy or Powys (or Lawrence). Hardy and Powys are both post-Wordsworthian. As mystics they have more in common with Chuang-tzu than Thomas Aquinas, more in common with Hui-Neng, Shankara and D.T. Suzuki than Augustine, St Francis and Teilhard. Hardy's and Powys's mystical thinking leans towards Lonergan, Merton, Watts, Huxley, Neumann and Jung. Among philosophers they incline more towards Plato than Aristotle. Hardy's major fiction charts the Empodeclean battle between Love and Strife. The Hardy novel opens with a calm world of Love and shows how it is torn apart by invading Strife. Powys leans more towards Heraclitus than Empodecles or Pythagoras. Heraclitean fire, fanned by Powys's cosmic winds, appears in *Wolf, Maiden Castle* and *Weymouth,* among others. The sayings of Heraclitus, with their vocabulary of fire, flux and souls, are bound to endear themselves to modern Western writers – from the Decadents to the latest feminists:

> Night-walkers, magicians, priests of Bacchus, and priestesses of the wine-vat; mystery-mongers. The mysteries practised among men are

---
85 In *Why I am not a Christian*, p. 48.

unholy mysteries…God is day and night, winter and summer, war and peace, surfeit and hunger…[86]

For modern writers the myths, dramas and philosophies of ancient Greece are hugely important. A cultural bond is kept alive among artists with Homer, Plato and Sophocles. Ancient and Hellenic Greece is a rich source of paganism, myth, learning and poetry. Modern artists recognise the Mediterranean as the seed-bed of Western life. Ancient Greece is the Golden Age, culturally and spiritually. It embodies the poetic way of life for modern artists. This sensual, pagan stance is found in Verlaine, Gide, Durrell, Klee, Picasso, Byron and Cocteau as well as Hardy and Powys. In the Greeks passion and intellect flower abundantly. The human-centred poetic paganism of Greece, rebirthed in the Renaissance, continues to intoxicate many artists today, such as the abstract painter Brice Marden whose serene upright canvas panels echo the architectonics and skies of pre-Byzantine Greece.

Thomas Hardy balances his folky, pagan Greek side with a sturdy rational-realism culled from 18th and 19th century empirical philosophers. Darwin, Mill, Bentham, Hume, Marx, Huxley, Spencer and Hegel counter the transcendent elements in Hardy's world-view. Passion and reason are constantly at war in Hardy's fiction. Passion forces action, the movement that culminates in marriage and then in tragedy. Reason is static – it means standing back and looking at every angle. With no passion there would be no more narrative. Reason comes too late in Hardy's world. His fools rush in – there are no angels, no angelic figures out of Blake, Rimbaud or Dionysius. Powys allows angels to walk in his world (in Christie, Wizzie, Elphin, etc) but they are out of kilter with the workaday world.

Hardy, despite his philosophic detachment, is an artist of passion. Passion sets his tales in motion, and also fires up his rage and rebellion. The revolt of Jude-the-obscure-man is against society, against 'man's inhumanity to man'. It is a passionate rebellion, stemming from personal pain. Jude does not understand that he is an outsider – he cannot articulate it, and neither can his Creator. Jude is not yet an existential modern artist, angst-ridden, with a slick facility for self-expression.

---

[86] In B. Russell, *A History of Western Philosophy*, pp. 61-62.

Hardy's philosophical inarticulacy is both frustrating and endearing. He is a poet, not a pamphleteer. The novel, the 'bright book of life' is his vehicle for his polemics. He would soon dry up if he had to write in the form of philosophical commentary. Powys loves writing in this way, like Lawrence, but Hardy is very bad at it. How much more powerful, though, is the polemical discourse in Jude for being couched in fiction. Hardy is one of those rare artists – Shakespeare, Dante and Petrarch are others – who can combine poetry with politics in drama without making either discourse suffer. His fiction is poetic, dramatic and powerful while also being pertinent socio-politically. In some writers ideas and narratives mix uneasily (in Aldous Huxley, Colin Wilson, Golding, Pynchon, Graves, Powys). In Hardy the ideas and discourses are mostly fully enmeshed with the narratives. Part of the joy of reading him is to tease those discourses out. We regret that Shakespeare did not write a philosophical treatise, setting out clearly his life-view. How boring it would be, though, to have a single statement to explain all the plays. Much better is the mass of contradictions, games, side-trackings and glories of the works. It is so much more authentic. Those who demand a single philosophic statement that must never change do not live in the real world in which everything is changing. Nothing is certain, except the organic essentials, and nothing remains the same. As Brecht says, things will change.

John Cowper Powys accepts plurality. Though his sensualisms are often monist, he advocates multiplicity. Hardy too wants a myriad of pathways in life – in love especially. Let us have, he says, lots of ways of living. No true artist can advocate just one of living. Artists continually cross boundaries and thresholds. They want the boundaries to be pushed back even further. André Gide in his *Paludes* crystallizes one of the modern artists' fundamental manifestos:

Once we take up an idea, we must carry it to the very end.[87]

This ethical extremism is (partly) what drives the modern artist, what made Ad Reinhardt spend the 1960s painting five-foot square black canvases, or made Proust write those many volumes in order to recapture Time Past, or made Nietzsche create his Superman. Passion here is pushed

---
87 *Marshlands*, Secker & Warburg, 1953, p. 86.

to extremes – it tips over the edge into mysticism, madness, genius and violence. The Romantic revolt culminates in Hitler and Stalin – in the sex, mind and war crimes of Russia, Germany, Japan, China, America, Africa and Europe.

Powys pushes things to extremes – he jumps into stones, using his multi-sensual technique, and extends his soul outwards to include distant suns. Hardy pushes events to tragic extremes and climaxes. In *Jude the Obscure* he want as far as he could. Little Father Time's death is the furthest his rage pushed him. For many critics he went too far – right over the edge. Everything changes, though – twenty years later the Great War astonished everyone with its mass atrocities. In literature, seventy years after Jude, we had William Burroughs. When *his* characters are hung, they scream manically and ejaculate multi-coloured venom everywhere. In the multi-secular post-Sadeian post-atomic world you can go as far as you like, because *nothing* is sacred. Two world wars have seen to that.

Thomas Hardy went as far as the could in fiction with *Jude*. His aim was not to shock but to draw attention to injustice and suffering. It is the same with Burroughs. Both writers tried to go one stage further than their contemporary worlds, just as Pasolini and Ferreri did in their Sadeian satiric films. In Hardy the individual struggles against society – this fight first appears forcefully in *The Return of the Native*, when the Promethean revolt of fire leaps out of the stagnant earth. Hardy sets fire above water – the human above the natural. His humans are on fire – they burn with passion, both sexual and social. The fire flickers above the still water of society. The individual is a Lawrencean flame, trembling, trying to reach up and away from the earthy, watery element below it. Earth tries to stifle humanity's flame. But fire also kills – and the fiery souls in Hardy (Eustacia, Tess, Jude) have to die. They burn too fast, too brightly. In *Tess of the d'Urbervilles*, as Tess rides off with Alec, just before she is raped, Car's mother says: "out of the frying pan into the fire!" (p. 113). 'Fire' is perfect here – it refers to the holy male element of sexuality and power, and also to the holy male right to napalm anything in its way.

In Powys there is more water than fire, and more earth than water. Filling in the gaps between the psychic structure of these sensual elements is his beloved Homeric/ætheric air. Powys's fire feeds his mythic sensualism. His target, ultimately, is the self, not other people. The deeper the Powys-character sinks into her/ his sensuality, the happier s/he is. The ultimate goal of Hardy's characters is an enriching relation with the beloved, with the family, with friends and neighbours, and with society. There are many ghosts to placate. Though Hardy's philosophical discourses are often buried under his carefully structured narratives, Hardy's ethics are quite clear. Altruism, compassion, dignity, work, love and integration are all stressed – and here Hardy chimes with most other writers. Not *live and let live*, but *live and love and help others to do likewise*. Hardy wants an ordered society, but one that is also open, that allows for many ways of living. Open structures, not closed strictures.

Thirteen

The Metaphysics of Style

The novel is the highest example of subtle inter-relatedness that man has discovered... The novel can help us to live, as nothing else can... the novel as a tremulation can make the whole man alive tremble... In the novel, the characters can do nothing but live... at its best, the novel, and the novel supremely, can help you.

D.H. Lawrence, *A Selection from Phoenix*[88]

---

[88] pp. 177, 181, 185, 187-8.

Thomas Hardy is, first and last, a poet. He did not regard the novel as the 'bright book of life', which Lawrence called it. Lawrence exalted the novel: 'The novel is the one bright book of life' said Lawrence; 'The novel is a perfect medium for revealing to us the changing rainbow of our living relationships.'[89] Lawrence reckoned that the novel could help us to live. For him writing novels was a matter of life and death – he wrote from a primæval, urgent sense of necessity. Certainly the novel has always aimed to circumscribe a vast chunk of life, to describe life in all its myriad experiences, from the trivial to the universal and mythical. Thus Francois Mauriac wrote: 'The ambition of the modern novelist is to apprehend the whole of human nature'.[90] This is the aim of Powys – to capture as much of life as possible. This is why Powys's book are so long – he is panoramic, he wants to include everything he can. He includes the banal, the trivial, the stupid. Often he just chugs along. There is quite a lot of time and space in a novel in which to wander. There's no rush. As André Gide said: 'The novel requires a certain slowness of progress that allows the reader to live with the characters and become accustomed to them.'[91] *A Glastonbury Romance* moves along at a slow pace. Sometimes it grinds to a halt through lack of energy and momentum. *Jude the Obscure*, on the hand, cracks along at a frenetic pace. Powys takes the slow-motion narrative too far. He will not prune. When he has it done for him, as with *Maiden Castle* and *Porius*, the results are even more unsatisfactory.

'One should not write' says Stendhal, 'unless one has important or profoundly beautiful things to say'.[92] Arthur Schopenhauer says the same thing; the first rule of style is to have something to say. Few writers adhere to this rule. Powys seems to write whenever he feels like it. Robert Graves, on the other hand, will re-write his poems endlessly, until they are as near-perfect as he can get them. For Powys writing is hugely enjoyable, while for Lawrence it is a religious act. It is part of his religious rebellion. Powys likes to tell stories, as Hardy does. Lawrence likes to rage in prose.

Thomas Hardy likes to present us with scenes, not to philosophize too much (Per, p. 114). Hardy reins in his desire to wander off-course. His

---
89 *A Selection from Phoenix*, pp. 180-1, 185.
90 Mauriac, *God and Mammon*, Sheed & Ward, New York 1930, v.
91 *The Journals of André Gide*, III, 1928-39, Knopf, New York 1949.
92 Letter, in Allott, ed., p. 128.

authorial intrusions are usually annoying. He is a story-teller, in the ancient, oral-poetic sense. He tells stories in a mythical-shamanic manner. *Once upon a time this happened, and then this happened,* and so on. His novels are Victorian versions of mediæval ballads. Hardy invites us to gather around the fire of his artistic talent to hear his stories of 'man's inhumanity to man – and woman'. His tales are set in the classically simple format of mythologies. Myths tell sacred stories, tell us of what is *really happening* in the world. Hardy stories (aim to) do just that. They tell us what is really happening underneath the calm veneer of social life. Under the skin, behind closed doors, in private places, extraordinary events are taking place. Even on a shabby, forgotten bit of heathland great aches and pains are felt among the inhabitants. *Gather round,* Hardy's narrative voice cries, *and hear ye of the Passions of Eustacia Vye, or the Victimization of Tess Durbeyfield.* Hardy begins with that age-old opening: *once upon a time a man was walking along...* etc. The classic opener. We could put *once upon a time* at the beginning of each of Hardy's novels and it wouldn't make them sound stupid. It fits, it works – Hardy's narrative style is traditional but powerful.

Thomas Hardy is best when he is simple and mythical. He is not good at discourse and conjecture. He soon gets confused and lost. Lawrence is one of the great Wanderers in prose. When Lawrence's Wanderings have been re-written and tightened up, as in *Lady Chatterley,* the result is compact and startling. When he intrudes upon the narrative with his silly remarks, the result is idiotic, as in *The Lost Girl.* Powys's intrusions are complex, because they are the very stuff of his fiction. His art is a Hardyan series of 'impressions' of philosophy and elementalism. Powys's Wanderings into the souls of stones of First Causes are all part of his discourse. Powys does go over the top at times. That opening passage of *A Glastonbury Romance* still reads really badly, even after repeated attempts at re-reading. Powys's choice of words helps to ruin his intention ('microscopic biped', for example, instead of 'man').

As well as being immensely cinematic, Hardy's style is also *architectural.* 'Architectural' because he uses spatial *mise-en-scène.* He places people together spatially. His sense of drama is spatial, as well as aural, symbolic, nature-soaked and cinematic. Hardy binds together his dramas with spatial and painterly configurations. Buildings are expressive in his art.

A brilliant example of this is at the end of *The Woodlanders*, with its lengthy panning and tracking-shot technique. This brings together, just as in theatre at the end of a play, the cast of characters. Melbury and his workmen search for Grace, who was seen with Fitzpiers. They meet Percomb, who opens the novel by buying Marty's hair. The lengthy tracking-shot continues as Melbury catches up with Grace and Fitzpiers. Like Tess, displaced in another hotel, in Sandbourne, Grace tells her father that her lover, Fitzpiers, is upstairs. Content that his daughter is safe, but restless about her future with Edred, Melbury and his neighbours retire to an inn for sustenance. Melbury muses at the door upon his daughter's fate; Hardy cuts to the rustic chorus inside the tavern for their views on the drama. They swop yarns about marriage and courtship. They walk back to the Hintocks passing the churchyard. Here Marty waits – the rustic chorus fades from view and Marty is left, standing centre-stage, ready for her passionate address of Giles' grave. How clever is Hardy's orchestration of drama and actors here. All the main characters, plus a handful of the rural chorus, are involved. Significantly, neither Mrs Charmond nor Fitzpiers (the outsiders) speak, although both are mentioned in the dialogue. This is, after all, a novel about the inhabitants of the Hintocks, and their relationships with the outsiders, not the other way around. The viewpoint, as always in Hardy, is selective but disguised. Grace has nothing much to say, but both Melbury and Marty have important views to express, generally of a resigned, wary nature. The workfolk echo this resignation. In the matter of love-relations things have not greatly changed since ancient times, the rustic chorus concludes.

If this scene was done in the theatre (the scene is very theatrical) the lights would dim gradually throughout the action, as they do in performances of Beckett. Marty would be left, a solitary figure, softly lit. A spotlight would serve as a moon, while behind her on the right there would the dark shadow of the church tower. The girl and her beloved grave would be downstage. She would face the audience and begin her soliloquy a few melancholy moments after the country folk have shuffled off into the wings. The lights fade to black at the end of her speech. Pause.

Applause.

Architectural style. Thomas Hardy spoke of an analogy between architecture and art and poetry (Life, p. 301). Hardy has a good, perceptive eye for architecture – his learning and his trade show through here. In simple instances, such as the depiction of Sherborne Abbey and the other buildings around it 'having the linear distinctness of architectural drawings' (Woodlanders, p. 75). In *Jude the Obscure* there is a much more complex discourse, a debate between Jude and his love of Gothic, mediævalism, Ruskinian æsthetics and stone-carving, and Sue with her preference for the modern, the secular, the functional – the railway station over the cathedral (p. 187). Oxford, seen early on as 'that ecclesiastical romance in stone' (76) turns out to be hollow, falling apart, and full of lies. Jude is one the other side of the wall – 'Only a wall – but what a wall!' (p. 132). These walls are rotting, however, and Jude literally helps to rebuild them. While rebelling against the colleges he also helps to rebuild them. While resenting the social and educational system, he still endorses it through his labour. The 'wall' is inside him, as it is inside us all. He can't destroy it, because he would destroy so much of himself. So he simply writes (in chalk – he's no vandal) a quote from the *Book of Job*.

Tess outside the cottage's hearthwall, Jude outside the universities, Giles outside his own shed – these Hardy characters cannot break down the defences that society puts up around itself. The social system, embodied in *Jude* by Oxford, is too vast for the natural boy to break down. But even when Tess is faced with a reasonably human-sized obstacle – such as getting in touch with Angel's father at the vicarage – she cannot do it. In Hardy so often the tragedy is accelerated by someone not confronting a potentially embarrassing situation. Thus the architectural realities – Clym's house, Alec's hotel, James Clare's vicarage – symbolize psycho logical barriers which the Hardyan protagonists cannot overcome. Hardy solidifies in stone human emotions. He makes distress and failure concrete. So the dispossessed hang around outside in the cold, like Cathy's spirit haunts Wuthering Heights house. They are like teenagers too shy to ask someone out. Can a full-blown tragedy hinge on such immaturity? Can a tragic story pivot on someone being afraid to lose a little of their social and self-esteem?

While Hardy's stories seem to be predetermined, controlled by fate, chance, accident and all kinds of novelistic conventions and dramatic contingencies, Powys's stories are typically open, in the modern, 20th century sense of the term. Bahktin wrote that 'the ultimate word of the world and about the world has not yet been spoken, the world is open and free, everything is still in the future and will always be in the future'.[93]

The world of the modern novel is open, indefinite, always changing. Nothing is certain and there are no ultimate mysteries or truths. This is the view of the fiction of Camus, Gide, Lawrence, Woolf, Durrell, Pynchon and Beckett. Powys says exactly the same thing in *A Glastonbury Romance* (p. 665). Powys reckons that no novelist has ever captured this changing, multi-dimensional life in writing:

> The composers of fiction aim at an æsthetic verisimilitude which seldom corresponds to the much more eccentric and chaotic disposition of Nature. Only rarely are such writers so torn and rent by the Demon within them that they can add their own touch to the wave-crests of real actuality as these foam up, bringing wreckage and seatangle and living and dead ocean monsters and bloody spume and bottom silt into the rainbow spray! (GR, p. 666)

This is a key statement of Powys's æsthetics. He wants actuality in fiction – the real feeling of myriad and elemental realities. So he tries to describe what things are really like (as he experiences them) – *that* particular tree, or *this* particular lake. For Powys 'the universe is crowded with levels, strata, planes, dimensions, altitudes, regions' (*Ducdame*, p. 288). The creative problem is: how to, first of all, get to those levels, then how to describe them.

The problem for John Cowper Powys was finding a suitable expression-language dynamic enough to accommodate such intense apperceptions. Lawrence is so much better at describing that particular wall. Powys takes so much longer to do it, but he invariably gets there eventually. Powys does not know when to stop, but Hardy, working initially for serial publication, knows how to edit his narratives. Stendhal and Graves both say that one should write only from inner necessity. Stendhal adds: 'I

---

[93] Mikhail Bahktin, *Problems of Dostoevsky's Poetics*, tr. Cary Emerson, Manchester 1984, p. 160.

know of only one rule: style cannot be too clear, too simple'.[94] Unfortunately, Powys did not follow this dictum. He gets increasingly difficult to read. In the later novels, his style becomes obtuse.

Thomas Hardy disliked the strictures of supplying what he called 'family fiction' (Life, p. 232). His novels developed not only under the usual influences of publishers, editors and readers, but also magazine editors and magazine readers. He felt his fiction had been damaged by serial publication, by the need to keep up the demand a particular kind of magazine fiction (Life, p. 183). Novel-writing became robotic (p. 189). Increasingly dissatisfied, Hardy felt the novel should move further into psychological analysis: 'Why not by rendering as visible essences, spectres, & c. the abstract thought of the analytic school?' (Life, p. 183). This is what *Tess* and *Jude* move towards. Hardy develops the novel towards the form of Lawrence, who wrote: 'the novel is the highest complex of subtle inter-relatedness that man has discovered' (*Study of Thomas Hardy*, p. 172). Hardy gravitates more towards Dostoievsky than Dickens, more towards Gide than James, more towards Powys than Conrad. In a note of 14 January 1888 Hardy wrote: 'A 'sensation-novel' is possible in which sensationalism is not causality but evolution; not physical but psychical...' (Life, p. 213). Hardy's movement away from novels towards poetry reflects this yearning for a deeper exploration of personal, subjective, psychological concerns.

Amongst the many factors that made Thomas Hardy stop novel-writing must have been the weary acknowledgement that books have only a limited value. Schopenhauer had come to the same conclusions earlier: it is the *subject*, not the *book*, that counts; books are only a reproduction of one author's thoughts; books must be read, not just bought.[95] Hardy must have thought something of the same. Poetry for him became the right kind of vehicle for his intimate, emotional concerns. In poesie he could celebrate the seasonal haunting of the beloved in a quietly passionate way:

> Upon a noon I pilgrimed through
> A pasture, mile by mile,
> Unto the place where last I saw
> <u>My dead Love's living</u> smile

---

[94] In Allott, p. 312.
[95] *Essays*, pp. 199-210.

And sorrowing, I lay me down
 Upon the heated sod;
It seemed as if my body pressed
 The very ground she trod.

...She smiled and went. Since then she comes
Oft when her birth-moon climbs,
Or at the seasons' ingresses,
 Or anniversary times.

But grows my grief. When I surcease,
 Through whom alone lives she,
Her spirit ends its living lease,
 Never again to be![96]

---

[96] 'Her Immortality'. CP, p. 55-56.

Fourteen

Thomas Hardy Goes To the Cinema

I find poetic links, the logic of poetry in cinema, extraordinarily pleasing. They seem to me perfectly appropriate to the potential of cinema as the most truthful and poetic of art forms…I love cinema…Cinema should be a means of exploring the most complex problems of our time, as vital as those which for centuries have been the subject of literature, music and painting.

Andrei Tarkovsky, *Sculpting in Time* (pp. 18, 80)

The film is only pictures, like pictures in the *Daily Mirror*. And pictures don't have any feelings apart from their own feelings. I mean he feelings of the people who watch them. Pictures don't have any feelings except in the people who watch them. And that's why they like them. Because they make them feel that they are everything.

D.H. Lawrence, *The Lost Girl* (p. 144)

Thomas Hardy wants us to be magiced away by his stories. He wants to be the shaman of the tribe who can guide souls over the edges of their well-known terrain, into stranger, distant regions. In 'The Profitable Rereading of Fiction' he speaks of how art can enable us to 'travel without moving'. He says that 'the shifting of scenes should manifestly be as complete as if the reader had taken the hind seat of a witch's broom stick' (Per, p. 111).

This is what cinema can do. It can change scenes for us suddenly, it can bend, fold and implode time and space. With the special effects out of Hollywood, cinema can take us to bizarre worlds. Hardy is cinematic because he presents scenes more than analyzing them. Lawrence is impossible to film because his fiction pivots around relationships and psychology and deep meanings that are invisible. Lawrence writes of emotions and relationships, primarily, and his prose is abstract, as well as immensely sensuous. You can't show 'darkness cleaving to darkness' on film. You *can* show Giles disappearing into the mist up a tree – and Hardy's *mise-en-scène* does the talking in that scene from *The Woodlanders*.

John Cowper Powys is also impossible to film. He goes even deeper than Lawrence into essences and abstractions. Hardy's third-person narratives are more suited to cinema. There are still many problems to overcome, however. The most obvious is time, editing and book-length – what to cut out and what to leave in. Depth is also a problem – how deep to go in the film version? Tense is important: film works in a continuous (eternal) present tense, while fiction is usually retrospective. Film has presence, while words have a different kind of presence. Books rely on the reader's imagination – here fiction wins out over film. One can read at one's own pace – one controls pace. In film everything is laid out for you. Film is didactic, as an experience. Then there is the problem of style, of putting a difficult lingual style into moving images. This is partly why Lawrence is nearly impossible to film. His prose style, with its strong sense of rhythm, its repetition of key-words and its intricate abstractions and metaphors, does not translate well into cinema. Films show you everything – books ask you to imagine everything. Then there are the problems of history and background. In books we are (often) given a good deal of history and background to a character or a situation. In film this can be done using flashbacks – but how unsatisfactory they are – or with a voice-over. Here's where film can imitate the novel, but again it is too obvious a solution. Viewpoint next: which viewpoint to take? A first-person subjective eye-witness account is immensely difficult to visualize on film. The distanced objective third-person is used most often, but this can't get inside characters' minds. The problem of literary cinema is that it is always looking at people from the outside. We see actors' faces, we have to rely on their ability to act, to express their inner natures. Actors then become a problem – especially in a period film, such as Hardy, Powys or Lawrence. They never look right. Film versions of classic novels are doomed to fail from the beginning.

Hardy's third-person narratives are more suited to cinema than many other writers' texts (such as Gide, Camus, Beckett, Lawrence, Powys, Woolf, Joyce). Hardy is visual, they say, but all writers are visual in some way. Even Beckett, who reduces people to mere consciousnesses floating above the earth is visual. Hardy uses a network of *looks* in his novels – people looking at other people. Cinema thrives on The Look. We perceive Hardy's characters through other characters' eyes. Meanings shift, perspectives are modulated through a series of personas. Durrell later explored such semantic shifting in his *Alexandria Quartet*. The dairymaids look at Angel from afar; Alec stares at Tess, Angel watches Tess on the white road; the cleaner sees Tess and Angel in bed; Angel and 'Liza-Lu watch the flag in Wintonchester. Jude falls in love with Sue's photograph before he meets her; Grace watches her princely lover (Fitzpiers) depart on horseback to be replaced by the dogged Giles; the network of fires and figures on Egdon Heath is mediated through an onlooker; Henchard trains his telescope on Maiden Castle, and so on. The instances in Hardy of observers are numerous. This is cinematic, and easily rendered in films. But this only deals with presentation and action, easy things to depict. What is lost in Hardy's film and television adaptions are the tragic themes, the themes of work and class and ambition, the themes of accident and fate and motive. There is a welter of psychological and emotional discourse in Hardy which is lost in the filmic adaptions.

Thomas Hardy uses cinematic framing, focussing, pull-focus, panning, tracking and montage. Powys uses the wide-angle view often. His fiction seems to have been visualized through a series of distorting lenses. The solitary walks Powys's characters go on would be best filmed with a hand-held camera in the technicolour of Matisse in his Fauvist phase.

Hardy is not always visual. To get a five-sense synæsthetic effect other sensations are needed, and Hardy uses sound a lot. In the poetry the one distinctive Hardyan sound is of a dress rustling, signalling the approach of the well-beloved (in 'She Did Not Turn', 'The Old Gown', 'The Revisitation', etc). Hardy uses many kinds of sounds – of animals, trees hissing, sighs, moans, people at work, rain, wind, the sea, rivers and so on. Hardy has a very heightened perception of sound. His country people are sensitive to sound – to the different noises of the trees, for example. They can tell where they are in the dark by the different sounds the grass underfoot makes. Filmmakers pull out certain sounds from a sound-picture and mix them high for particular effects – think of the jangling keys at the beginning of Spielberg's E.T., for example, or the really peculiar creaking of a curtain in Tarkovsky's *The Sacrifice*. Hardy too isolates one sound. A powerful instance is when Wildeve and Clym hear the distant splash of Eustacia falling into the wier. Typically particular, Hardy states: 'Its origin was unmistakable – it was the fall of a body into the stream in the adjoining mead' (*Return*, p. 436).

The network of looks – the voyeuristic look, the primacy of the gaze and the eye – all these are found in Thomas Hardy's art. Perception in Hardy is highly imaginative, and, as with the mediæval courtly 'love from afar', much of Hardy's way of seeing is erotic. Hardy tries to make the inner and the outer eye work together. In Hardy, seeing is being. The apotheosis of being for him passive observation – in the stance of the rural 'waker'. He is cinematic partly because much of his drama centres on observers and the observed. In Hardy, the object of desire is fetichized – Tess's mouth, for example, or Eustacia's eyes. As pornography hinges on the visual, so Hardy concentrates on it more than other means of description. Hardy's erotic discourse is traditional – it deals with distance and desire, with the longing of an observer for the sexualized object. Desire is not to be easily gratified, however. As in conventional popular 'romances', the lovers must be kept apart until the end of the book. Only then can sexual union occur. In Hardy, of course, consummation is fraught with problems, and if it does take place, it never lasts long. The sexual climax is postponed – the characters, and fore the reader. Hardy delights in using Roland Barthes' *jouissance*, the 'tecstasy' of postmodernism. For Hardy, as for most love-poets, desire is everything.

Thomas Hardy knows, like Graves, Shakespeare and Petrarch, that the satisfaction of Desire kills the narrative. The thrust, in patriarchal literature, is ever onward. Orgasm is endlessly delayed. You mustn't let the audience touch the characters, as the lovers are not allowed to touch each other in the text. It is all tantalizing anticipation. A full-blown consummation weakens everything. The drama falls flat. So in Hardy, and Powys and Graves and Lawrence and a mass of other writers, maximum love-union is rare. Desire must be kept intense. The aim is to keep pushing, never arriving – becoming, not being. Otherwise, why carry on writing? Why not accept the Oriental code of actionless activity? Why not sit under the Tree of Idleness, planted in the Infinitude, and bliss away into Nothing. No. The Western way is to keep on moving, to keep on pushing and trying. Hence each novel of Hardy's gets stronger and stronger, more and more passionate, until only the poetry could carry the full electric charge, the heavy current of polemic and emotion.

Certainly the TV and movie versions of Hardy that exist – the BBC's *Mayor*, Schlesinger's *Madding Crowd* or Polanski's *Tess* look marvellous. The landscape in these versions is superbly photographed. But then, it would be difficult to point a camera at a piece of landscape and *not* get a decent image. This is because we see so little greenery in our television broadcasting – most of the programmes come out of urban environments, and refer to the cityscape – all that concrete, strip-lighting and grey faces. A little green landscape goes a long way, as TV advertizers know well. Any rural view will do – it doesn't matter where you grab it from, as is demonstrated in Ridley Scott's Hovis advert, which used Shaftesbury's famous Gold Hill as the backdrop to its mishmash of Yorkshire olde worlde 1930s Depression nostalgia and post-industrial values.

Film directors can make Hardy and Dorset look good. It's more difficult to make it sound good too. The modern attempts at Dorset dialect fail hilariously. The modern faces don't work, either, like the modern accents. Julie Christie and Nastassia Kinski are too modern, too well-known, too Hollywood, too film-starrish to be believable as Hardyan heroines. 'Fine English actors', such as Alan Bates, are caricatures of themselves. It is a case of Alan Bates or whoever playing at playing Hardy. Big theatrical gestures don't work, and nor does the studied introspection and passivity of Kinski's Tess. Only Robert Bresson's non-actorish non-theatrical style could work with Hardy. Bresson was the only director who could do Arthurian material well (in his *Lancelot du Lac*, 1974, France). Tarkovsky might have given us a decent reading of Hardy. Beautiful scenery, exquisite attention to period detail and verbatim dialogue is not enough. The opening of *The Return of the Native*, with its grand visions of Egdon Heath, is very cinematic. It calls for the trashy epic treatment of Cecil B. de Mille. Hardy is so visual at these moments, we don't need a film version. We picture Eustacia dancing in the moonlight, or Susan and Elizabeth-Jane coming into Dorchester so vividly, the dictatorial way of seeing of cinema is not necessary. Hardy is supremely visual on his own. A straight, close adaption is bound to fail.

There have been a number of versions of Hardy's fiction: the BBC have made *Jude the Obscure* and *The Woodlanders* (both dramatized by Harry Green, 1970-1). They made *The Mayor of Casterbridge* in 1978 with Alan Bates (David Giles director). In 1986 the BBC made *A Day After the Fair*, with Sammi Davis in the lead role, from the short story *On the Western Circuit*. The credits for this piece of television were impressive – photography by Kenneth Macmillan, music by Rick Wakeman, directed by Anthony Simmons, but the final result was a watered-down interpretation. Despite the big production values – the set-dressing, costumes, choice actors and exquisite locations – it does not escape being insipid melodrama. Thomas Hardy is turned into trivial Cartlandesque 'romance'. Instead of bitterness and heartfelt emotion we get strained acting and gorgeous lighting. Where's the passion? Not here, not on television. The most famous film renderings are Schlesinger's *Far From the Madding Crowd*, and Polanski's *Tess*. Schlesinger's movie is really bland – Hardy turned into Hollywood schmaltz. Polanski's *Tess* is worth considering in more detail.

It was made in France in 1979 with Natassia Kinski in the lead role. Leigh Lawson and Peter Firth are merely adequate as Hardyan males. Polanski fills his film with a clutch of bizarre faces. He relishes the re-creation of Hardy's Wessex. *Tess* tries to be as close to the book as possible. The sets, costumes, lighting, photography and the look of the film are lovingly produced. Polanski creates a rather dumb, passive Tess, quite different from the sparky country girl of the novel. He picks up the pagan elements in the story – these are exalted over the Christian aspects. Thus the film opens with the May club-walking and ends with Stonehenge. As Tess/ Kinski is led away in a dark scarlet dress, Polanski cuts back to the stone circle. The sun rises behind the stones, and the music of the beginning of the film is reprised. For Polanski *Tess* is a cyclical story, a disaster that is repeated like the seasons. Tess is depicted as a passive victim of male aggression and misunderstanding. Tess is silenced in the film even more than she is in the book. The film omits the horse's death, the baptism, Alec becoming a preacher, and, most importantly, Tess's passionate speech delivered to Alec before she murders him. Polanski radically alters the character and the narrative. He plays down the family curse, but exalts the paganism and fatalism. He picks up on the solar and red colour imagery. When we first see Tess/ Kinski in close-up she has the setting sun right behind her. This is Polanski's major motif in the film. The sun crashes into Tess/ Kinski's life again when she climbs up the ladder to discover that Angel has not read her letter. This comes at the end of a very touching scene: Tess/ Kinski slips into Angel's room and puts flowers everywhere. She leaves, climbs down the ladder, turns, and pulls out the letter from under the carpet. The camera cranes down slightly, Tess/ Kinski leans back into the sun. Brilliant white shatters the lens for a few moments. The music which swells up loudly at this point is not necessary: the visuals have done all the talking here. As Tess/ Kinski moves back down the ladder, the world suddenly changes, it becomes windy and shadowy. Polanski uses wind in the long opening scene, in a very delicate touch. The camera pans away from the dancing girls to show the three Clare brothers walking up the lane. As it moves the camera tracks past a bush on a wall, which the wind rustles. Wind blows into Tess/ Kinski later on as she sits in the boat with the parasol. Later the storm breaks as Tess/ Kinski stands in her bedroom in the Stoke-d'Urberville house and Alec bangs on the door outside.

Polanski envisions *Tess of the d'Urbervilles* as a love-story, as a record of intolerance, and as 'the film of my mature years'.[97] Polanski makes the connections, as Hardy does, between sexuality and materialism, between spiritual purity and bodily cleanliness, between class and integrity, between silence and expression, between bogus, classist statues and true, ontological nobility. Class is underlined in the scene where Angel visits his family. Materialism is portrayed in the long shot of Tess's destitute family underneath the church window. There are many looks in the film – looks of power and sexuality: Tess watches Angel, Angel watches the maidens, they stare at him as he stares at the sunset, Alec stares at Tess, the horse looks at the rape, and so on. A powerful filmic look occurs when the farmer in the cart sneers at Tess/ Kinski and calls her a 'fancy-woman, a trollop'. The language, much as it is in the novel, is modernized. Instead of 'clipping and colling' Tess's friend speaks of having no men around 'to give you a squeeze'.

Tess of the d'Urbervilles is a *Cinderella* story. There is the ineffective Lear-like father, the pushy mother, the false prince (Alec) and the true (but blind) prince (Angel). Tess, like Cinderella, works with poultry, with birds. She has the opposite of the glass slippers – the muddy boots (later picked up by the ugly sister/ rival, Mercy Chant). Like Cinderella, and other fairy tale heroines, Tess is deeply associated with animals – birds, cows, horses and so on.

Polanski fills the film with a vast array of natural sounds. Tess is associated with cows, dogs, birds, deer – all kinds of animal noises. When she is raped the forest is alive with bird-sounds, as exotic as a jungle. In the extended honeymoon scene, some fifteen or so minutes long, there are two or three ticking clocks – filmmakers' shorthand for mortality (later on the sound of shears clipping away at a hedge plays throughout the scene in the Sandbourne hotel; there is also the sound of bells tolling, and wood being chopped). Some of the motifs are cartoon-like.– very obvious. As when a hunting party of horses and dogs crosses directly in front of Tess/ Kinski as she plods along. Mistletoe is thrown

---

97 In Wexman, pp. 118, 125.

on a fire. Angel prods the ashes the following morning. It also rains. Polanski here is blindingly obvious in his mise-en-scène.

There are many twilit scenes in the film. The characters move through a ghostly half-light. There are many images, too, of people on lonely roads. More positive images occur with the women in the film. The images of female solidarity are very encouraging – at Talbothays, and when Tess finds sanctuary later on at Flintcomb-Ash. Polanski describes things visually here. There are long passages of action accompanied by silence of natural sounds. The music, when it occurs, is lushly orchestrated in the Hollywood style. At times the music is crude – as when Tess/ Kinski buries her baby and the soundtrack features the lullaby *Bye, Bye Baby Buntin'* played on quivering strings. This is embarrassingly bad. Polanski plays with the viewer visually: when Izz Huet appears, struggling along with her bags, in the distance, we imagine first to be Tess. Earlier, Polanski positions three maidens to balance and contrast with the three Clare brothers. The acting is often quite difficult to accept – especially Firth's po-faced Angel, and Kinski's sombre Tess. Kinski is the biggest problem. Any film version of *Tess of the d'Urbervilles* pivots around the actress's ability to portray the heroine. The question is, can anybody portray Tess convincingly? No. The Tess of Kinski as directed by Polanski is the most disappointing aspect of the film. The film depends upon her so much. Polanski changed her character. He made her more passive. In the book she is lively, noble, and quietly passionate. In the film she is dour. We simply do not believe that Kinski can go through everything as she does. Polanski makes an even more crucial change in the rape-scene.

Hardy called Tess's rape a 'fatal experience' (Preface to *Tess of the d'Urbervilles*, p. 37). Feminists use rape as a demonstration of patriarchy-in-action. Susan Brownmiller calls rape 'a conscious form of intimidation by which all men keep all women in a state of fear' (in Kramarae, p. 380). Mary Daly and Andrea Dworkin have exposed many of the lies at the powerbase of patriarchy. Dworkin writes:

> Being owned and being fucked are or have been virtually synonymous experiences in the lives of women. He owns you; he fucks you. The fucking conveys the quality of the ownership; he owns you inside out. (*Intercourse*, p. 76)

What Polanski does is to change the rape-scene dramatically. There are many problems with this scene. It occurs in total darkness, for a start. Polanski instead lights the forest as if for a *Dracula* film, with shafts of light slanting down through smoke and mist. Birds sing wildly. The horse looks on dumbly. Tess/ Kinski kisses Alec/ Lawson back at first, then she struggles. As she writhes, we are not sure if this is a rape or a seduction. Hardy is not ambiguous, but Polanski is. The music sweeps in at this point, as does the theatrical fog. The whole thing is fraught with problems. Firstly, Hardy does not describe the actual rape. He leads up it, as he takes Alec and Tess deeper into the ancient forest on The Chase. Alec leaves Tess to try to find out where they are; he returns, leans down to her; there are tears on her cheeks; then Hardy cuts away from this intimate description to a wide view of abstractions and moralizing. Why is it, intones the authorial voice, that so many girls like Tess are treated thus by men such as Alec? The rhetoric continues to the end of the Phase 'The Maiden'. The act of the rape is allowed to grow in our minds. How clever Hardy is here. Victorian standards might have censored him from showing the rape, but it actually does not need to be depicted. Cinema, however, thrives on visual images – without them it is nothing. We have to *see* what goes on. The audience cannot be defrauded at this dramatic moment. We cannot cut to a new scene and back-announce the rape, as it were. Polanski's film aims to be as close as possible to the drift of the text. So we must *see* the rape. A rape-scene must be one of the most difficult of all scenes to act and to film. Total body invasion is an extraordinary psychological experience. Cinema focusses on the body and frames it, but it cannot move inside the body. So the mass of terror and pain experienced during rape must be expressed through acting, and here is where everything breaks down. Cinema remains always on the outside of things. It dwells on surfaces, not on essences. Acting is not enough, nor is montage, *mise-en-scène*, voice-over or music. A film can be patched up in so many ways, but no film has yet depicted the hideous violence and psychological damage of rape. Polanski's *Tess* is no exception. And because the narrative pivots on just such an incident, the film must fail. It fails for many reasons. It tries to be close to the book but misses out so much important material. Many of the book's themes are jettisoned. Characters are not developed. Dialogue is shortened and dialect is ruined. Hardy's polemic is reduced to whimpers and gorgeous scenery. The closer Polanski tries to get to Hardy's *Tess of the d'Urbervilles*, the farther away he actually is in the film. He distorts the spirit of the book at key-moments. He gags his heroine when she is bursting to speak. He simplifies the characters to stereotypes. The film is too long. It looks wonderful at times, but most people can get a good picture from a piece of postcard-quality landscape. Polanski says all he has to say in the opening and closing sequences. The glowing summery light in the dance-field contrasts superbly with the brooding, lowering clouds over the Stonehenge set. Tess appears in white, with a red face and red ribbon; she leaves the film with a dark red dress, white face and no ribbon but lace and a hat. Polanski's stylization here works well. It fits in with the rest of the film, which is crude in its symbolism, as in the sudden cut to the speeding train after Tess tells Angel she has killed Alec. Polanski's *Tess* is the most impressive adaption of Hardy yet, even though it fails.

Thomas Hardy's fiction is difficult to translate onto the screen. Though he uses a relatively objective viewpoint, a wealth of intriguing characters and a lot of dramatic incident, filmmakers have so far failed to capture the spirit of his fiction. They do not seem to be able to grapple seriously with Hardy's themes and concerns. Dickens gets a better treatment, with Lean's and Reed's film versions, and in the BBC *Bleak House*. Brontë, Trollope and Austen have also fared quite well, though no satisfying film version can ever made of *Wuthering Heights*, perhaps for the same reasons as with Hardy's books. Some novels are so fully realized in prose – *Wuthering Heights, The Rainbow, Tess of the d'Urbervilles, The Unnameable, The Alexandria Quartet*, for example – they simply cannot be turned into films. Filmmakers would do better to leave some of the 'classics' alone, and write their own original material. The results are far more satisfying, being conceived in cinematic terms – think of the films of Tarkovsky, Bergman, Godard, Chaplin, Fellini, Allen and Bertolucci. The two filmmakers who could have given us spirited versions of Hardy – Bresson and Tarkovsky – are dead. Few other directors could render

Hardy authentically. Bresson's quiet, precise intensity is well suited to the tone of Hardy's fiction. Imagine, then, a radical rendition of *Tess of the d'Urbervilles* in the style of Bresson's *Mouchette* (1967, France) or his *Diary of a Country Priest* (1950, France), combined with Bergman's passion around the time of his *The Virgin Spring* (1959, Sweden).

Fifteen

Conclusion: Thomas Hardy, John Cowper Powys and D.H. Lawrence

Some true lover's instinct must indeed have drawn you in your present mood to D.H. Lawrence's extraordinary works... Yes: you use the word congruity in its precisely correct sense when you speak of the strange affiliation between persons and landscapes – the very chemistry of the elements around those figures of his.

John Cowper Powys, *Letters to Sven-Erik Tackmark* (p. 49)

This is the wonder of Hardy's novels, and gives them their beauty. The vast, unexplained morality of life itself, what we call the immorality of nature, surrounds us in its eternal incomprehensibility, and in its midst goes on the little human morality play, with its queer frame of morality and its mechanized movement.

D.H. Lawrence, *Study of Thomas Hardy* (p. 29)

John Cowper Powys is no tragedian, like Thomas Hardy, nor a religious polemicist, like D.H. Lawrence. His style is wayward, Like Miller he veers from the brilliant to the terrible. His elemental prose never reaches the heights of Lawrence's rhythmic, dense, ecstatic writing – in Lawrence's descriptions of the rose-red snow in *Twilight in Italy*, for instance. Like Lawrence, Powys believed too that 'we must get back into relation, vivid and nourishing relation to the cosmos and the universe'.[98] In figures such as Wolf, Sylvanus and Uryen, Powys espoused a Lawrencean version of 'the quick and the dead'. Powys lacked the form, unity, structure and discipline of Hardy, and the focussing power of Lawrence. Powys exaggerates, he spools out time, he expands episodes. A gesture is endlessly extended. Lawrence, when he's burning up with his poetic, religious and social polemical fire, 'outworks and kills' all other British writers, as Turner outworked and killed all other painters.

Powys's gift is for bringing out the strangeness of people. Lawrence's goals are a return to instinct, to the body, to relationship. Hardy's goals are tenderness and the abolition of societal hypocrisies. Powys's goals are more difficult to define. He tries to maximize self-integrity through an ecstatic sense of sensualism and mythology. Powys is detached, like Hardy. Lawrence does not play around. He is wholly committed, he is serious and plangent. Powys is the most playful of the three. The lack of humour in Hardy is frustrating. He does not use humour enough. Neither does Lawrence. They are united by their love of landscape and the energies that course through it. They are united by their belief in what Hardy called 'the intensity of experience' (Blue Eyes, p. 260). For Lawrence. 'actual living' was 'a question mostly of direct contact'.[99] For Powys this intense, direct contact is most fruitful between self and Nature, between the self and the mythical elements, not between the self and other people. This goal of a six-sense intensification is most fully worked through in the character of Wolf Solent. No Jude he, orchestrating his life to reproduce maximum ecstasies from minimum resources. Tea and bread for him, and he glories in them. Powys's characters are trying to be shaman, working on the magnification of their souls. The result might be what Taleissin called in *Porius* 'The beginning of the Peace paradisic' (P,

---

98 'A Propos of *Lady Chatterley's Lover*', in *A Selection from Phoenix*, p. 355.
99 'Insouciance', *Selected Essays*, p. 105.

p. 417).

John Cowper Powys goes beyond Thomas Hardy and D.H. Lawrence and most British writers in his depictions of the self alone. Tess Alone, like Ursula Alone, is a majestic conception. But she gains much of her majesty from her relationships with others. The Powys self-alone is truly alone (or at least, far more alone than most fictional characters – Beckett's protagonists are probably the most isolated people in modern fiction). Sensual solitude is Powys's special province. He writes best there. His characters possess a holy kind of isolation. They are unique, self-sufficient, complete in themselves (Zoyland, Elphin, Porius, Evans, Gaunt, Thuella).

John Cowper Powys is difficult. Sometimes Joyce and Woolf are difficult to follow, but Powys overwrites much more than they do. The wanderings, the diffuseness, the oblique allusions, the awkward metaphors – it is not easy for the reader of Powys's Wessex tetralogy. His biggest fault is the use of the *longueur*, the long sentence. Fourteen-line sentences are not uncommon (on page 457 of *Weymouth Sands*, for example). Powys is the Whitman of prose – big visions require big writing. But Powys does not write simple long sentences. Instead we get pleonasms, convolutions, whimsicalities and irrelevancies. Powys's mind teems when he writes. He makes intuitive connections too fast for his pen. The thin, spidery hand tries hard to encompass a big vision of the world. Always on the edge, Powys often falls off it. Of *Porius* he wrote:

> It suits my weaknesses, badnesses, all my whimsies and quimsies and de quincies, all my superstition, prejudices, blasphemies and blissphemies, my hoverings round and my shootings off, my divings down and poppings up...[100]

Like Joyce, Powys tries to expand the events of one day over hundreds of pages. The results – in *Porius* and *Owen Glendower* in particular – are badly organized. Powys needs structure and discipline. Instead he lets himself rant like a dervish. He did not revise much, unfortunately (ib, p. 9). The multiple viewpoints in *Porius* are confusing. Of the Wessex novels *Wolf Solent* begins tamely enough but soon becomes a catalogue of altered states of consciousness. Nevertheless, the intensity renders it readable.

---

[100] March 1944, in Wil, pp. 142-3.

Weymouth Sands is the most approachable. *Maiden Castle* is already becoming diffuse and misty, like the later Welsh histories. But *A Glastonbury Romance* is the most difficult. That opening sentence! Ouch! How much better is the terse, dry style of the opening sentences of E.M. Forster ('They were all at Charing Cross...')[101] or Evelyn Waugh ('"I have been here before,' I said...')[102] or, more recently, Jeanette Winterson ('He liked me because I am short').[103] In comparison with the stately, sonorous simplicity of Hardy ('On an evening in the latter part of May a middle-aged man was walking homeward...' [*Tess*, p. 43]) Powys is erratic and obscure (see the opening lines of *Wolf Solent, Weymouth Sands* and *The Brazen Head*, for example).

John Cowper Powys's time-dilated spatially-shifted prose style is an attempt at post-Proustian spiritual realism. In the spiritualized world, nothing is quite as it seems. In Powys fairy tale-like mythic world, most things *are* as they seem. That patch of moss on that wall *is that patch of moss on that wall*. And nothing else. In the elemental Powys-scape, everything can be reduced to elements. The complex vision must leave no stone unturned. Every stone is worthy of turning so Powys patiently turns over every stone on the beach of his fictive world (this is of course Chesil Beach in his Wessex). He snips every blade of grass, collects every species of flower, sketches every kind of cloud. However, even the dedicated follower gives up after turning over the five hundred thousand two hundred and eighty fourth stone, even if Christ, the Logos, the Essence, the *Nous*, the living Spirit or the Tenth Sephiroth lies under it.

Powys has many annoying habits. One is the breakdown of speech and thoughts... in his characters... expressed... like... this. Another is the sudden concentration on utterly insignificant incidents (a moth flies out of Dud's clothes into the air above Mai-Dun Castle, for instance – gosh!). Another is the lack of verisimilitude. Another is his use of far-fetched metaphors. Another is his long chapters. Another is archaic colloquialisms and nicknames. Another is his repetitiousness. Hardy's faults include awkward phraseology, bad sentence-structure, authorial intrusions, vagueness, moralizing, repetitions, oversimplification and

---
101 *Where Angels Fear to Tread*, Penguin 1959, p. 5.
102 *Brideshead Revisited*, Chapman & Hall 1949, p. 150.
103 *The Passion*, Penguin 1988, p. 3.

intellectual snobbery.

The surprises in Powys's fiction are worth waiting for: the eidetic landscaping, the ecstasies, the elementalism, the bizarre characters. Sometimes Powys manages to a pull out a succulent metaphor from the erratic flood of his prose, as in *Maiden Castle* when Uryen's voice is described as 'so low and yet so intense that it was like the wind lifting the tapestry in a royal death-chamber' (MC, p. 455) Marvellous imagery, this, but used so few and far between. It conjures up the right mixture of the Past and the præternatural, absolutely correct for Uryen's personality. It is quite ordinary, though – a tapestry lifting up in the wind. But in a *royal death-chamber* – that's the great touch.

Most authors have at least one annoying fault – Brontë's stridency, Greene's Catholicism, Durrell's studied cosmopolitanism, Dickens' detailed scene-setting, Miller's and Mailer's egotism, Woolf's introspection, Lawrence's reductionism and Waugh's upper classism, for example. Powys's slow-motion style is certainly frustrating. Seldom does he accelerate up to normal speed. Reading him is like walking through water, against the incoming tidal flow.

Apolitical, culturally ostracized and ideologically ambiguous, John Cowper Powys is disliked partly because he evades classification and analysis. He is a gargantuan in an age which exalts slick, stream-lined 250-page materialist authors who write about shopping and fucking in Hampstead. What has a middle-aged Celtic wimp staring at a bit of moss on a wall in the country-bumpkin provinces got to do with the real world, the urban world of the early 21st century? Precious little. But Hardy writes of adultery, marriage and divorce – and adultery is pretty much *the* subject of bourgeois fiction. Hardy is a guaranteed winner, because (on the surface at least) he idealizes the country life. In Hardy you can ignore the fierce polemic and concentrate on the story. *Story story story* – how the Western world thrives on *story* – in movies, in soap operas, in newspapers. What happened in last night's edition of the Grumps soap? everyone asks. Not theme, *mise-en-scène*, emotion, production team, actors, discourse, ideology – but *story*. Naturally Powys fails to deliver compelling narratives. He is not populist, he is not popular. Hardy is, because along with everything else, he delivers a good story – and simply.

From his dug-out halfway up a rain-sodden Welsh mountain, Powys aims his guns not at society or ethics but at mythology, inner space and the soul. Powys is not political like Lawrence, Tolstoy, Conrad or Faulkner; he is not existentialist like Camus, Hamsun, Musil, Mann or Sartre; he is not epic like Cervantes, Dante or Sophocles; he is no social portraitist like Flaubert, Balzac, Dickens or Austen; and his stream-of-consciousness discourse does not have the bite of Proust, Joyce or Woolf. Powys is out on his own, out in his own mythopoeic world, like Graves – and he enjoys it there.

Like his mythical God-Fish, John Cowper Powys is slippery. he changes colour and shape and will *not* be speared, caught and eaten. He struggles free of the clamps on the cultural vivisector's laboratory table. Powys is vast, like Hardy. He overflows conventional boundaries. he will not be categorized, just as Lawrence, Brontë, Rimbaud and Petrarch will not be. Like Hardy, Powys wants to the 'other ways' of living to be within the reach of all. Every pathway is worth exploring.

John Cowper Powys followed his bliss, and we can follow the trajectory of this bliss by moving from book to book. In this Grail-Quest Powys knew that 'you are the only one who can do it'.[104] Few of his characters did it – still less of Hardy's. The magicians in Powys come closest to fusing the excitement of ecstasy, escape and excrement. Powys advocates life-enhancement, as does Hardy, although the latter freights his with a Schopenhauerian renunciation. Going back – or forward – to the mythic Centre means going through it all again.

Powys approached Wessex like some vast tidal essence, flowing in from the subaquatic depths of Atlantis to surrounded the decayed harbour of Weymouth; flowing on further inland, to flood the ancient walls of the city of glass; moving onwards and deeper down through the fenlands of Somerset, towards the seething plantlife and underlife of the Dorset–Somerset border; and finally, trickling softly but surely into the clear streams of Dorchester, the capital of Hardy's Wessex.

Thomas Hardy, meanwhile, charted Wessex at a stolid walking pace. His landscape is profoundly *humanized*. Hardy records the human touch carefully – his Wessex is, like *Tess* the novel, 'faithfully presented'. Hardy

---

[104] J. Campbell, *Myths to Live By*, p. 73.

is circumspect, thoughtful, poetic – he is on a countrywide ramble, but fully attentive, watchful. Lawrence, meanwhile, steps restlessly through the world. He is eternally dissatisfied. Mexico, Australia, Italy – these wild places are still not big or wild enough for him. Back to the savage zones of England then? No, there is no answer for alienated souls. Hardy and John Cowper Powys are tranquil in comparison to Lawrence's feverish ontological questing.

While Hardy and Lawrence died two years apart – in 1928 and 1930 – Powys was to carry on writing for another thirty years. When they died he was just starting to write his best works.

Bibliography

All books are published in London, England, unless otherwise stated.
Abbreviations appear after each entry

John Cowper Powys

Wolf Solent, Penguin 1964 [WS]
A Glastonbury Romance, Macdonald 1955 [GR]
Weymouth Sands, Picador/Pan 1980 [Wey]
Maiden Castle, Cassell 1937 [MC]
Maiden Castle: The First Full Authoritative Edition, University of Wales Press, Cardiff 1990
Rodmoor, Macdonald 1973 [R]
Ducdame, Village Press 1974 [D]
Wood and Stone, Village Press 1974 [Wood]
Atlantis, Macdonald 1954
Morwyn, Village Press 1974
The Inmates, Macdonald 1952
All or Nothing, Village Press 1973
Up and Out, Macdonald 1957
Owen Glendower, The Bodley Head 1941 [OG]
The Brazen Head, Macdonald 1956 [BH]
Homer and the Aether, Macdonald 1959
Autobiography, Macdonald 1967 [A]
A Philosophy of Solitude, Cape 1933 [Sol]
In Defence of Sensuality, Gollancz 1930 [Def]
The Complex Vision, Village Press 1975 {Com]
The Pleasures of Literature, Village Press 1975 [PL]
Suspended Judgements, Village Press 1975 [SJ]
Visions and Revisions, Macdonald 1955 [VR]
The Art of Happiness, Bodley Head 1935 [Hap]

In Spite Of, Macdonald 1953
Rabelais, Village Press 1974
Dostoievsky, Bodley Head 1946
Confessions of Two Brothers, Sinclair Browne 1982
Selected Poems, ed. Kenneth Hopkins, Macdonald 1964
Mandragora: Poems, Village Press 1975
Lucifer, Macdonald 1956
Obstinate Cymric: Essays 1935-47, The Druid Press, Carmarthen 1947
Mortal Strife, Cape 1942 [MS]
Letters 1937-54, ed. Iorwerth Peate, University of Wales Press, Cardiff 1974
Letters to Louis Wilkinson 1935-56, Village Press 1974 [Wil]
Letters of John Cowper Powys to C.Benson Roberts, Village Press 1975
The Letters of John Cowper Powys to G.Wilson Knight, ed. Robert Blackmore, Cecil Woolf 1985
Letters of John Cowper Powys to Sven-Erik Tackmark, ed. Cedric Henstschel, Cecil Woolf 1983
The Diary of John Cowper Powys 1930, ed Davis, Greymitre Books 1987

Thomas Hardy

Jude the Obscure, ed. C.H.Sisson, Penguin 1978/85
Jude the Obscure: An Authoritative Text, Backgrounds and Sources, Criticism, ed. Norman Page, W.W.Norton & Co, New York 1978
Tess of the D'Urbervilles, ed. David Skilton, Penguin 1978/85
Tess of the D'Urbervilles: An Authoritative Text, Hardy and the Novel, ed. Scott Elledge, W.W.Norton & Co, New York 1965/79
The Return of the Native, ed. George Woodcock, Penguin 1978
The Woodlanders, ed. James Gibson, Penguin 1981
The Mayor of Casterbridge, ed. Vivian de Sola Pinto, Macmillan 1934/61
Far From the Madding Crowd, ed. James Gibson, Dent 1984
Under the Greenwood Tree, ed. Simon Gatrell, Oxford University Press 1985
A Pair of Blue Eyes, ed. Alan Manford, Oxford University Press 1985
The Well-Beloved, ed. Tom Hetherington, Oxford University Press 1986
Two on a Tower, ed. F.B.Pinion, Macmillan 1975
A Laocidean, Heron/Macmillan 19877
The Hand of Ethelberta, ed. Robert Gittings, Macmillan 1975
The Trumpet-Major, St Martins Library, Macmillan 1962
Complete Poems, ed. James Gibson, Macmillan 1981 [CP]
Selected Poems, ed. Walford Davies, Dent 1982

Selected Short Poems, ed. John Wain, Macmillan 1966/75
The Gates Along the Path: Poems, Terra Nova Editions 1979
Hardy's Love Poems, ed. Carl J.Weber, Macmillan 1983
The Short Stories of Thomas Hardy, Macmillan 1928
The Literary Notebooks of Thomas Hardy, ed. Lennart A.Bjork, 2 vols, Macmillan 1985
The Collected Letters of Thomas Hardy, eds. Richard Little Purdy & Michael Millgate, 7 vols, Clarendon Press 1978-88
Thomas Hardy's Notebooks, ed. Evelyn Hardy, Hogarth Press 1955
The Personal Notebooks of Thomas Hardy, ed. Richard H.Taylor, Macmillan 1978
The Life of Thomas Hardy, Macmillan 1962 [Life]
The Life and Work of Thomas Hardy, ed. Michael Millgate, Macmillan 1984 [Life]
Personal Writings, ed. Harold Orel, Macmillan 1967 [Per]

Others

Peter Ackroyd: *First Light,* Abacus 1990
Robert Martin Adams: *After Joyce,* Oxford University Press, New York 1977
John Alcorn: *The Nature Novel from Hardy to Lawrence,* Macmillan 1973
Walter Allen: *Tradition and Dream*, Phoenix House 1964
Marc Alexander: *British Folklore, Myths and Legends,* Weidenfeld & Nicolson 1982
Geoffrey Ashe: *Mythology of the British Isles*, Methuen 1990
D.F. Barber, ed. *Concerning Thomas Hardy,* Charles Skilton 1968
John Bayley: *An Essay on Hardy,* Cambridge University Press 1978
Patricia Beer: *Wessex,* Hamish Hamilton 1985
Ean Begg: *The Cult of the Black Virgin*, Routledge 1985
J.H.Betley: *The Landscape of Wessex*, Moonraker Press, Wiltshire 1980
Andrew Bingham: *Dorset: Ordnance Survey Landranger Guidebook,* Ordnance Survey/ Jarrold Colour Publications, Norwich 1987
R.L.Blackmore, ed. *Philobiblion: The Journal of the Friends of Colgate University,* New York 1966
— ed. *The Powys Newsletter,* 1-3, Colgate University, New York 1971-3
Haskell M.Bloch & Herman Salinger, eds. *The Creative Vision: Modern European Writers,* Grove Press, New York 1960
Ronald Blythe: *Characters and Their Landscapes,* Harcout Brace

Jovanovitch, New York 1983
Janet & Colin Bord: *Ancient Mysteries of Britain*, Paladin 1987
John Brebner: *The Demon Within*, Macdonald 1975
Richard Breckon: *John Cowper Powys: The Solitary Giant*, K.A.Ward, Loughton 1969
Jean Brooks: *Thomas Hardy: The Poetic Structure*, Elek 1971
Douglas Brown: *Thomas Hardy*, Longmans, Green & Co. 1954
Peter L.Brown: *Megaliths, Myths and Men*, Blandford Press, Poole 1976
J.B. Bullen: *The Expressive Eye: Fiction of Perception in the Work of Thomas Hardy*, Clarendon Press 1986
David Burnett: *Dorset Before the Camera 1855-1974*, Dovecote Press, Wimbourne, Dorset 1974
Lance St.John Butler, ed. *Thomas Hardy, After Fifty Years*, Macmillan 1977
— ed. *Alternative Hardy*, Macmillan 1989
— *Thomas Hardy*, Cambridge University Press 1978
Robert Cafritz, Lawrence Gowring & David Rosand: *Places of Delight: The Pastoral Landscape*, Weidenfeld & Nicolson 1989
Glen Cavaliero: *John Cowper Powys, Novelist*, Clarendon Press 1973
— *The Rural Tradition in the English Novel 1900-1939*, Macmillan 1977
Joseph Campbell: *The Power of Myth*, with Bill Moyers, ed. Betty Sue Flowers, Doubleday, New York 1988
— *The Hero With a Thousand Faces*, Paladin 1988
— *An Open Life*, Larson Publications, New York 1988
— *Myths To Live By*, Paladin 1985
— *The Hero's Journey: Joseph Campbell on his Life and Work*, ed. Phil Cousineau, Harper & Row, San Francisco 1990
Albert Camus: *The Outsider*, tr. Stuart Gilbert, Penguin 1961
— *A Happy Death*, tr. R.Howard, Penguin 1973
Richard Carpenter: *Thomas Hardy*, Macmillan 1978
Norman T.Carrington: *The Mayor of Casterbridge*, Pan 1976
David Cecil: *Hardy the Novelist*, Constable 1943
Tom Chetwyd: *A Dictionary of Symbols*, Collins 1982
Herschel B.Chipp, ed. *Theories of Modern Art*, University Press of California, Los Angeles 1968
R.C.Churchill: *The Powys Brothers*, British Council/Longman 1962
J.E.Cirlot: *A Dictionary of Symbols*, Routledge 1981
Kenneth Clark: *Landscape into Art*, Reader's Union 19653
C.A.Coates: *John Cowper Powys in Search of a Landscape*, Macmillan 1982
— *John Cowper Powys: A discussion of the implications of his use of Nature and Nature imagery in selected works* [unpublished thesis]
H.P. Collins: *John Cowper Powys: Old Earth-Man*, Village Press 1974
Martin Collins: *South-West Way*, Cicerone Press, Cumbria 1989
Vere H. Collins: *Talks With Thomas Hardy at Max Gate*, Duckworth 1972
J.C. Cooper: The Aquarian Dictionary of Festivals, Aquarian Press, Northants 1990

—*An Illustrated Dictionary of Traditional Symbols*, Thames & Hudson 1978
—*Fairy Tales*, Aquarian Press, Northants 1983
Michael Cox: *Mysticism*, Aquarian Press, Northants 1983
R.G. Cox, ed. *Thomas Hardy: The Critical Heritage*, Barnes & Noble 1970
Cecil N. Cullingford: *A History of Dorset*, Phillimore 1980
Gail Cunningham: *The New Woman and the Victorian Novel*, Macmillan 1978
David Daiches & John Flower: *Literary Landscapes of the British Isles: A Narrative Atlas*, Paddington Press 1979
Mary Daly: *Pure Lust: Elemental Feminist Philosophy*, Women's Press 1984
—*Beyond God the Father*, Women's Press 1985
Michael Dames: *The Avebury Cycle*, Thames & Hudson 1976
H.C.Darby & R.W. Finn: *The Domesday Geography of South-West England*, Cambridge 1967
Jagdish Chandra Dave: *The Human Predicament in Hardy's Novels*, Macmillan 1985
Donald Davie: *Thomas Hardy and British Poetry*, Routledge & Kegan Paul 1979
Carol Dix: *D.H. Lawrence and Women*, Macmillan 1990
Margaret Drabble, ed. *The Genius of Thomas Hardy*, Weidenfeld & Nicolson, 1976
—ed. *A Writer's Britain*, Thames & Hudson 1979
R.P. Draper, ed. *Thomas Hardy: Three Pastoral Novels*, Macmillan 1987
—ed. *Hardy: The Tragic Novels*, Macmillan 1975
H.C. Duffin: *Thomas Hardy*, Greenwood Press, Conn., 1978
Maureen Duffy: *The Erotic World of Faery*, Cardinal/Sphere 1989
Lawrence Durrell: *The Durrell-Miller Letters 1935-80*, ed. Ian MacNiven, Faber 1988
—*Spirit of Place*, Faber 1971
Andrea Dworkin: *Intercourse*, Arrow 1988
—*Pornography: Men Possessing Women*, Women's Press 1984
—*Our Blood*, Harper & Row, New York 1976
Dorothy Eagle & Hilary Carnell, eds. *The Oxford Illustrated Literary Guide to the British Isles*, Oxford University Press 1977
Roger Ebbatson: *Lawrence and the Nature Tradition*, Harvester Press, Brighton 1980
Anne-Marie Edwards: *Discovering Hardy's Wessex*, BBC 1978
Mircea Eliade: *Ordeal by Labyrinth*, University of Chicago Press 1984
—*A History of Religious Ideas*, I, Collins 1979
—*Patterns in Comparative Religion*, Sheed & Ward 1958
—*Symbolism, the Sacred and the Arts*, Crossroad, New York 1985
Ralph W.V. Elliott: *Thomas Hardy's English*, Basil Blackwell 1984
Julius Evola: *The Metaphysics of Sex*, East-West Publications 1985
Neil Fairbairn & Michael Cyprien: *A Traveller's Guide to the Kingdoms of*

Arthur, Evans Brothers 1985
H.W. Fawkner: *The Ecstatic World of John Cowper Powys*, Associated University Press
John Ferguson: *An Illustrated Encyclopaedia of Mysticism*, Thames & Hudson 1976
John Fowles & Jo Draper: *Thomas Hardy's England*, Cape 12984
G.S. Fraser: *The Modern Writer and His World*, Penguin 1964
J.G. Frazer: *The Golden Bough*, abridged edition, Macmillan 1922/59
Alan Friedman: *The Turn of the Novel*, Oxford University Press 1966
Simon Gatrell: *Hardy the Creator: A Textual Biography*, Clarendon Press 1988
James Gibson & Trevor Johnson, eds. *Thomas Hardy: Poems: A Casebook*, Macmillan 1979
André Gide: *Fruits of the Earth*, tr. Dorothy Bussy, Penguin 1970
— *Strait Is the Gate*, tr. Dorothy Bussy, Penguin 1969
— *The Journals of André Gide*, vol.II, tr. Justin O'Brien, Secker & Warburg 1948
Robert Gittings: *The Older Hardy*, Heinemann 1978
Wolfgang Goethe: *The Sorrows of Young Werther*, tr. Michael Hulse, Penguin 1989
Robert Goldwater & Marco Treves, eds. *Artists on Art*, John Murray 1975
John Goode: *Thomas Hardy*, Basil Blackwell 1988
Robert Graves: *The White Goddess*, Faber 1961
— *Mammon and the Black Goddess*, Cassell 1965
— *Collected Poems 1975*, Cassell 1975
— *Between Moon and Moon: Selected Letters of Robert Graves 1946-72*, ed. Paul O'Prey, Hutchinson 1984
— *Conversations with Robert Graves*, ed. Frank Kersnowski, University of Mississippi Press, Jackson 1989
R.P. Graves: *The Powys Brothers*, Routledge & Kegan Paul 1983
Ian Gregor: *The Great Web*, Faber 1974
Albert J. Guerard, ed. *Hardy: A Collection of Critical Essays*, Prentice-Hall International, New York 1963/86
F.E. Halliday: *Thomas Hardy*, Adams & Dart, Bath 1972
Reginald J. Hammond & K.E. Lowther: *Complete Dorset and Wiltshire*, Ward Lock 1976
Knut Hamsum: *Mysteries*, tr. Bothmer, Picador/Pan 1988
F.C.Happold, ed. *Mysticism*, Penguin 1970
Evelyn Hardy: *The Countryman's Ear*, Tebb House, Padstow, Cornwall 1982
G.B.Harrison, ed. *A Book of English Poetry*, Penguin 1950
Desmond Hawkins: *Hardy's Wessex*, Macmillan 1983
— *Hardy: Novelist and Poet*, David & Charles, Devon 1976
Stephen Hazell, ed. *The English Novel*, Macmillan 1978
Cicely Hill: *Life, Death, Books & Heroes*, Powys Society paper 1975

F.S.Hinchey: *Dorset Today and Yesterday*, Blandford 1965
Jeremy Hooker: *John Cowper Powys and David Jones*, Enitharmon Press 1979
—*John Cowper Powys*, University of Wales Press, Cardiff 1973
Kenneth Hopkins: *The Powys Brothers*, Phoenix House 1967
Grahamn Hough: *The Last Romantics*, Methuen 1961
Irving Howe: *Thomas Hardy*, Macmillan 1985
Howard E.Hugo, ed. *The Portable Romantic Reader*, Viking Press, New York 1957
Belinda Humfrey, ed: *Essays on John Cowpoer Powys*, University of Wales Press 1972 [Hum 72]
—ed. *John Cowper Powys's 'Wolf Solent': Critical Studies*, University Press of Wales, Cardiff 1990 [Hum 90]
—ed. *Recollections of the Powys Brothers*, Peter Owen 1980 [Hum 80]
—ed. *The New Welsh Review*, Vol.III, no. 3, Winter 1990-1
Virginia R. Hyman: *Ethical Perspectives in the Novels of Thomas Hardy*, Kenniket Press, New York 1975
Patricia Ingham: *Thomas Hardy*, Harvester Wheatsheaf, Hemel Hempstead 1989
Arlene M. Jackson: *Illustration and the Novels of Thomas Hardy*, Macmillan 1981
A.Norman Jeffares: *A Review of English Literature*, vol. 4, no. 1, Longmans 1963
Michael Jenner: *A Traveller's Companion to the West Country*, Michael Joseph 1990
B. Jones: *John Cowper Powys*, Dorset Natural History & Archaeological Society, Dorchester 1962
R.L.P. & Dorothy M. Jovitt: *Discovering Walks in Wessex Towns*, Shire publications. Bucks 1974
C.G. Jung: *Memories, Dreams, Reflections*, Collins 1967
Denis Kay-Robinson: *The Landscape of Thomas Hardy*, Webb & Bower 1987
—*Hardy's Wessex Reappraised*, David & Charles, Newton Abbot, Devon 1972
Patrick J. Keane: *A Wild Civility: Interactions in the Poetry of Robert Graves*, University Press of Missouri, Columbia 1980
John Keats: The *Complete Poems*, Penguin 1977
W.J. Keith: *Regions of the Imagination: The Development of the British Rural Tradition*, University of Toronto Press, Toronto 1988
—*The Poetry of Nature: Rural Perpsectives in Poetry From Wordsworth to the Present*, University of Toronto Press, Toronto 1980
G. Wilson Knight: *The Saturnian Quest: John Cowper Powys*, Harvester Press, Sussex 1978 [Sat]
—*Neglected Powers*, Routledge & Kegan Paul 1972 [Neg]
—*Visions and Vices: Essays on John Cowper Powys*, ed. John D.Christie,

Cecil Woolf 1990
Cheris Kramarae & Paula A.Treichler, eds. *A Feminist Dictionary*, Pandora Press, 1987
Morine Krissdottir: *John Cowper Powys and the Magical Quest*, Macdonald & Jane's Publishing Group 1980
Weston La Barre: *The Ghost Dance*, Allen & Unwin 1972
— *Muelos*, Columbia University Press, New York 1985
Jacques Lacan and the Ecole Freudienne: *Feminine Sexuality*, ed. Juliet Mitchell and Jacqueline Rose, Macmillan 1982
Derek Langridge: *John Cowper Powys: A Record of Achievement*, The Library Association 1966
Marghanita Laski: *Ecstasy*, Cresset Press 1961
Albert J.LaValley,ed. *Tess of the D'Urbervilles: A Collection of Critical Essays*, Prentice-Hall, New Jersey 1969
D.H. Lawrence: *Study of Thomas Hardy and Other Essays*, ed. Bruce Steele, Cambridge University Press 1985
— *A Selection from Phoenix*, ed. A.A.H. Inglis, Penguin 1971
— *The Rainbow*, ed. John Worthen, Penguin 1981/6
— *The Complete Short Novels*, ed. Sagar & Partridge, Penguin 1982/7
— *Selected Essays*, Penguin 1950
— *Lady Chatterley's Lover*, Penguin 1960
— *The Letters of D.H. Lawrence*, ed. Aldous Huxley, Heinemann 1934
— *The First Lady Chatterley*, Penguin 1973
— *John Thomas and Lady Jane*, Penguin 1973
— *The White Peacock*, Penguin 1982/7
— *The Lost Girl*, Penguin 1950
— *The Letters of D.H. Lawrence*, vol.III, Cambridge University Press 1984
— *The Letters of D.H. Lawrence*, vol.IV, Cambridge University Press 1987
— *Selected Literary Criticism*, ed. Anthony Beal, Heinemann 1967
— *The Complete Poems*, ed. Vivian de Sola Pinto & Warren Roberts, 2 vols, Heinemann 1972
— *Sons and Lovers*, ed. Keith Sagar, Penguin 1981/6
Herman Lea: *Thomas Hardy's Wessex*, Macmillan 1977
Glenda Leeming: *Who's Who in Thomas Hardy*, Elm Tree 1975
Lawrence Lerner, ed. *Shakespeare's Tragedies*, Penguin 1968
David Lodge: *Language of Fiction*, Routledge & Kegan Paul 1966
Bernard Lonergan: *Method in Theology*, Darton, Longman & Todd 1971
Longman's Bookshop: *Thomas Hardy: A Selected Bibliography, for the 1988 Thomas Hardy Festival*, Dorchester 1988
Louis Marlow: *Welsh Ambassadors*, Chapman & Hall 1936
Roland Mathias: *The Hollowed-Out Elder Stalk: John Cowper Powys as a Poet*, Enitharmon Press 1979
John Matthews, ed. *An Arthurian Reader*, Aquarian Press, Northants 1991
Ellen Mayne: *The New Mythology of John Cowper Powys*, New Atlantis Foundation, Surrey 1969

Arthur Mee: *Dorset,* Hodder & Stoughton 1967
Patricia Merivale: *Pan the Goat-God: His Myth in Modern Times,* Harvard University Press, Mass., 1969
J.C.J. Metford: *Dictionary of Christian Lore and Legend,* Thames & Hudson 1983
Michael Millgate: *Thomas Hardy: His Career as a Novelist,* Bodley Head 1971
Michael Millgate: *Thomas Hardy: A Biography,* Oxford University Press 1982
Rosemarie Morgan: *Women and Sexuality in the Novels of Thomas Hardy,* Routledge 1988
V.S.Naipaul: *The Enigma of Arrival,* Penguin 1987
Erich Neumann: *The Great Mother,* Princeton University Press, New Jersey 1972
John Newman & Nikolaus Pevsner: *Dorset,* Penguin 1972
Shirley Nicholson, ed. *The Goddess Re-awakening,* Theosophical Publishing House, New York 1989
Friedrich Nietzsche: *Beyond Good and Evil,* tr. Zimmern, Allen & Unwin 1907/67
—*A Nietzsche Reader,* ed. R.J.Hollingdale, Penguin 1977
Timothy O'Sullivan: *Thomas Hardy: An Illustrated Biography,* Macmillan 1981
Norman Page: *Thomas Hardy,* Bell & Hyman 1980
Geoffrey Parrinder: *Mysticism in the World's Religions,* Sheldon Press 1976
Walter Pater: *The Renaissance,* Oxford University Press 1980
John Peck: *How to Study a Thomas Hardy Novel,* Macmillan 1983
F.B.Pinion: *Thomas Hardy: Art and Thought,* Macmillan 1977
—*A Hardy Companion,* Macmillan 1968
Llewelyn Powys: *Somerset and Dorset Essays,* Macdonald 1957
John Press: *The Fire and the Fountain,* Oxford University Press 1955
Alan Proctor: *A Visitor's Guide to Somerset and Dorset,* Moorland Publishing, Derbyshire 1983
John Rabbets: *From Hardy to Faulkner: Wessex to Yoknapatawpha,* Macmillan 1989
Jeremy Mark Robinson: *Love and Tragedy: A Study of Thomas Hardy,* Crescent Moon 1989
—*The Poetry of Landscape in Thomas Hardy,* Crescent Moon 1990
—*The Light Eternal: A Study of J.M.W.Turner,* Crescent Moon 1989
—*Glorification: Religious Abstraction in Renaissance and 20th Century Painting,* Crescent Moon 1990
—*Sensualism and Mythology: The Wessex Novels of John Cowper Powys,* Crescent Moon 1990
—*Blinded By Her Light: The Love-Poetry of Robert Graves,* Crescent Moon 1991

Royal Commission on Historical Monuments: *England: An Inventory of the Historical Monuments in Dorset*, vols I-V, West, Her Majesty's Stationery Office 1952
John Ruskin: *Works*, ed. E.T.Cook & A.Wedderburn, 39 vols, Allen 1903-12
Bertrand Russell: *A History of Western Philosophy*, Allen & Unwin 1971
— *Why I am Not a Christian*, Allen &Unwin 1963
— *Bertrand Russell's Best*, Allen & Unwin 1971
Keith Sagar: *A D.H. Lawrence Handbook*, Manchester University Press 1982
— *The Art of D.H. Lawrence*, Cambridge University Press 1966
Richard Sale: *Dorset*, Hitchinson 1985
C.H.Salter: *Good Little Thomas Hardy*, Macmillan 1981
Arthur Schopenhauer: *Essays and Aphorisms*, Penguin 1970
Eric Shanes: *Turner's Rivers, Harbours and Coasts*, Chatto & Windus 1981
— *Turner's Picturesque Views in England and Wales 1825-38*, Chatto & Windus 1979
G.W.Sherman: *The Pessimism of Thomas Hardy*, Associated University Press, New Jersey 1976
Penelope Shutle & Peter Redgrove: *The Wise Wound*, Paladin/Grafton 1978/86
Anne Smith, ed. *The Novels of Thomas Hardy*, Vision Press 1979
F.R.Southerington: *Hardy's Vision of Man*, Chatto & Windus 1971
Marlene Springer: *Hardy's Use of Allusion*, Macmillan 1983
Peter Stainer: *Dorset*, Shire County Guide, Shire Publications, Bucks 1986
R.J.Stewart, ed. *The Book of Merlin*, Blandford Press, poole 1987
Rosemary Sumner: *Thomas Hardy: Psychological Novelist*, Macmillan 1981
Dennis Taylor: *Hardy's Poetry, 1860-1928*, Macmillan 1981
Richard H.Taylor: *The Neglected Hardy*, Macmillan 1982
Andrei Tarkovsky: *Sculpting in Time: Reflections on the Cinema*, tr. Kitty Hunter-Blair, Faber 1989
Dante Thomas: *A Bibliography of the Writings of John Cowper Powys*, Paul P.Appel, New York 1975
J.M.W. Turner: *Collected Correspondence of J.M.W.Turner*, ed. John Gage, Clarendon Press 1980
— *The Sunset Ship: The Poems of J.M.W.Turner*, ed. Jack Lindsay, Scorpion Press 1966
Humfrey Welfare: *Wessex: National Trust Histories*, Collins 1984
Virigina Wright Wexman: *Roman Polanski*, Columbia Books 1987
R.J. White: *Thomas Hardy and History*, Macmillan 1974
Edward C. Whitmont: *Return of the Goddess*, Routledge 1987
Peter Widdowson: *Hardy in History: A study in literary sociology*, Routledge 1989
Merryn Williams: *Thomas Hardy and Rural England*, Macmillan 1972
Raymond Williams: *Marxism and Literature*, Oxford University Press 1971

George Wing: *Hardy*, Oliver & Boyd 1963
Ralph Wightman: *Portrait of Dorset*, Robert Hale 1983
J.H. Wilks: *Trees of the British Isles in History and Legend*, Frederick Muller 1972
Colin Wilson: *The Sexual Misfits: A Study of Sexual Outsiders*, Collins 1989
— *Mysteries*, Granada 1979
— *The Occult*, Granada 1971
— *The Craft of the Novel*, Gollancz 1975
Ludwig Wittgenstein: *Tractatus Logico-Philosophicus*, tr. D.F.Pears & B.F.McGuiness, Routledge & Kegan Paul 1974
David Wright, ed. *English Romantic Verse*, Penguin 1968
Terence Wright: *Tess of the D'Urbervilles*, Macmillan 1987
T.R.Wright: *Hardy and the Erotic*, Macmillan 1989
R.C.Zaehner: *Mysticism Sacred and Profane*, Oxford University Press 1957

J.R.R. Tolkien
The Books, The Films, The Whole Cultural Phenomenon

by Jeremy Mark Robinson

A new critical study of J.R.R. Tolkien, creator of Middle-earth and author of *The Lord of the Rings, The Hobbit* and *The Silmarillion*, among other books.

This new critical study explores Tolkien's major writings (*The Lord of the Rings, The Hobbit, Beowulf: The Monster and the Critics, The Letters, The Silmarillion* and *The History of Middle-earth* volumes); Tolkien and fairy tales; the mythological, political and religious aspects of Tolkien's Middle-earth; the critics' response to Tolkien's fiction over the decades; the Tolkien industry (merchandizing, toys, role-playing games, posters, Tolkien societies, conferences and the like); Tolkien in visual and fantasy art; the cultural aspects of The Lord of the Rings (from the 1950s to the present); Tolkien's fiction's relationship with other fantasy fiction, such as C.S. Lewis and *Harry Potter*; and the TV, radio and film versions of Tolkien's books, including the 2001-03 Hollywood interpretations of *The Lord of the Rings*.

This new book draws on contemporary cultural theory and analysis and offers a sympathetic and illuminating (and sceptical) account of the Tolkien phenomenon. This book is designed to appeal to the general reader (and viewer) of Tolkien: it is written in a clear, jargon-free and easily-accessible style.

754pp   ISBN 1-86171-057-7   £25.00 / $37.50

THE SACRED CINEMA OF ANDREI TARKOVSKY

by Jeremy Mark Robinson

A new study of the Russian filmmaker Andrei Tarkovsky (1932-1986), director of seven feature films, including *Andrei Roublyov, Mirror, Solaris, Stalker* and *The Sacrifice*.
This is one of the most comprehensive and detailed studies of Tarkovsky's cinema available. Every film is explored in depth, with scene-by-scene analyses. All aspects of Tarkovsky's output are critiqued, including editing, camera, staging, script, budget, collaborations, production, sound, music, performance and spirituality. Tarkovsky is placed with a European New Wave tradition of filmmaking, alongside directors like Ingmar Bergman, Carl Theodor Dreyer, Pier Paolo Pasolini and Robert Bresson.
An essential addition to film studies.

Illustrations: 150 b/w, 4 colour. 682 pages. First edition. Hardback.

Publisher: Crescent Moon Publishing. Distributor: Gardners Books.

ISBN 1-86171-096-8 (9781861710963) £60.00 / $105.00

The Best of Peter Redgrove's Poetry
The Book of Wonders

by Peter Redgrove, edited and introduced by Jeremy Robinson

Poems of wet shirts and 'wonder-awakening dresses'; honey, wasps and bees; orchards and apples; rivers, seas and tides; storms, rain, weather and clouds; waterworks; labyrinths; amazing perfumes; the Cornish landscape (Penzance, Perranporth, Falmouth, Boscastle, the Lizard and Scilly Isles); the sixth sense and 'extra-sensuous perception'; witchcraft; alchemical vessels and laboratories; yoga; menstruation; mines, minerals and stones; sand dunes; mud-baths; mythology; dreaming; vulvas; and lots of sex magic. This book gathers together poetry (and prose) from every stage of Redgrove's career, and every book. It includes pieces that have only appeared in small presses and magazines, and in uncollected form.

'Peter Redgrove is really an extraordinary poet' (George Szirtes, *Quarto* magazine)
'Peter Redgrove is one of the few significant poets now writing... His 'means' are indeed brilliant and delightful. Technically he is a poet essentially of brilliant and unexpected images...he never disappoints' (Kathleen Raine, *Temenos* magazine).

240pp   ISBN 1-86171-063-1   2nd edition   £19.99 / $29.50

Sex–Magic–Poetry–Cornwall
A Flood of Poems

by Peter Redgrove. Edited with an essay by Jeremy Robinson

A marvellous collection of poems by one of Britain's best but underrated poets, Peter Redgrove. This book brings together some of Redgrove's wildest and most passionate works, creating a 'flood' of poetry. Philip Hobsbaum called Redgrove 'the great poet of our time', while Angela Carter said: 'Redgrove's language can light up a page.' Redgrove ranks alongside Ted Hughes and Sylvia Plath. He is in every way a 'major poet'. Robinson's essay analyzes all of Redgrove's poetic work, including his use of sex magic, natural science, menstruation, psychology, myth, alchemy and feminism.
A new edition, including a new introduction, new preface and new bibliography.

'Robinson's enthusiasm is winning, and his perceptive readings are supported by a very useful bibliography' (*Acumen* magazine)
'*Sex-Magic-Poetry-Cornwall* is a very rich essay... It is like a brightly-lighted box. (Peter Redgrove)
'This is an excellent selection of poetry and an extensive essay on the themes and theories of this unusual poet by Jeremy Robinson' (*Chapman* magazine)

220pp   New, 3rd edition   ISBN 1-86171-070-4   £14.99 / $23.50

THE ART OF ANDY GOLDSWORTHY

COMPLETE WORKS: SPECIAL EDITION
(PAPERBACK and HARDBACK)

by William Malpas

A new, special edition of the study of the contemporary British sculptor, Andy Goldsworthy, including a new introduction, new bibliography and many new illustrations.

This is the most comprehensive, up-to-date, well-researched and in-depth account of Goldsworthy's art available anywhere.

Andy Goldsworthy makes land art. His sculpture is a sensitive, intuitive response to nature, light, time, growth, the seasons and the earth. Goldsworthy's environmental art is becoming ever more popular: 1993's art book *Stone* was a bestseller; the press raved about Goldsworthy taking over a number of London West End art galleries in 1994; during 1995 Goldsworthy designed a set of Royal Mail stamps and had a show at the British Museum. Malpas surveys all of Goldsworthy's art, and analyzes his relation with other land artists such as Robert Smithson, Walter de Maria, Richard Long and David Nash, and his place in the contemporary British art scene.

The Art of Andy Goldsworthy discusses all of Goldsworthy's important and recent exhibitions and books, including the *Sheepfolds* project; the TV documentaries; *Wood* (1996); the New York Holocaust memorial (2003); and Goldsworthy's collaboration on a dance performance.

Illustrations: 70 b/w, 1 colour. 330 pages. New, special, 2nd edition.
Publisher: Crescent Moon Publishing. Distributor: Gardners Books.

ISBN 1-86171-059-3 (9781861710598) (Paperback) £25.00 / $44.00

ISBN 1-86171-080-1 (9781861710802) (Hardback) £60.00 / $105.00

CRESCENT MOON PUBLISHING

ARTS, PAINTING, SCULPTURE

The Art of Andy Goldsworthy: Complete Works(Pbk)
The Art of Andy Goldsworthy: Complete Works (Hbk)
Andy Goldsworthy in Close-Up (Pbk)
Andy Goldsworthy in Close-Up (Hbk)
Land Art: A Complete Guide
Richard Long: The Art of Walking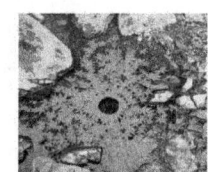
The Art of Richard Long: Complete Works (Pbk)
The Art of Richard Long: Complete Works (Hbk)
Richard Long in Close-Up
Land Art In the UK
Land Art in Close-Up
Installation Art in Close-Up
Minimal Art and Artists In the 1960s and After
Colourfield Painting
Land Art DVD, TV documentary
Andy Goldsworthy DVD, TV documentary
The Erotic Object: Sexuality in Sculpture From Prehistory to the Present Day
Sex in Art: Pornography and Pleasure in Painting and Sculpture
Postwar Art
Sacred Gardens: The Garden in Myth, Religion and Art
Glorification: Religious Abstraction in Renaissance and 20th Century Art
Early Netherlandish Painting
Leonardo da Vinci
Piero della Francesca
Giovanni Bellini
Fra Angelico: Art and Religion in the Renaissance
Mark Rothko: The Art of Transcendence
Frank Stella: American Abstract Artist
Jasper Johns: Painting By Numbers
Brice Marden
Alison Wilding: The Embrace of Sculpture
Vincent van Gogh: Visionary Landscapes
Eric Gill: Nuptials of God
Constantin Brancusi: Sculpting the Essence of Things
Max Beckmann
Egon Schiele: Sex and Death In Purple Stockings
Delizioso Fotografico Fervore: Works In Process 1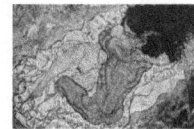
Sacro Cuore: Works In Process 2
The Light Eternal: J.M.W. Turner
The Madonna Glorified: Karen Arthurs

LITERATURE

J.R.R. Tolkien: The Books, The Films, The Whole Cultural Phenomenon
Harry Potter
Sexing Hardy: Thomas Hardy and Feminism
Thomas Hardy's *Tess of the d'Urbervilles*
Thomas Hardy's *Jude the Obscure*
Thomas Hardy: The Tragic Novels
Love and Tragedy: Thomas Hardy
The Poetry of Landscape in Hardy
Wessex Revisited: Thomas Hardy and John Cowper Powys
Wolfgang Iser: Essays
Petrarch, Dante and the Troubadours
Maurice Sendak and the Art of Children's Book Illustration
Andrea Dworkin
Cixous, Irigaray, Kristeva: The *Jouissance* of French Feminism
Julia Kristeva: Art, Love, Melancholy, Philosophy, Semiotics and Psychoanalysis
Hélène Cixous I Love You: The *Jouissance* of Writing
Luce Irigaray: Lips, Kissing, and the Politics of Sexual Difference
Peter Redgrove: Here Comes the Flood
Peter Redgrove: Sex-Magic-Poetry-Cornwall
Lawrence Durrell: Between Love and Death, East and West
Love, Culture & Poetry: Lawrence Durrell
Cavafy: Anatomy of a Soul
German Romantic Poetry: Goethe, Novalis, Heine, Hölderlin, Schlegel, Schiller
Feminism and Shakespeare
Shakespeare: Selected Sonnets
Shakespeare: Love, Poetry & Magic
The Passion of D.H. Lawrence
D.H. Lawrence: Symbolic Landscapes
D.H. Lawrence: Infinite Sensual Violence
Rimbaud: Arthur Rimbaud and the Magic of Poetry
The Ecstasies of John Cowper Powys
Sensualism and Mythology: The Wessex Novels of John Cowper Powys
Amorous Life: John Cowper Powys and the Manifestation of Affectivity (H.W. Fawkner)
Postmodern Powys: New Essays on John Cowper Powys (Joe Boulter)
Rethinking Powys: Critical Essays on John Cowper Powys
Paul Bowles & Bernardo Bertolucci
Rainer Maria Rilke
In the Dim Void: Samuel Beckett
Samuel Beckett Goes into the Silence
André Gide: Fiction and Fervour
Jackie Collins and the Blockbuster Novel
Blinded By Her Light: The Love-Poetry of Robert Graves
The Passion of Colours: Travels In Mediterranean Lands
Poetic Forms
The Dolphin-Boy

POETRY

The Best of Peter Redgrove's Poetry
Peter Redgrove: Here Comes The Flood
Peter Redgrove: Sex-Magic-Poetry-Cornwall
Ursula Le Guin: Walking In Cornwall
Dante: Selections From the Vita Nuova
Petrarch, Dante and the Troubadours
William Shakespeare: Selected Sonnets
Blinded By Her Light: The Love-Poetry of Robert Graves
Emily Dickinson: Selected Poems
Emily Brontë: Poems
Thomas Hardy: Selected Poems
Percy Bysshe Shelley: Poems
John Keats: Selected Poems
D.H. Lawrence: Selected Poems
Edmund Spenser: Poems
John Donne: Poems
Henry Vaughan: Poems
Sir Thomas Wyatt: Poems
Robert Herrick: Selected Poems
Rilke: Space, Essence and Angels in the Poetry of Rainer Maria Rilke
Rainer Maria Rilke: Selected Poems
Friedrich Hölderlin: Selected Poems
Arseny Tarkovsky: Selected Poems
Arthur Rimbaud: Selected Poems
Arthur Rimbaud: A Season in Hell
Arthur Rimbaud and the Magic of Poetry
D.J. Enright: By-Blows
Jeremy Reed: Brigitte's Blue Heart
Jeremy Reed: Claudia Schiffer's Red Shoes
Gorgeous Little Orpheus
Radiance: New Poems
Crescent Moon Book of Nature Poetry
Crescent Moon Book of Love Poetry
Crescent Moon Book of Mystical Poetry
Crescent Moon Book of Elizabethan Love Poetry
Crescent Moon Book of Metaphysical Poetry
Crescent Moon Book of Romantic Poetry
Pagan America: New American Poetry

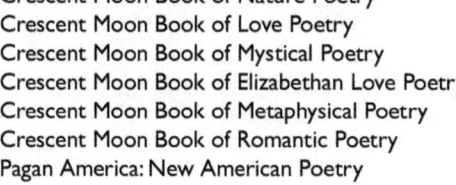

MEDIA, CINEMA, FEMINISM and CULTURAL STUDIES

J.R.R. Tolkien: The Books, The Films, The Whole Cultural Phenomenon
Harry Potter
Cixous, Irigaray, Kristeva: The *Jouissance* of French Feminism
Julia Kristeva: Art, Love, Melancholy, Philosophy, Semiotics and Psychoanalysis
Luce Irigaray: Lips, Kissing, and the Politics of Sexual Difference
Hélene Cixous I Love You: The *Jouissance* of Writing
Andrea Dworkin
'Cosmo Woman': The World of Women's Magazines
Women in Pop Music
Discovering the Goddess (Geoffrey Ashe)
The Poetry of Cinema
The Sacred Cinema of Andrei Tarkovsky (Pbk and Hbk)
Paul Bowles & Bernardo Bertolucci
Media Hell: Radio, TV and the Press
An Open Letter to the BBC
Detonation Britain: Nuclear War in the UK
Feminism and Shakespeare
Wild Zones: Pornography, Art and Feminism
Sex in Art: Pornography and Pleasure in Painting and Sculpture
Sexing Hardy: Thomas Hardy and Feminism

In my view *The Light Eternal* is among the very best of all the material I read on Turner. (Douglas Graham, director of the Turner Museum, Denver, Colorado)

The Light Eternal is a model monograph, an exemplary job. The subject matter of the book is beautifully organised and dead on beam. (Lawrence Durrell)

It is amazing for me to see my work treated with such passion and respect. (Andrea Dworkin)

Sex-Magic-Poetry-Cornwall is a very rich essay... It is like a brightly-lighted box. (Peter Redgrove)

CRESCENT MOON PUBLISHING
P.O. Box 393, Maidstone, Kent, ME14 5XU, United Kingdom.
01622-729593 (UK) 01144-1622-729593 (US) 0044-1622-729593 (other territories)
cresmopub@yahoo.co.uk www.crescentmoon.org.uk

www.ingramcontent.com/pod-product-compliance
Lightning Source LLC
Chambersburg PA
CBHW062154080426
42734CB00010B/1688